END-USER SEARCHING
Services and Providers

edited by

Martin Kesselman
and
Sarah B. Watstein

AMERICAN LIBRARY ASSOCIATION
Chicago and London 1988

Cover designed by Marcia Lange

Composed by Point West in
Times Roman on Compugraphic
Quadex 5000

Printed on 50-pound Glatfelter
Natural B-16, a pH-neutral stock,
and bound in 10-point Carolina cover stock
by Edwards Brothers

Library of Congress Cataloging-in-Publication Data

End-user searching.

   Includes index.
   1. Reference services (Libraries)—Automation.
2. Information services—User education.
3. Bibliographical services—user education.
4. On-line bibliographic searching. 5. Data base
searching. I. Kesselman, Martin. II. Watstein, Sarah.
III. American Library Association.
Z711.E55 1988   025.5'24   87-37444
ISBN 0-8389-0488-2

Contents

v

Preface

End-User Searching in Libraries was written to aid librarians as they confront the challenges of direct searching by patrons. The vast growth in sales of personal computers for all segments of the market has affected the way electronic data can be retrieved in libraries. It has turned users of electronic information into end users, people who search for information themselves. Such rapid growth raises the question of how to guide others who could be end users. What directions should libraries take in working with end users? How can administrative support be acquired for directions taken and roles assumed? What issues and concerns are involved in the training of end users? What end-user services are available, and to which target audiences are they marketed? What books, journals, and journal articles can assist librarians and end users in these decisions?

Currently, there are several popular books on the market addressed directly to the needs of end users. In addition, there are several new magazines and newsletters and numerous articles in the increasingly popular microcomputer literature. However, as of this writing, there are no books on the market that deal with the topic of end-user searching from the perspective of librarians.

Typically, most online services in libraries, be they academic, public, school, or special, are performed by librarians as intermediaries. Librarians, having undergone a great deal of training, have knowledge of online searching. They are familiar with advantages and disadvantages of online searching; online search commands; database-indexing vocabulary, thesauri, and other user aids; search strategy formulation; and database selection. Because of the increasing interest by end users in doing their own searches, libraries are now grappling with the challenge of identifying the best ways to serve this kind of patron. The thought and care that need to go into the process of identifying the best ways to serve this new population of end users open up new and exciting challenges and new roles for librarians and libraries.

The sales growth of personal computers and modems and the increasing number of databases available online is stimulating the growth of end-user searching. Other contributing factors include the development of user-friendly—i.e., simplified—searching systems, such as *BRS After Dark* or *Knowledge Index,* and front-ends, such as *Sci-Mate, Search Helper,* or *Searchware.* With advances in artificial intelligence techniques, systems will offer even more features and greater ease of use, providing additional options for users with varying levels of sophistication.

So far, the paradoxical experience of libraries with an end-user program has been to cause constant or even increasing demand for online services. To meet this demand, librarians must act as teachers, consultants, and problem solvers for the end users, as well as assist them with document delivery and SDIs. End-user programs, then, will extend the range of librarians' functions as well as that of library services. The function for libraries, however, remains one of putting patrons in contact with the information resources they need as quickly and as easily as possible.

The potential of the resources librarians have to offer end users is the focus of this book. If librarians neglect to make their resources available, the end user will likely make a less productive search.

The first three chapters deal with some of the basic topics involved with end-user searching. Chapter 1, "Toward End-User Searching in Libraries," considers the reasons why end-user searching demand is increasing, as well as the rationales and issues for libraries considering an end-user program. Chapter 2, "Starting an End-User Service," reviews the factors to consider, such as staffing, costs, and marketing, in establishing an end-user program with the greatest chances of success. Chapter 3, "Training End Users," provides a sound overview of training options for home or office users, for users within an in-library program, and for individual users through such means as presearch consultations or computer-assisted instruction.

The next six chapters focus on both specific end-user search systems and on services in specific subject areas. Chapters 4, 5, and 6 focus on end-user search services available from BRS, DIALOG, H. W. Wilson, and the Information Access Company. These three chapters detail the special features of each service, as well as discuss case studies that demonstrate the usefulness of these services for end users. Chapters 7 and 8 focus on end-user services in specific subject areas, such as business and related fields, and science and health, providing information on services aimed at special populations. Chapter 9 focuses on the large "online supermarket" services, such as *CompuServe* and *The Source,* targeted for the general consumer market. These three chapters should help librarians become familiar with the services that are of interest to some of their users.

Chapters 10 and 11 focus on front-end and gateway software and laser disc-based services for end users, all of which have led to the increased acceptance of end-user searching today. Chapter 10 discusses software-based services that aid users with search commands and database selection without extensive training. Chapter 11 reviews how databases on CD-ROM and other optical media, many with easy-to-use menu-driven search options, allow users to search inhouse at a fixed cost, without the "online clock ticking away." Both chapters discuss several services currently available and their utility for end-user searching.

The final part of the book and the Appendix consist of three sections that list resources to consult for further information. A literature review of timely articles and conference papers on the topic of end-user searching constitutes the first section. In the second section, books, journals, and user aids for end users are discussed. The third section contains a directory of services discussed within the book, with names, addresses, and telephone numbers.

Many thanks are due, and we now gratefully offer them: to the staff at ALA Books for their valuable help; to our colleagues at Rutgers, Hunter College, and New York University for their encouragement and support; and to the cited end-user system vendors and distributors for their cooperation.

Chapter 1

Toward End-User
Searching in Libraries

Martin Kesselman, Priscilla Kronish, and Sarah B. Watstein

Whether we are in public, technical, or administrative services, we are at a marvelous time in history with regard to the planning of information services. Roger K. Summit writes:

> Development in three primary technologies—communications, publishing, and data processing—has come together in a manner that allows the accumulation, selection, and transfer of knowledge in today's world on a scale so vast and [at a] cost so low that virtually any literate person can easily and conveniently become familiar with society's collected knowledge in any area that piques his or her professional interests. Pause for a moment to consider the profound nature of such a phenomenon.[1]

Pause for a moment also to consider the impact of this joining of technologies on the information services we in libraries can offer our users.

In his 1984 article "Online After Six: End-User Searching Comes of Age," Richard Janke concludes, "The question to be asked is no longer: is end-user searching here to stay? for it certainly is."[2] Today, end-user searching has been tested and found feasible in a number of settings. Throughout North America, and in academic, public, school, and special libraries, end-user activities are taking place with the support, involvement, and cooperation of the library. It is no longer appropriate to expect users to turn to intermediaries in all search situations. Indeed, with the advent of user-friendly systems such as *Lexis/Nexis, Dow Jones News/Retrieval, Easynet, BRS After Dark,* and *DIALOG's Knowledge Index,* as well as programs such as *ProSearch* and *Wilsearch,* libraries have

1

a responsibility to seriously consider giving patrons direct access to information available online.

This chapter is concerned with decision making and the processes that accompany the decision to establish an end-user search service or program. Such decision making is a multifaceted process involving, among other components, awareness—of the history of end-user searching and of factors that have contributed to its rise; knowledge—of the stages of decision making, relevant alternatives, and dilemmas; and advocacy—in the form of a service or program proposal.

This chapter begins with a review of the history of end-user searching and a consideration of some of the factors that have contributed to its rise. Discussion then turns to consideration of the following question: What is involved in the process of deciding whether or not to establish an end-user service or program? The stages of decision making are then highlighted, and alternatives to setting up a program are reviewed. Dilemmas with which decision makers must grapple are also discussed. The chapter concludes with a review of the components of a well-thought-out proposal to establish an end-user service or program.

HISTORICAL PERSPECTIVE

Any discussion of the history of end-user searching has its roots in the late 1970s, when the "nerve center" of the online industry was the librarian responsible for online searching. Within their communities, organizations, or institutions, librarians played a pivotal role in the promotion and provision of online services, serving to link the information with the person who wanted it. The following characteristics enabled librarians to function as the catalysts for online action: library background; technical search instruction in system commands and file content; information sensitivity; technological awareness; and service orientation. Throughout the 70s, the online bibliographic industry consisted of three principal markets: the library market, the professional market, and the business and technology market. Each of these markets had several segments, with varying levels of acceptance and usage of online searching. Users themselves were usually inexperienced, with needs ranging from the simplest to the most complex. Users had various needs, but they did not know how to obtain what they needed.

The computer industry in the 70s was small, and sales consisted mostly of mainframe computers until the introduction of microcomputers in the late 1970s. These first microcomputers were both expensive and had limited memories and capabilities, but the market for them was vast.

The value of personal computers shipped to all market segments in 1986 approached $14.6 billion, compared with $1.9 billion in 1981. In

1986, 6.6 million personal computers moved from manufacturers to business, science, education, and home customers. Business customers bought 362,000 personal computers in 1981; whereas in 1987, the number of units approached 3.25 million. In 1981, only 151,000 PCs were purchased for home use, contrasted with 1986's estimated 2.2 million.[3]

Orientation to the technology, skills, and decision-making processes needed for dependent information retrieval and management constituted one major component of online services in libraries in the 1970s. The second major component of these services consisted of service provision. As the 70s drew to a close, computerized search services were increasingly widespread in all types of libraries. Characteristically, the stages of online training during this period dealt with two areas: (1) capabilities of major retrieval systems, and (2) topic analysis and strategy formulation. Online protocols and database-specific idiosyncracies were not generally introduced to new users. Users did not need to worry about understanding terms such as *command, default, mnemonics, prefixes, suffixes, offline, SDI, sorting, stop words, classification, controlled vocabulary, descriptor, thesaurus, hierarchical, natural language, textword,* or *free text.* In all, there was very little active involvement on the part of users in information management activities.

Service provision was the domain of librarians or information specialists. Indeed, training materials and database documentation, along with online products and services, were designed with this professional market in mind. Lack of accessibility and language clarity were common criticisms of training and search manuals. Service provision was nearly always accompanied by a presearch interview or a consultation in which such concepts as primary and secondary sources, citations, database, abstract, and log time were painstakenly introduced, and samples of output from a variety of databases were reviewed. Librarians, synonymous with "online searchers," were expected to keep up with the state of the art in online searching and major subject areas. Discussions and presentations at professional meetings in the 1970s focused on the pivotal role of information specialists in making online information available to users. Such speculation on the future as there was did not encompass the notion of users searching a database themselves.

FACTORS IN THE RISE OF END-USER SEARCHING

The rise of end-user searching can be attributed to numerous factors, including the evolution of the role of the librarian in the promotion and provision of online services, and the change in and growth of the online industry. Other factors discussed here are the increasing recognition of an end-user market, marketing strategies that reflect this awareness, the changing nature of library collections and services, and the tremendous increase in the sales of personal computers.

The future shape of the market will be determined by the current focus of database firms on developing end-user products and services. This activity reflects the evolution of end users from a mere concept into a sharply defined, well-known market that will gradually provide more cost-effective, simple, and flexible online services.

Broadly defined, this market consists of individuals who can and will make use of online services. This market is not homogenous or close-knit. End users may include "hackers," students, researchers, investors, marketers, chemists, lawyers, or data processing professionals. End users also may consist of individuals who may or may not be library users, or who may or may not ever have searched online, with or without an intermediary. People become end users for several reasons. Some need to increase job skills, others need to meet academic requirements, others recognize the additional uses of a PC and modem, and still others can solve problems by searching a database. These different users constitute a single market pursued by all the components of the information industry, an industry that is very interested in expanding the use of online services as a primary means of gathering information.

It naturally follows that the rise of end-user search services can be attributed, amongst other things, "To aggressive marketing directly to end users by both DIALOG and BRS, which have been advertising regularly in popular computing magazines; to widespread discussion and advertising of end-user searching in popular magazines...; to the fact that BRS has taken early criticisms of the initial *BRS After Dark* service to heart and greatly improved the system's ease of use; and finally, to the ever growing awareness amongst librarians that end-user searching is, in fact, here to stay, whether they are willing to become directly involved in it or not."[4]

The changing nature of library collections and services has also contributed to the rise of end-user searching. As bibliographic instruction has expanded in libraries, end-user instruction has increasingly been seen as a responsibility of libraries. Librarians have traditionally assisted patrons with the selection and use of printed indexes and abstracts, and will continue to help patrons with online databases, which, on the whole, contain more information than most libraries could individually obtain. Another factor that has made end-user instruction more urgent is the increased presence of public access online catalogs and circulation systems in libraries. Many of the techniques and strategies required for accessing online catalogs and circulation systems are the same as those needed for online services aimed at end users.

A final factor contributing to the rise of end-user searching is the tremendous increase in the sales of personal computers. In the past decade, advances in hardware and software technology and decreased costs have made the personal computer commonplace in homes as well as in the workplace. The current growth rate is expected to continue until the year 2000, when a large percentage of library users and office workers will have a desktop computer. The sales of modems, particularly those offering faster speeds, are also increasing. Such broad dissemination of this equipment, which enables users to directly access a database, will require librarians to find new ways to assist users and to develop public service programs to help them.

ISSUES FOR END-USER SEARCHING

A key to the success of any service or program is to enter the planning process knowing what you want and how to gain approval for your plan. The planning process is not a framework within which end-user issues are routinely discussed and systematically resolved. If the process is used in this way, you are avoiding the matter of purpose. You must be more interested in producing an actual planning document that clearly defines the program's goals. In attempting to win approval from management, staff, or a key target group, you must include the interests of others. Of course, holders of power dictate to a large degree what your objectives for the planning effort will be, but to get the most out of the effort it is important to externalize and rank each of the objectives that you feel is important to achieve.

The planning process, when applied to online information systems, must begin with evaluating the demand for access. When deciding whether or not to start an end-user program, a library must weigh the alternatives carefully. The easiest alternative would be to continue the online service as it exists, i.e., accessible only through intermediaries, with no additional resources allocated. However, as demand increases, delays in delivery of service will occur, thereby diminishing one of the greatest advantages of online searching—speed and timeliness. In order to continue the same level of service, the library must substantially increase its expense budget to obtain more equipment and hire new personnel. Large budget increases are usually very hard to obtain, particularly when there are more cost-effective solutions to the growing demand for online information. One solution is establishing an end-user program.

Several topics should be discussed by staff involved in the decision-making process of whether or not to establish an end-user service or program. Issues discussed briefly in this section include: (1) pricing, (2) the role of the librarian, (3) service selection, and (4) end-user interface.

Thinking about these topics requires consideration of various questions. What are all your possibilities? What are all the options among the possibilities? What can be learned from the literature? How do choices relate to the library's established priorities? The goal of the discussion should be to choose a single course of action within each topic.

Pricing

In her review "Toward a Decade of Personal Information Products," Spigai comments:

> Only a small proportion of database publications are profitable, yet online prices are too high for growth into new markets and these prices are increasing. How will this problem be solved? Will a more information/computer literate society provide a large enough market to support lower prices? Will lower prices attract a larger market?[5]

Spigai's remarks frame the economic question in the pricing issue. Librarians considering the issue of pricing must also ask: Do the economics of online services consider the life of online publications? Will new end-user markets require a higher level of support than do other markets? How can libraries determine which prices are low enough to attract end users while maintaining the financial viability of the online service?

Role of the Librarian

What position will librarians occupy if the availability of end-user services and programs in their communities and organizations becomes widespread? Will the instruction required for online searching diminish, thereby encouraging widespread and occasional business, professional, or consumer use? Will librarians re-assume their role as information reviewers and educators for some significant segment of electronic publications, or will they continue in their role as intermediaries? Will their role of promoter or distributor gain prominence? In considering this issue, it is useful to learn about the environment of products and people involved in the transfer of online information to end users.

Service Selection

As we embark on the years spanning from 1987 to 2000, database service selection will become increasingly complex. That the number of end-user systems and services will increase is certain. This increase will be caused by a number of factors, including: the rapid shift in technologies; a rise in the number of electronic publishers; and changes in the packaging and segmentation of databases as on-demand publishing becomes more common. Faced with an increase in the number of end-user systems and services, librarians will have to develop system- and service-selection criteria, in much the same manner as such criteria were developed for the selection of public access catalogs.

Consideration of what to do about disk-based products naturally follows the discussion of the service-selection dilemma, for, indeed, consideration of these products involves applying selection criteria. Developing separate product-by-product selection criteria may not be deemed necessary or desirable by all libraries, however. As CD-ROM and CD-I products penetrate the online market, new services and systems will come onto the market. Librarians must follow the maturing and consolidation processes of database providers, as well as keep up with technologies associated with online information systems, e.g., E-mail, teletext, videotext, interactive systems, robotics, reprographics, etc., so that they will be ready to select products that are the most cost effective, simple, and flexible.

Librarians need to be mindful of which online vendors provide easy access to their services by improving their software and gateways. (Gateways permit communication by the user with the databases of different vendors.) Such flexibility will certainly be demanded by fee-paying end users. Other questions to consider include: Which suppliers offer improved methods for retrieving and manipulating data? Has any software been written for the purpose of allowing more opportunities for using information captured from online services?

The Online Interface Issue

The online interface poses several obstacles for end users. The online interface, defined as the point of interaction between the end user and the online database, risks restrictiveness if users cannot exploit the search offered by the medium.

End users often neglect presearch preparation, viewing the use of a computer as a "quick" way to get at information. Although they likely will have expertise in the topic to be searched, they often lack the analytical searching techniques of the information specialist. A failure to master searching methods leads to false evaluation of the search results. One type of user perceives online database searching as fast and infallible, and may rush through the search and be satisfied with incomplete or erroneous results as long as something is found. Others will be totally dissatisfied with a search if a citation they know of is not retrieved. If the end user thinks computers always make mistakes, he or she may not trust the search process and honestly attempt a viable search.

End users searching for specific information or for a few items on a current topic may have a more successful experience than those searching for a comprehensive bibliography. The physical ease of doing an online search while comfortably seated at a terminal, as opposed to the annoyance of locating all the necessary volumes of an index and repetitively performing the same search in each volume, for each term, also should not be discounted. The online search may be perceived as better simply because it was easier, or more comfortable. Conversely, for those who are distrustful of or made anxious by computers, more discomfort, therefore less satisfaction, may be felt in undertaking an online search than a manual search.

The nature of the information sought affects the results, as does the correct choice of database to be searched. The effectiveness of a search; the relevance and utility of the retrieved information; and the efficiency, cost, and time of the search strongly influence user satisfaction. End-user searching thus will be more satisfactory for the regular rather than the occasional searcher. The regular user will take time to read the search manuals and review specific citations in order to learn which index terms are used to retrieve the needed information. Libraries, in establishing an end-user search service, can best deal with end users' misconceptions about searching and with their tendency to be satisfied with less than they should be. Librarians can provide assistance by examining and clarifying users' information needs and counseling users on the best access and use of online information resources.

Beyond counseling for specific needs, there is a need for training that covers file access in a systematic way. The online interface will pose obstacles for end users who are not familiar with the use of Boolean logic; database content, organization, or indexing vocabulary; and other system parameters, such as command languages and access protocols, broadening or narrowing a search strategy, or choosing an appropriate database to search. Simplifying the search process, however, does not compensate for a user's lack of knowledge of database indexing principles or of the search system software. In an online database, the index structure is invisible to the end user; by contrast, the user can readily view the access points in a print index and conduct a search accordingly.

These obstacles can be overcome by general training of the end user, but in particular situations the end user must be alerted to the number of options available in selecting a search system. Menu-driven systems, for example, prompt the end user through a search step by step. Each prompt gives the user the option of going forward in the search and displaying the results. The advantage of a menu-driven system is that there is no need to learn commands or remember strategies. Menu-driven systems are recommended for the infrequent or novice user. For more experienced users, menu-driven systems tend to be slow and frustrating after a while. Command-driven systems necessitate learning the basic commands before one is able to enter a search strategy, to display or print results, and to switch from one database to another. Although some learning time is needed before one can use a command-driven system, the searches are usually faster, and more complex strategies can be developed.

The end user also must be alerted to the range of database indexing features. Often lacking knowledge of these features, end users have trouble putting their search request into the terminology of the databases they wish to search. An additional obstacle to end users is the lack of standardization among the various types of indexes and with indexing policies, procedures, quality, and comprehensiveness, resulting in a great deal of variation from one database to the next.

Some database indexes provide complete text access, which allows the end user to search for every word of the document. The disadvantage of this type of index is that the end user must match terms of interest to those terms used by the document's author, usually necessitating the use of many synonyms for each term or concept searched. Other databases are indexed with controlled vocabularies, using thesauri that are usually available in print and sometimes online. Controlled vocabulary systems ensure greater consistency in the assignment of subject descriptors to documents and greater control in the retrieval of relevant citations for these concepts. But even a controlled vocabulary is not foolproof, as some papers may be indexed with incorrect terms, indexed too broadly or narrowly, indexed by too few descriptors. For these reasons, documents may not be retrieved if the searcher relies on controlled descriptors alone. Fortunately, most databases provide access through a basic index in which the user does not specify an index field. In these cases, the user will access the title, abstract, descriptor, and identifier fields. Although some search precision may be lost, there is an increased chance that end users will retrieve some items of interest.

As a third method of surmounting interface obstacles, end users must be alerted to the fact that many databases offer additional access options that may make searching more productive. For example, with access to the full text of databases such as electronic journals, encyclopedias, and handbooks, there is a greater chance that users will find items of interest, but there is also a greater chance of retrieving inappropriate references. The adept use of Boolean logic and proximity searching will help prevent these "false drops." Therefore, it is usually necessary to offer first-time searchers an extensive introduction to Boolean operators. The understanding and application of Boolean logic for narrowing and broadening search statements is a vital factor in the successful retrieval of information from an online system. Additional database index and online features advantageous for end users include searching by codes, expanding terms, truncation, searching by non-subect parameters such as language and year, and the use of online thesauri.

In the future, artificial intelligence may provide more effective methods for online searching by end users. Artificial intelligence attempts to mimic the knowledge and reasoning processes as well as the "rules of thumb" or heuristics of human experts. Two areas of artificial intelligence that hold the greatest promise for end users are expert systems and natural language processing. An expert system, acting as the librarian, could assist with the selection of a database and search service, the selection of search terms, and the development of an appropriate search strategy. Natural language processing allows users to state their search request in their native tongue, which the system translates into the appropriate descriptors and format for the search.

PROPOSING AN END-USER PROGRAM

The basis of a successful end-user service or program is the belief of the library in the necessity of the service, together with the institution's financial support. The key to securing the institution's support is a carefully prepared proposal, the importance of which increases as it circulates to higher echelons of management. After all, the proposal is often the only vehicle for communicating the staff's message to the approving agency. The purpose of this section is to discuss the composition of such a proposal, first, in general, and then specifically regarding an end-user program.

To achieve maximum impact, a proposal to establish any new service or program should begin by stating how the service or program will advance the library's goals. The proposal should then explain in detail the nature of the new service or program and the steps that will be taken to implement it. The proposal should include the following parts: statement of the problem, service or program outline, evaluation, staff or personnel, budget, impact of the new service or program, and calendar.

A statement of the problem of managing information is first given, and the mission of the library is framed as the solution. The general mission of libraries is to provide those services that will allow users to gain access to information. These services may include catalog assistance, reference, interlibrary loan, and referrals, among others. The information provided may range from a single fact to comprehensive references on a specific topic. Libraries have a responsibility to teach users how to be information literate, especially because of "information overload," the fact that information resources are increasingly available in a variety of formats and offer many new access options. An end-user search service could be a library's first step toward offering the special skills and guidance it is organized to provide, such as helping patrons learn about and use online information resources.

An outline follows the statement of the problem and may include a description of the objectives of the new service. The activities planned to accomplish each objective are described in a well-articulated working plan. In addition, the proposal must relate the goals of the new service or program to the stated problem, and it must outline the plan's implementation. The proposal should also include a detailed timetable for installing the service.

The proposal then should explain in detail the nature of the proposed service or program. A clear statement of the problem, documented with facts, figures, and appropriate references to the literature, constitutes the first step of this explanation. A needs assessment may be substituted for the statement of the problem. Approval of the new service or program will utlimately depend on management's agreement that the stated problems can best be solved with the service or program proposed. Indeed, management will be primarily interested in how implementation will ameliorate or even solve the problems. Therefore, each step of the implementation process must achieve a realistic goal, which is the most effective way to convince management (and those responsible for implementation) that the whole project is feasible.

A method of evaluation is the third part of the proposal. The instrument used to conduct an evaluation is discussed at the end of Chapter 2.

The fourth part of the proposal should be a list of people responsible to the director of the library for setting up and managing the end-user search service or program. Involving the right people in the planning and implementation processes goes a long way toward increasing the chances for a successful outcome. Selection of personnel depends on answers each library has to the following questions: On what organizational level should planning occur? Would the process benefit from the involvement of representatives of market audience groups or from the involvement of a consultant? How broad should the group of planning and implementing participants be? Involving the right people from outside (and inside the library) is easier said than done, and requires skill and a creative approach.

A detailed account of the budgetary requirements constitutes the fifth part of the proposal. What does an end-user service or program cost? Funds must be allocated in at least five areas. First, there is the initial cost of the equipment, which includes furniture, hardware, and software. The minimum equipment required is a computer terminal with a modem, which can cost about $400. A more flexible and efficient set-up consists of a personal computer with a modem and a printer, which will cost at least $2,000. The amount of memory available in the microcomputer, the types of disk drives and modems, the speed and quality of the printer, the software programs, as well as the number of workstations made available, all will affect the cost. Although equipment must be maintained, this is basically a one-time expense. Therefore, you should choose equipment with a view to future developments. A microcomputer can be upgraded and offers many alternative set-ups and possible uses, while a terminal can only connect you to another computer.

Making documentation available to patrons is another budgetary requirement. At least one copy of the systems' manuals and guides, as well as specific database manuals, thesauri, etc., must be purchased and provisions made for keeping the collection up to date. Supporting books must also be purchased, and standing orders to supporting journals must also be set up.

A third expense will be programs for training personnel and patrons. Online charges for this purpose can be kept down by taking advantage of demonstration passwords, as well as training contracts offered by many services at special discounted prices. Vendor-supplied teaching materials may help offset the costs of developing such materials inhouse. Currently, the staff time needed to support an end-user program in, say, a moderately sized library is not unreasonable.

Finally, funds must be allocated for online subscription and connect charges. These costs will vary depending on the systems used, as well as the software used to access them. The relatively low cost involved in offering access to some of the online services, such as *BRS After Dark* or *Dow Jones News/Retrieval,* should allow libraries to provide them at no cost to the user or at a fairly moderate fee.

The initial outlay for equipment, documentation, and training is costly and hard to obtain. Grants are the best and easiest way to start any program. In fact, once you prove a program's usefulness, the funding institution feels an obligation to keep it going. However, grants are usually given to pioneering projects, and unless you plan to develop your own expert system for online information retrieval, or something of the kind, grants will be hard to obtain because end-user programs are becoming more the norm than the exception. In this case, you can obtain institution support simply by pointing out that yours may be the only institution of its kind not offering its patrons access to information online.

To keep the program going, some libraries fully subsidize searching, either through grant funding or library allocations. Some receive departmental contributions, while others charge flat hourly rates, or fees based on a cost recovery schedule.

The Law Department of Baruch College felt so strongly about having access to *Lexis* for both faculty and students that they strongly recommended the library spend half its allocation for law books on a subscription to this online service. This event has set the pattern for how online services are viewed at this institution. At present, online services at Baruch College are totally subsidized by the library, and subscription and usage charges are paid from the book budget. Online services through intermediaries, as well as the end-user program, were initially funded by grants from the federal government.

Conclusion

In evaluating the end-user search service, it should be made clear to what extent the program's objectives have been realized. Evaluation should also consider how the new service has affected the library, its staff, and its services. There are payoffs and pressures that libraries can expect with the establishment of an end-user search service. Because users will undoubtedly appreciate the service, providing it will have a positive effect on the librarian's role, which will expand to include serving as advisor to and teacher of end users. The boundaries of professional supportive services provided will also expand. Manual reference, traditional intermediary-based online searching, and bibliographic instruction services will be complemented and enriched by the arrival of end-user searching. A final payoff is that providing the service allows online searching to be introduced to users on a large-scale basis.

Overall, libraries should keep in mind that end-user searching is fun and keeps the library at the hub of information searches. With an in-house online service, end users will not bypass the library but will instead really begin to appreciate what it does, as well as the knowledge and experience its staff can provide users in their research endeavors.

In addition to benefits, libraries considering whether or not to establish an end-user search service or program should be aware of what pressures to expect. First, in spite of ease of use, end-user systems require a considerable amount of staff time to monitor the service. Demands for help by end users may place a burden on traditional reference services, making it necessary to schedule appointments for search counseling sessions. Second, while the amount of intermediary-based searching may initially decline, it may ultimately increase as patrons realize the limitations of end-user systems and recognize the need to search databases not available through these systems. There will be a continuing need for intermediaries to perform online searches for those library users who do not want to do their own searching, for comprehensive searches, or for an end user unfamiliar with a particular database. Third, after users become familiar with the available systems, they will also demand greater access to these services within the library and a wider variety of systems from which to choose.

Once an end-user search service is established, libraries are faced with the dual challenge of ensuring its continued development and availability, while at the same time integrating it effectively into the spectrum of existing reference services. The first challenge can be met by the development of questionaires and other evaluation methods that will allow libraries to obtain information on patron satisfaction and search effectiveness and to determine whether the service needs expansion or refinement, as well as whether further training is needed. Effectively integrating the end-user service with existing reference services may be accomplished by any of the following: marketing the service and training sessions through existing and ongoing bibliographic instruction classes; scheduling search appointments from the reference desk; requiring that students attend, before searching, a workshop on the service or that students go through a self-paced workbook or computer-assisted instruction package to gain familiarity with the service; and referring unsuccessful end-user searchers to make an appointment for a strategy counseling session.

APPENDIX

OCCASIONAL PAPERS

Constance R. Miller, Editor   Number 1

Planning for End-User Searching: A Checklist of Questions

Prepared by the MARS Direct Patron Access to Computer-based Reference Systems Committee (Nancy Crane, chair; Susan Brynteson, Sharon D. Cline, James E. Crooks, Louis Drummond, Barbara Goodman, Dennis Hamilton, Elliot Kanter, David King, Sarah Loken, Deborah Masters, and Victoria Ann Reich)

I. Introduction

This *Checklist* was developed to assist librarians planning for end user searching within libraries. All of the items may not be necessary in the evaluation process. The items are not arranged in any priority. A positive or negative answer to a particular question may not impact on your final decision. The general principles used in materials selection for the library collection should be observed in selecting electronic information resources. Of particular importance is the experience of others who have used the services, software, and programs offered. In addition, recommendations found in descriptive and evaluative review sources should be consulted.

II. Needs Assessment

A. What is the demand for end user searching? Are users establishing their own searching contracts? Are other units within the organization providing end user services? What volume of use do they receive?

B. Are consulting services wanted? Are users seeking advice on how to evaluate and select databank services, gateways, front-ends, and/or hardware? Is there a market for training programs?

C. What is the potential volume of use by and composition of the clientele? Is there a particular group of users being targeted?

D. What are the information needs? What are the levels of expertise and sophistication of the users?

E. What are the subject areas served?

F. Are mediated searches currently available? How many of these searches are currently performed and for whom?

G. Does the library envision itself as playing an active role in developing computer and technology literacy among its clientele?

III. Administrative Issues

A. Service Considerations
1. Who will be responsible for teaching the public how to select and use the systems? Will the staff advise users on selection?
2. What is the quality of the documentation and materials describing the search process, commands, strategies, etc.? Will library staff develop materials and documentation for users?
3. What does the library consider its educational role, opportunities, and obligations? How will any new programs fit into existing user education programs?
4. How does end user searching relate to existing reference services? Will the manager of the service be the Head of the Reference Department?
5. Is there strong administrative support? What is the commitment of the reference staff?
6. What locations for search stations are feasible? What are the advantages/disadvantages of each in terms of staffing, availability of experienced searchers, costs for renovation, installation, and displacement of other activities?

B. Staff Resources
1. What staffing is needed to support the use of the system? What hours will desk, telephone, or electronic reference service be available to help users? Will all staff or a dedicated staff be involved?
2. What existing activities will undergo change so that staff can be reallocated to this new activity?
3. Who will maintain the equipment and order supplies? Who will be responsible for the daily operation of the public's work area?

C. Cost Factors
1. What are the start-up costs, if any? Is there a one-time start-up fee? What are the total start-up costs for purchase or lease of hardware and software needed?
2. What are the ongoing search costs? Is there a contract for minimum usage per month or per year? Is there an annual subscription or licensing fee? Are funds expended for a product for outright

purchase, or for leasing of the information (i.e. who will own the information)? Are there additional costs for membership in a network in order to gain access to the system?

3. What kind of contract or billing arrangement is possible? Can a group contract together at a reduced rate? Is payment by check, credit card, coin box, or deposit account? Is a group contract itemized by account and subaccounts?

4. Will the library, users, or a combination of library and users pay costs?

5. What bookkeeping functions are available? What management reports are generated by the system?

6. How are users apprised of ongoing search costs? Is there an accounting system for end users with automatic online cost estimates? Is it possible to get subtotals for multiple database searches? Does software set maximum expenditure per search session and prohibit further interaction if amount exceeded?

7. Can charges to the user be overridden when there is an error or system problem?

8. Are there additional costs for software upgrades?

9. Are there additional costs for documentation and/or training?

10. What funding is required for ergonomic furniture, space renovation, and installation?

D. Vendor Characteristics

1. Are a warranty and maintenance contract available?

2. What is the reliability of the system? How much down time does it have? Are the scheduled hours of availability acceptable?

3. Is there responsive service from the company? Is there a toll-free, 24-hour number for help? Is there an experienced customer service staff? What is the local support?

4. Is there a commitment to upgrading or revising the software when necessary? How much technical support will the vendor provide? Will the package interface with more than one system?

5. Is a training program offered? How effective is it?

6. Is it possible to do local modifications on the system? Can you get the source code? Are there licensing restrictions on this type of activity?

7. Is software copy-protected? Can working copies be made if you do not sell or give them away?

8. Where has the product been reviewed? Is it reviewing the current version? Will the vendor give names of current users as a reference check? Is there an active users' group or newsletter? How long has the vendor been in business? What are the company's dependability and reliability factors?

IV. Scope of System Being Evaluated

A. Which systems or databases can be accessed?

B. How frequently are the databanks updated?

C. What subject areas are covered?

D. What relevant subject areas or specific databases are not included?

E. Can the system also access updated information or other databanks via telecommunication networks?

F. Does the user of the software decide which database or system to search?

V. Software

A. Log-on Features

1. How much of the log-on process is automatic?

2. Is dial-up access to databanks via telecommunication networks possible?

3. Can users change or add to the configurations?

4. What security is provided for the password? Is it masked during printing?

B. Searching and Retrieval

1. Is the system menu-driven, command-driven, or a combination of both? Can the end user make that decision?

2. Are function keys available and appropriate? Can they be reprogrammed to meet local needs?

3. What kind of command structure is available?
   a. What are the available commands?
   b. What are the possible ways to limit a search?
   c. Can the commands be renamed?

4. Are Boolean operators available? Which ones? Can you specify the order of Boolean operations? Nest? Are there limits on the number of operators? Is set building supported? Is there a limit on the number of sets?

5. What other search features are available?
   a. Wild card characters
   b. Truncation (right, left, specified number of characters)
   c. Proximity (word adjacency, within N words, within field, within sentence, within paragraph)
   d. Range searching

6. Are non-Boolean search features supported?
   a. Term weighting
   b. Highlighting search words in context
   c. Similarity: "Find me a document like this one"

7. Can the search strategy be uploaded? Can it be modified online during the search? How many different search statements can be uploaded? Is there a limit on the total number of characters?

8. What kind of display and printing capabilities does the system offer? Can citations be reviewed before printing? Are there any limitations on, or added charges for, the number of citations printed or formats selected?

9. Is authority control offered through the system? How does the command structure facilitate use of controlled vocabulary? Is there an online thesaurus from which terms can be selected? Is automatic switching to appropriate terms provided? If so, does the system inform the user of this automatic mapping feature?

10. Can the text be manipulated, edited, downloaded, and sorted as ASCII files? Will downloaded results be compatible with local database management software?

C. User Interface

1. How effective are user aids and/or help screens? Does the documentation include illustrations,

detailed examples, an index, glossary, and summary charts? Is the documentation included in the software and can it be displayed?

2. Can screen messages be altered by user?
3. What kind of assistance, if any, is needed to help first-time users, experienced users? How easy is it for users to interact with the software program and system?
4. What kind of language is used by the system? Does it use English language or jargon?
5. Is the software available in languages other than English?
6. Does the system match the intended clientele in its level of sophistication? Is it suitable for the audience? Does it offer more than one level?
7. Can you interrupt the online process (e.g. break function, switching back and forth to software while online)?

VI. Hardware

A. Is the system hardware specific? Is a specific brand of hardware required to operate the system? Can the hardware be used for other applications or is it dedicated to the system?
B. Is the hardware supplied as a part of the contract for the system? Are all necessary peripherals included (e.g., printer, compact disk controller, etc.)? Can the hardware be leased or purchased?

C. What size memory is required to use the system? Does the system require a single floppy disk drive, double drives, or a hard disk?
D. Does the hardware offer buffering capability? What is the buffer size?
E. Are the American Library Association character set and non-Roman alphabets available?
F. Can the hardware display non-Roman characters, graphics, and color?
G. What are the physical characteristics of the hardware? Does the terminal use a keyboard, function keys, a separate number pad, a tough screen, a light pen, a mouse? Does the screen offer good resolution for display of the textual or graphic information?
H. What are the implications of public access to the equipment such as security, durability, lighting, noise, and number of work stations?
I. What kind of communication requirements does the system have? Are dedicated telephone lines needed? If needed, is a modem included with the computer? How does access to the system interface with other telecommunications protocols in the institutional setting? What is the transmission speed?
J. Is the equipment portable?
K. What is the print quality and speed of the printer?
L. Are the keyboard and screen adjustable? Is there any problem with screen glare?

RASD sections, committees, other units, and individual members occasionally prepare documents that are potentially very useful to practicing reference and adult services librarians but do not fit the established editorial guidelines for RQ and are longer than the usual *RASD Update* item. "RASD Occasional Papers" provides a forum for sharing these documents to improve communication between the division and its members.

NOTES

1. Roger K. Summit, "Online Information: A Ten-Year Perspective and Outlook," *Online* 11 (Jan. 1987): 61.
2. Richard V. Janke, "Online After Six: End User Searching Comes of Age," *Online* 8 (Nov. 1984) 22.
3. Stephen E. Arnold, "End-Users: Dreams or Dollars," *Online* 11 (Jan. 1987): 71.
4. Dennis A. Lewis, "The Next Decade...," *Online* 11 (Jan. 1987): 57.
5. Fran Spigai, "Toward a Decade of Personal Information Products," *Online* 11 (Jan. 1987): 58.

BIBLIOGRAPHY

Elmore, Barbara. "End-User Searching in a Public Library." In *Online '85 Conference Proceedings,* edited by Jean Paul Emard, 98–101. Weston, Conn.: Online, Inc., 1985.

Janke, Richard V. "Presearch Counseling for Client Searchers (End-Users)." *Online* 9 (Sept. 1985): 13–26.

Jaros, Joe, Vicki Ander, and Geri Hutchins. "Subsidized End-User Searching in an Academic Library." In *National Online Meeting Proceedings—1986,* comp. by Martha E. Williams and Thomas H. Hogan, 223–29. Medford, N.J.: Learned Information, 1986.

Snow, Bonnie, "Self-Help Tips for End-Users." In *National Online Meeting Proceedings—1986,* comp. by Martha E. Williams and Thomas H. Hogan, 427–31. Medford, N.J.: Learned Information, 1986.

Teitelbaum-Kronish, Priscilla. "Relationship of Selected Cognitive Aptitudes and Personality Characteristics of the Online Searcher to the Quality of Performance in Online Bibliographic Retrieval." Ph.D. diss., New York University, 1984.

Tenopir, Carol, "InfoTrac: A Laser Disc System." *Library Journal* 111 (Sept. 1, 1986): 168–69.

_____. "Online Searching in Schools." *Library Journal* 111 (Feb. 1, 1986): 60–61.

Vigil, Peter J. "End-User Training: The Systems Approach." In *National Online Meeting Proceedings—1984,* comp. by Martha E. Williams and Thomas H. Hogan, 419–24. Medford, N.J.: Learned Information, 1984.

Wood, Sandra M., Bonnie Snow, and Ellen Brassil Horak. "End User Searching in the Health Sciences." *Medical Reference Services Quarterly* 5 (Summer 1986): Special issue.

Woolpy, Sara, and Nancy Taylor. "Enduser Searching: A Study of Manual vs. Online Searching by Endusers and the Role of the Intermediary." In *Online '84 Conference Proceedings,* edited by Jean Paul Emard, 243–45. Weston, Conn.: Online, Inc., 1984.

Chapter 2

Starting an End-User Service

Ida B. Lowe

Once a proposal for an end-user service is accepted, the challenge facing staff responsible for the proposal is implementing it. Setting up and managing an end-user service or program are multifaceted processes that can vary amongst different institutions and individuals. Discussed here are some components of these processes that are common to institutions, such as establishing policies and procedures; selecting hardware, software, and services; marketing and promotion; and support programs such as training. Evaluating each of these components is the main part of managing an end-user service.

Setting up an end-user service or program that is responsive to patron needs and interests requires the use of surveys and questionnaires, which serve the multiple purposes of helping staff identify the size, composition, and level of interest of the potential market audience. This audience may be narrow and consist of patrons who use a business, health, science, law, or other specialized library; or this audience may be broad and consist of an entire university, college, or community population. The market audience may be composed of researchers and students with access to equipment; researchers with subject expertise; or the general public with a need for specific information or with a curiosity about online searching. The broad question is to determine the most suitable database for your institution. *Dow Jones News/Retrieval* might be appropriate for a business school, and *Sci-Mate* for a science library.

When considering the various end-user services you can subscribe to, you should keep in mind the following questions: How easy are the systems to use? How satisfied are patrons with such systems? Do they provide access to the information needed? Ease of use is related to the demands the system places on the library staff for assisting users. Costs must include the costs to the library aside from staff time, including those of passwords on the service(s) selected; online time for in-house training; and books, journal subscriptions, and teaching materials. Other costs include those of microcomputers, modems, software and phone lines, and staff to assist with logon and equipment use and maintenance.

The surveys and questionnaires should also be used to determine patrons' level of interest in online searching in general and in doing their own searching in particular. These surveys can show if potential end users are interested in conducting their own searches. They can indicate whether or not information seekers have been increasingly exposed to online searches as well as to the marketing efforts of search services and database producers. Surveys can also show whether patrons have complaints about intermediaries not always being within easy reach or about a search taking too long due to an overloaded information department. In addition, surveys can document whether or not users show a preference for the convenience and speed of searching directly for discrete information needs. Finally, surveys can document whether patrons are interested in individual contracts with the various databanks.

Undertaking an assessment of market audience, needs, and interests early in the implementation of a new end-user service or program will contribute to successfully identifying the types of service programs that are best suited to the library's patrons. Failing to undertake such an assessment will result in decisions based only on the reference librarian's point of view.

POLICIES AND PROCEDURES

Policies and procedures must be formulated before the service is implemented. In this section, the policies and procedures common to most online search services will be discussed. All policy statements must determine who may search, types of searches, and reimbursement of costs.

Who can search depends on whom the library serves. It is much easier to control usage in an academic or special library than in a public library, and this is probably the reason why end-user programs have flourished in the former environments. It is useful to spell out the groups of users qualified by training for online access. At Baruch College, access to *Dow Jones* is open to all students, faculty, and staff, while access to *DIALOG* and *BRS* is open only to faculty and graduate students. In order to qualify for use of direct-access databases such as *DIALOG, BRS,* and *Orbit,* attendance at an introductory workshop should be mandatory. This requirement is necessary, in part, to avoid the tremendous expense that can be incurred if a novice is allowed to access these databases in an undirected, futile search. However, time and personnel constraints can make it very hard to schedule and provide basic training for all interested users, so it may be better to allow untrained users access to simpler-to-use services such as *Dow Jones News/Retrieval,* which provides good search aids and tutorial diskettes.

Appropriate end-user searches should be defined. End-user searching can be carried out successfully when there is a need for specific information, such as an author's name, a stock quote, an annual report, a title, a specific chemical compound, etc. End users should perform subject searches when only a few answers are required. Comprehensive searches should be discouraged. In fact, when a thorough subject search is required, an intermediary should be consulted. If the search is on a specific subject requiring expertise in the field, and the patron's knowledge of a subject is so comprehensive that there is no time for explaining the request to an intermediary, the search may be performed by the end user, in consultation with the intermediary.

Some of the other common policies and procedures concern password distribution, time and searching limitations, patron responsibility and agreement forms, payment, strategy approval, and scheduling. A discussion of each of these areas follows. Should passwords be freely distributed to anyone requesting one, or should they be closely controlled? Control of passwords is absolutely imperative. When passwords are given out, patrons must sign an agreement in which each party's responsibilities for expenses incurred and for proper usage are outlined. In an environment where equipment and support are readily available, passwords are entered in the software programs and hidden from the users. If an end user expresses an interest in doing searching at home from his or her own microcomputer, encourage the user to get his or her own subscription. Offer all the support needed in terms of contact people, services available, costs, hardware and software needed, and, of course, training, but do not deal with uncontrolled environments (i.e., when online searching is done outside the library, the library is not responsible).

The number of searches a patron is entitled to during a specified period of time, the amount of time a user can stay online, and the number of citations retrieved must also be clearly spelled out. Good rules of thumb to follow include limiting users to one search per day, two searches per week, and 30 minutes per search, and forbidding offline printouts. Time online may also be limited if there is a lineup of patrons waiting to use services that the library subscribes to as opposed to services for which patrons have their own passwords.

Some libraries have devised a "patron agreement form" in which the library's policies and user's responsibilities are outlined. Patrons must sign this form before using the service. This waiver might include a warning to the effect that end-user systems have certain limitations, and that if patrons wish, they may progress to more capable systems with the use of intermediaries later. When a fee for the service is involved, these forms are necessary. Patron agreement forms can also be used to keep statistics on systems and database usage.

Any library intending to offer end-user searching needs to devise regulations for payment that are suited to its own operating environment. Key points in these regulations for may include requiring users to be familiar with the fee structure; requiring users to surrender an ID card to ensure that they will pay for their searches, and not just dash off with the printout; requiring payment in the form of cash only; allowing payment by check with one or more forms of currently validated identification; etc.

Last, libraries may also elect to require that users have their strategy approved or discussed with a librarian before the search and in the event of an unsuccessful search. At the very least, this service should be made available on an optional basis.

Scheduling of end-user searching is necessary to ensure appropriate staff support and equipment availability, as well as to provide control over usage and expenses. The existence of scheduling policies and procedures contributes to the efficient operation of the service or program. Sign-up sheets are an easy way to schedule appointments. For instance, patrons can sign up in person beginning at 8:00 a.m. for that day only and appointments for the weekend can be made starting Friday at 8:00 a.m. Online sessions can be scheduled for every 30 minutes, with the user typically spending about 20 minutes online. If a patron is more than 10 minutes late, the appointment will need to be rescheduled. This set-up is the most efficient and least time consuming. When consultation with a professional librarian is needed, appointments can be scheduled ahead of time, over the telephone or in person. This set-up will vary depending on the level of support, type of online systems, and services offered to end users.

STAFFING

While nearly all service or program proposals include a discussion of staff needed, provide a list of people responsible for carrying out the proposal, and document the qualifications of those involved, they often do little more. Administrators implementing these proposals must review the staffing requirements and specific staff proposed, must outline specific responsibilities of such staff, and must plan for the impact that increases in staff workload will have on the institution.

Increases in staff workload can be expected with the addition of any new reference or information service. It is often reference or other public service staffs who provide the general assistance and training. The workload of this staff is thus a factor that influences the ease and time required to set up and maintain an end-user search service or program. The time commitment for seminars, workshops, and demonstrations, for example, may range from twice during the academic year to once per month. In academic libraries, graduate student employees often contribute to the provision of general support by reference or other public service staff. In public and school libraries, library assistants or other employees who are familiar with microcomputers or trained in their use contribute to the provision of general assistance and training.

The reference staff has two major responsibilities regarding end-user programs: general assistance and training. These functions are fundamentally no different from the traditional reference role. Tasks such as record keeping, system security, basic system instruction, and advice regarding database content are essentially already performed at the reference desk, and can be performed by non-professional staff or even by adept students. The areas requiring additional expertise—and therefore more staff training—are specific system and database structure, and search strategy formulation. These tasks rely more heavily on professional staff with online skills.

When in-house equipment is available, at least one staff member must be posted at the workstation because end users generally require assistance before, during, and after searching. (Allocating staff can be difficult during evening and weekend hours, when most end-user searching is done.) The staff member can be either a professional librarian or a non-professional employee familiar with microcomputers. Besides assisting end users with their searches, logging onto the system, and acting as a troubleshooter for common problems, the staff member must monitor proper equipment functioning, make sure that the appropriate forms (patron's agreement, log sheet, evaluation, etc.) are filled out and statistics collected, and refer users to others when necessary. The time the staff needs to devote to these activities will eventually decline as patrons become more knowledgeable and systems become more user friendly, but the intermediary will always be needed for consultation and training— tasks the library has always had.

It is advisable, money and personnel permitting, to create a unit responsible for the service in particular, and online systems in general. Sometimes called "Computerized Information Services," this unit would handle all the managerial aspects (budgeting, staffing, training, purchasing equipment, etc.) concomitant with overseeing any new and growing program.

HARDWARE, SOFTWARE, AND SERVICE SELECTION

The minimum equipment required for an end-user workstation is a printer, terminal, modem, and telephone line. The best alternative is a personal computer with at least 256K of memory and a double disk drive. Such a system offers versatility, and its hard disk lets you store in one place all the programs and passwords needed for online searching, allowing you to avoid the hassle of dealing with numerous diskettes. A fast modem, 1200 or even 2400 baud, will lower communication costs. The printer need not be letter quality, but it should be fast, again at least 1200 baud, and as quiet as possible, particularly if the workstation is located in a public area. It is advisable to get an internal modem and some kind of security pad or enclosure to prevent theft and vandalism.

Workstations should be housed in appropriate sites, which should be selected during the early planning stages. Workstations can be located in either the main library, the branch library, or even in a non-library such as a computer center or dormitory. Next the in-house location should be considered. Should the stations be put in an isolated area, or be placed near the existing reference desk? Should online terminals be placed next to CD-ROM and videodisc services, thus creating an automated reference area?

It is very practical to establish one area that can accommodate all end-user searching, instruction, and training. This area should also be able to handle additional equipment, such as an overhead projector, a blackboard, and a computer projector with a parabolic screen for better image resolution. The computer projector is particularly useful in demonstrating the instructor's progress through software packages and online searches, as it displays the instructor's screen.

Besides the hardware and software needed for online searching, each site should be equipped with the appropriate number of electrical outlets and telephone lines, preferable with direct access, i.e., a line that does not go through a central exchange.

Librarians can assist end users by directing them to gateways and front-ends that allow users to bypass the specific differences of database systems, command languages, vocabularies, and access protocols. Advances in technology are making it easier for end users to gather their own information online. Several products and services have been introduced to the online searching market, featuring offline selection of appropriate databases and search strategy formulation, as well as software interpretation and the reformatting of search statements into command strings acceptable to the database vendor. The best-known programs are *ProSearch* (Menlo Corporation), *Wilsearch* (H.W. Wilson), *Sci-Mate* (Institute for Scientific Information), and *Searchmaster* (SDC). Also, both DIALOG and BRS offer low-cost evening access aimed directly at end users (*Knowledge Index* and *BRS After Dark,* respectively). These front-end and gateway programs not only simplify the search interface, but they also allow end users to plan their search offline without worrying about online costs: users can even have the search reviewed by the librarian before going online. Basic communications software usually includes the following features: offline search strategy formulation, or uploading; automatic dial-up and logon procedures, including storing and masking of passwords, allowing librarians to avoid the problem of issuing passwords to end users; modification of preliminary search results; immediate offline printing of results, or downloading; and ease of programming batch files to reduce logging on to a system, such as by pressing one key. *Smartcom* and *Crosstalk,* the most popular communications programs, offer all these features.

MARKETING AND PROMOTION

The implementation of a new end-user service or program requires the development of a marketing plan. The purpose of this plan is to ensure the success of the new product, i.e., end-user searching. The components of the plan must include the following: (1) a description of the current online information services, (2) a statement of goals and objectives, (3) the overall strategy and specific action programs for achieving the goals, (4) budgets, and (5) controls to be applied to monitor the plan's progress.

There are four main variables that influence the customer's acceptance or rejection of a project: (1) the product itself, (2) the place or location where it is available, (3) the price, and (4) the promotion or advertising. All of these variables require allocation of resources to favorably influence the customer's decision. The product is end-user searching, but the level of service and support will affect the nature of the product. The place should be easily accessible to users of the library, convenient to consulting staff, and offer an efficient and pleasant environment to work in. The price can be calculated to recover costs. However, at least in the beginning, the library should never consider offering this service free or at a minimal heavily subsidized fee. Finally, the introduction of a new library service requires some promotional activity. The level and intensity of promotion usually depend on the amount of support the service requires and on the resources available. Promotion should be directed at those groups you expect to provide a better response. Flyers are generally posted in the library, as well as sent to specific target groups.

Caution should be maintained in promoting end-user services, because you could quickly become a victim of your own success and have demand exceeding the ability to deliver. You want to make sure that you can handle the demand, and give the supporting staff a chance to learn what to expect. At the beginning, promotion should therefore be limited. Most libraries have found that word of mouth, together with the training workshops, has been enough to get the program going.

PROGRAM SUPPORT

Setting up an end-user service or program also involves creating appropriate documentation and providing appropriate training. End-user documentation consists of two basic types of materials. The first type of material concerns the online systems and is generally available from vendors and database producers. The second type of user documentation concerns the library's specific set-up and must be developed locally.

Reference guides to each service must be available at each workstation. Many systems have developed short and simple guides summarizing systems features, such as how to get on the systems, basic commands, database coverage, etc. Multiple copies of these guides are usually available at very little or no cost to subscribers. Whenever vendor documentation is available, use it. You can also create your own search planners, which should include illustrations of Boolean logic, search tips, examples of search strategies, and basic troubleshooting advice. Handouts on the library's policies and how to use the available equipment also have to be developed locally. Focus on clear and well-presented handouts; they should be simple to follow and written in step-by-step format, starting with how to turn the machine on and what keys to press to get on a system, and describing basic commands, printing functions, downloading to a disk, and logging off. It is very helpful to include an illustration of the terminal keyboard, pointing out such things as how to backspace and the location of the "enter" key. Policy statements should clearly outline the services available to end users; requirements for using them, appointment scheduling, forms to be filled out, user responsibilities, etc.

At Baruch College, copies of all materials are stored on diskettes, making it easy to edit, update, and reproduce materials at any time. Hard copies are available at the reference desk and at the end-user station. The college also has copies of selected articles on online searching in general, and on specific services, for those patrons who would like to read more about it.

Planning for the initial training of librarians and for the ongoing training of end users is an essential component of setting up a quality end-user service or program. Any library considering offering an end-user search service should encourage librarians to practice online before service start-up. Training should be required of both librarians with online experience and of those with little or no previous searching experience. Training seminars or sessions should be followed by the opportunity to run practice searches on the system—on different databases—in order to become sufficiently familiar with system content and search protocols. Librarians who are aware of the intricacies of the system before service start-up will be much better prepared to assist end users in pre- and postsearch counseling or when they run into difficulties online.

Planning for the ongoing training of end users cannot be ignored in the early stages of service or program implementation decision making. Today, users need to know something about system features, commands, and databases in order to obtain consistently good and reliable results as discussed earlier.

The training process is the subject of Chapter 3. Suffice it to say here that training does not replace the counseling role described in Chapter 1. That role consists of presearch and postsearch counseling. The librarian needs to build the end user's confidence by being a careful, helpful advisor and explaining all the steps of the search process. During a presearch interview, the librarian not only should encourage the end user who wants to perform his or her own search, but also screen searches that are very complex and should be performed, at least initially, by a librarian. This type of presearch counseling should be available both to patrons who are going to perform a search in the library on library equipment and to patrons who will be doing searches on their own equipment outside the library.

The librarian should also provide postsearch counseling. The end user must be given guidelines to evaluate the efficiency and effectiveness of the search performed. When the instructor-student relationship is established between the librarian and the end user, the library is no longer seen as only a repository of information and the librarian as the locator of information. The library, instead, becomes an active learning center, and the librarian the teacher of technical and decision-making skills that are needed for independent information retrieval.

One of the most important components of effectively managing an end-user service or program is evaluation, the method of which should be planned for at the proposal stage, as stated in Chapter 1. There is little doubt that the introduction of a new program such as end-user searching can have a profound effect on the organization. Therefore, continuous assessment of the programs and services is a required function in all organizations. Evaluation of the program must be carried out by surveying not only users, but librarians and staff as well. Appraisal instruments must be designed to measure patron and staff satisfaction, and to collect feedback that can be used to improve the program. The following data should be gathered by means of questionnaires filled out by patrons and staff, and a log kept by the supervisor:

1. Statistics on usage, consisting of demographics of users, class level, major field of study, age, sex, purpose of the search, prior computer experience, prior searching experience, prior library experience;
2. Statistics on patterns of use, i.e., date, starting time, length of session, resources used (e.g., databases, vendors, systems), and citations retrieved;
3. Assessment of user satisfaction with the system, training, documentation, and general support; and
4. Assessment of user independence, i.e., time spent with supervisor and types of questions asked by user.

These evaluations, coupled with logs of users, will provide valuable insight into end-user searching patterns. Evaluation studies to date have shown that end users can search with some success, albeit not at the levels of efficiency and comprehensiveness provided by professionally mediated searches. Although end users reported having relatively easy search experiences, professional staff indicated that considerable assistance was required for a search to be successful. In general, staff indicated that end users were able to deal with the more friendly systems after a minimal amount of experience, and the ratings on difficulty experienced declined with repeated usage.

BIBLIOGRAPHY

Arnold, S. "End Users: Old Myths and New Realities." In *National Online Meeting Proceedings—1986,* comp. by Martha E. Williams and Thomas H. Hogan, 5-10. Medford, N.J.: Learned Information, 1986.

Association of Research Libraries. Office of Management Studies. Systems and Procedures Exchange Center. *End-User Searching Services.* Kit 122. Washington, D.C.: ARL, 1986.

Corcoran, M., R. Copeland, and D. Clayton. "Subject Specialists Searching Chemical Abstracts on SDC." In *Proceedings of the 43rd ASIS Annual Meeting,* 345-47. White Plains, N.Y.: Knowledge Industry, 1980.

Dodd, J., C. Gilreath, and G. Hutchins. *Final Report from the Public Services Research Projects—Texas A&M University: A Comparison of Two End User-Operated Search Systems.* Washington, D.C.: Assn. of Research Libraries, Office of Management Studies, 1985. ERIC ED 255 224

Gordon, D. W. *"Online Training for the End User or Information Consumer."* (Paper presented at the mid-year meeting of the American Society for Information Science, Lexington, Ky., May 1983). ERIC ED 245 697

Eisenberg, M. *The Direct Use of Online Bibliographic Information Systems by Untrained End Users: A Review of Research.* Washington, D.C.: National Institute of Education, 1983. ERIC ED 238 440

Evans, N., and H. Pisciotta. "Search Helper: Testing Acceptance of a Gateway Software System." In *National Online Meeting Proceedings—1985,* comp. by Martha E. Williams and Thomas H. Hogan, 131–36. Medford, N.J.: Learned Information, 1985.

Haines, J. S. "Experiences in Training end User Searchers." *Online* 6 (1982): 14.

Hubbard, A., and B. Wilson. "An Integrated Information Management Education Program...Defining a New Role for Librarians in Helping End Users." *Online* 10 (1986): 15–23.

Hunter, J. A. "What Did You Say the End-User Was Going to Do at the Terminal, and How Much Is It Going to Cost?" In *National Online Meeting Proceedings—1983,* comp. by Martha E. Williams and Thomas H. Hogan, 223–29. Medford, N.J.: Learned Information, 1983.

_____. "When Your Patrons Want to Search—The Library as Advisor to End-users...A Compendium of Advice and Tips." *Online* 8 (1984): 36–41.

Kirk, C. L. "End-User Training at the Amoco Research Center." *Special Libraries* 77 (1986): 20–27.

Ojala, M. "End User Searching and Its Implications for Librarians." *Special Libraries* 76 (1985): 93–99.

Richardson, R. J. "End User Online Searching in a High Technology Engineering Environment." *Online* 5 (1981) 44.

Walton, K. R., and P. L. Dedert. "Experiences at Exxon in Training End-Users to Search Technical Databases Online." *Online* 7 (1983) 42–50.

Chapter 3

Training End Users

Laura M. Osegueda

As a consequence of increasing end-user activity, librarians can expect greater demand for their services, including assisted online searching and document delivery. Librarians can play the roles of consultants, guides and facilitators, and instructors. As consultants, librarians serve as experts who can perform the more difficult searches and who are up to date on developments in the information field that affect the end user's needs. As guides and facilitators, librarians work closely with faculty, academic departments, campus computer centers, or other personnel to ensure that people use end-user searching to its full potential. One of the most significant roles librarians play is that of instructor, for, clearly, the groundwork for end-user searching is laid in classes, workshops, or tutorials taught by librarians, and then reinforced by printed guides, computer-assisted instruction, and other materials developed by librarians.

This chapter focuses on the role the library and librarians take in educating and updating end users. In particular, the components of training are discussed. The discussion begins with the initial task of planning. Factors such as user and librarian motivation are highlighted as part of the planning process. The determination of the library's role in the training of end users is established as an important component of the planning process. A variety of roles and levels of training are described and accompanied by considerations of market audience skills and training needs, and cost and level of support for training available to the library. Developing aims and objectives for the training programs is also considered. In addition, the factors influencing the level of training provided are noted. The chapter reviews several instructional techniques and includes a short selection on evaluating training. General tips for training end users and the benefits of developing a library-based end-user training program are highlighted in the conclusion.

THE CONTEXT OF PLANNING

Planning is a time-consuming process, and therefore it is important to have a rationale for everyone involved in the process. The desire to reduce the cost of searches is a major reason for training end users, but it is a reason that offers benefits to users and to the library as well. Benefits to the library of a training program include: (1) rewarding users who supported the online search service since its inception; (2) broadening an institution's base of users by responding to expressed or perceived needs; (3) improving and enhancing the library's image and the librarian's role; (4) economizing on librarians' time by decreasing their workload, which increases when they mediate searches; (5) convincing faculty of the benefits of bibliographic instruction; and (6) taking advantage of the presence of the microcomputer in the workplace, school, and home. A training program can benefit users by dispelling computer anxiety; introducing a new, fun, and fast element to bibliographic instructional sessions; and simply saving time spent in research.

Structuring the planning process involves designating who will be responsible for decisions about training. Responsibility can fall under the scope of an existing library committee or special interest group on bibliographic instruction, online searching, or reference services. A new ad hoc or permanent committee or special interest group can be created to assume planning responsibilities. Depending on the organization of the library and its size, planners can be drawn from one library unit, division, or department, or include personnel representing diverse areas of the library. Staff with search intermediary, search consultant, or online searching experience are helpful resource persons, but the library may wish to include those with no searching skills as well. Generally, it is helpful to have several people work on the planning portion of an end-user training program in order to share responsibilities, spread out the time taken from each regular job assignment, represent diverse library groups and interests, and consider the various needs of users to be trained.

Assessing what physical library resources can be devoted to the project is the next step of the planning process. What kinds of equipment and facilities can be devoted to the project? What kinds of technical, audiovisual, and bibliographic instruction support services are available?

Following the assessment of the library's own ability to support the project, external human and financial support should be cultivated. If the library has started out with a minimal training program, it should try to obtain additional support by setting up local user groups and by contacting corporations. Funding sources to explore include university minigrants and state library LSCA funds. Successfully developing support requires that the coordinators of the training program keep abreast of new technologies, including system and database changes, software upgrades, and new search systems as they become available. The library may need to subscribe to a few computer-related instructional or training journals for staff. Setting up a network of knowledgeable contacts to call on to answer questions about the search system, equipment, and search strategies, and to serve as referrals for information not available in the library provides support to both program coordinators and librarian consultants. Key contacts may include customer service people for the search system, database producers, computing center or library systems staff, or any staff experienced with troubleshooting to save the expense of a service call.

Knowing the skills and training needs of potential end users is clearly an essential aspect of planning the implementation of any service. Finding out skills and needs can be achieved by administering a survey to library patrons, but the survey must be so structured as to reveal the intellectual interests of patrons and especially their level of computer "literacy" (including familiarity with bibliographic databases). The results of the survey will be a major help in deciding what materials to include in training sessions and the length of each session.

Considering the training needs and practice time for library staff involved in training for the first time or when introducing a new system is as important a factor in the planning process as assessing the skills and training needs of end users. Libraries need to allow for the online costs and time involved for staff to learn how to use and experiment with the various end-user services so that these staff members will be better able to instruct end users effectively.

Planning must also encompass an allocation of staff time for mediated searches. Although the installation of an end-user service will lessen the role of the librarian as search intermediary, that role will not be eliminated. There will also be patrons who do not wish to conduct a search themselves, and some complicated searches will require the assistance of a specialist.

SETTING THE OBJECTIVES OF TRAINING

Thus far, the planning process has been discussed in contextual terms. The next step in this process is a critical one—identifying the objectives of the training program. The objectives for establishing an end-user search are not the same as those for the training program. For example, the former might aim to enable untrained users to perform specific, cost-effective searches of bibliographic databases without the assistance of intermediaries and provide enhanced access to the periodical collection which comprises a significant portion of the library's collection and is not accessible via the online catalog. On the other hand, the goals for the training program will concern specific goals for end users, for instance, to teach students skills and concepts necessary for searching bibliographic databases and ones which they can transfer to other online systems and approach them with confidence; to evaluate the effectiveness of the program in achieving its objectives.

Identifying training objectives begins with the level of training the library would like to provide. Fjallbrant breaks down online instruction into two levels; orientation and instruction. Orientation generally acquaints the user with computerized retrieval systems, various services, and databases, and how to get access to these systems. Instruction teaches the user in detail how to carry out computerized information retrieval.[1] There is also an intermediate level concerned with teaching users enough about online searching so that they know how to access online systems, how to conceptualize a computer search, and how to choose amongst possible search strategies without having the more comprehensive knowledge of the expert searcher. Three factors must be considered to determine what level of training to provide: (1) what search system to select, (2) audience composition and motivation, and (3) the staff time available for instruction.

Training end users has been simplified by the introduction of searching software and other front-end systems. These items provide menu-driven searching and a single set of commands for searching several systems. Front-end systems have made access easier for the user with respect to knowing search protocols for specific systems, but more progress is needed in providing simple instruction in search strategy and Boolean logic. If these techniques and principles are obvious to the user, searching will be easy. However, if no information is provided to make the user aware of search strategies and of the underlying organization of a system, the library may wish to supplement system documentation to prevent errors, wasted search time, and user misconceptions. Generally, the simpler systems take less time to learn to use.

The second set of factors to consider are the varying computer search needs and motivations of the market audience. Young and inexperienced computer users will need more time than experienced users to become proficient in online searching. Microcomputer users may know about their machines, the mechanics of downloading, and using a modem for access to remote sources, yet they still may need instruction in search strategy formulation and search commands. Research needs of users may vary from wanting to keep up in broad areas of interest and finding references for term papers on a wide variety of topics to tracking financial information for personal investments. The motivation to learn about online searching also varies. Microcomputer owners may want to expand the use of their computers. Some faculty members, less familiar with new technologies, may see online searching as a less threatening way to learn something about computers. Others may want to cut down on the time spent on library research, and still others like the flexibility and independence end-user searching offers.

The third factor in determining what level of training to provide is the amount of time given to the librarian by teachers (for class-related instruction) and by library administrators. In general, the greater the time allotted the librarian, the more detailed, advanced, and comprehensive the level of training. In an experiment with biology students at Stanford University, a great deal of variation in lecture content was pointed out, with a bare minimum of 20 minutes devoted to lecturing as compared with two hours of class time.[2] An experiment in a Pennsylvania high school showed a large amount of time (over 40 hours) devoted by one librarian to training students using the BRS search service.[3] Sufficient time must be set aside to introduce users to the basics of online searching as well as to provide an overview of search mechanics. End users will then be equipped with sufficient knowledge to explore online services on their own, reinforcing what has been learned through training.

After deciding what level of training to provide, the library should then select the training methods to use in orientation and instruction. Training aids at the orientation level may include: brochures and other promotional materials from database vendors and producers; library-produced handouts or information packets containing comparisons of various systems (databases available, costs, hours available for use, etc.); bibliographies of current books and magazine articles, and of equipment needed to access online systems; transparencies, slide/tape programs, or videotapes to be used with training sessions or made available in library media departments for self-paced instruction; one-to-one consultations; short library workshops; information fairs; and lectures or demonstrations given in conjunction with existing library instruction. Training options at the instruction level may include: purchased materials, including books, system manuals, database thesauri, and brochures; customized materials developed by the library; slide/tape or videotape programs; instructional manuals, signs, or flipcharts located near end-user systems; workbooks; computer-assisted instruction; individualized instruction; workshops and seminars; simulations of online searches; lectures or demonstrations; and course-based instruction.

Generally, given the limited amount of time most librarians have, successful training programs must have well-defined objectives, provide information in a manner that is suitable and comfortable for the library and the user, and include some type of framework or model in order for the user to know how and where end-user search systems fit into his or her information needs. The Direct Patron Access Committee of the Machine-Assisted Reference Section (MARS) of the Reference and Adult Services Division (RASD) of the American Library Association has prepared an excellent set of objectives for user education in online systems.[4] These objectives are broad enough to be applicable to all types of libraries and may be used both for classroom or individual instruction as well as in the development of instructional materials. This document has been reprinted as an appendix to this chapter.

THE DESIGN OF THE TRAINING

Within the three levels of training, librarians may fashion particular roles. Not all of these roles are active. Some of the role options from which librarians may choose include search advisor, search liaison, search consultant, and search trainer. As a search advisor, the librarian serves as an advisor to end users, providing advice and tips. This is probably the most passive approach and might take place at the library reference desk. As a search liaison between end users and online services, the librarian basically passes the "training buck" to the online services. The librarian may also serve as the liaison between end users and local libraries that have the time and expertise for training, or between end users and local computer stores who will, no doubt, be glad to greet potential customers. As a search consultant, the librarian actively assists users in the use of online systems. Printed materials can be made available to users and include systems manuals, database thesauri, step-by-step instructions for using various online systems, brochures, flipcharts, and other handouts. If computer equipment is available in the library, staff may be stationed at terminals to aid end users before, during, or after their search. As a search trainer, the librarian can teach users to perform their own online searches. Training, in the form of new workshops, lectures, slide/tape programs, classes for credit, and so on, may be integrated into current bibliographic instruction services or developed separately. Printed instructions can be incorporated into already existing printed materials, or new ones may be developed. Individual instruction may be scheduled by appointment or be made available on demand. Resources available will influence the choice of training roles, with their attendant systems and learning materials. Needs of library users will determine which system(s) to include in instruction. Because budgetary limitations placed on many libraries require end-user systems to be self supporting yet provide access to as many users as possible, administrative support is essential to subsidize the end-user training program. Academic libraries may work with campus departments to use pre-existing computer facilities for training sessions and to share some of the costs of training. Some libraries have purchased equipment to have in the library for users. However, it is possible to instruct users without providing equipment. There is no reason why starting an end-user training program need be outrageously expensive. Costs will depend on the type of training planned (individual instruction, workshops, lectures, course-based instruction, CAI, AV programming), equipment needed, database search subscriptions required, personnel costs, etc.

ACTIVE TRAINING ROLES

The remainder of this discussion describes the more active training roles and the level of library participation, as well as the costs related to each method. Examples of actual library programs are also provided for purposes of illustration. The training methodologies discussed are individualized instruction; group instruction in the form of workshops, lectures, and demonstrations; full-length courses; programmed instruction; and audiovisual instruction.

Individualized instruction is more personal than other methods. For example, over the past eleven years, librarians working with medical researchers in the School of Pharmacy and the Department of Pathology at the University of Maryland have provided individual instruction at terminals located within the school and work areas but not in the library.[5] Individualized instruction requires staff knowledgeable in online systems and in microcomputer applications; such instruction can be time intensive for staff on a continual basis. Hands-on practice with end users provides more tangible experience for students. Performing online searches with the user present is another way to begin instructing library users about online searching. If the librarians are not knowledgeable in certain areas, it is important either to obtain additional training or to limit consultations to particular systems and subjects. In order to keep control of the time, some librarians set up consultation appointments. This method can also assist in the evaluation of the service by providing a record of the amount of time spent on the service.[6] Besides staff time, other costs for individual instruction can be incurred. The library may need to purchase additional books on computer searching and additional system manuals for services not available in the library. The library also may need to develop supporting instructional materials and guides. These guides should provide quick, relevant instruction for the user. Their format may vary, but the content should be concise, clear, and free of library and computer jargon. Library-produced materials require planning and preparation time. In-house graphics, and layout and design talents are especially helpful. Libraries should also consider the costs of paper, printing, and copying, as well as budget for reprinting and revisions.

Workshops, lectures, and demonstrations may be customized to a particular group, but the basic content of the session may be replicated in full or in part for a variety of groups. Workshops may be offered in a series, with each session lasting about one to two hours. Options for longer training time include full-day seminars or half-day workshops. The level of these sessions can range from an introduction to using a microcomputer or searching online databases, to instruction in the use of a particular search service, or an overview of online search strategies and advanced sessions on databases in certain subject areas. When possible, it is best to allow students time to become acquainted with searching by performing their own searches as part of the training process. Simulated searches can also provide good experience for the beginner. Lectures and demonstrations are usually incorporated into regular library instructional sessions given to research and technical writing classes. Lecture content may be developed for a group of academic or school classes, providing a wide variety of search examples to cover all subject areas, or it may be general and leave discussion of the subject-related material to the librarian giving the lecture. If possible, librarians should involve classroom teachers in the development of content, scope, and specific examples used in the lecture in order to tie the online instruction sessions to the rest of the class. Collaborative planning will provide the librarian with an idea of the course objectives, as well as allow the students to draw upon what they have learned throughout the course. Research methods classes and courses dealing with computer applications in a particular discipline have most successfully incorporated end-user search training effectively.[7]

Cost factors involved with workshops, lectures, and demonstrations include staff time to develop the content of the sessions, the length of training, instructional materials used, AV supplies, handouts, flyers, and evaluation materials. It is useful to note that several online vendors will supply free time for online demonstrations. Costs for developing and inserting an online component into existing library instruction sessions are similar to those encountered when offering introductory workshops but may involve more librarians and more sessions; therefore, costs for materials would increase, but initial planning and some instructional materials can be used for several courses.

Several academic libraries, including those at Penn State, San Jose State University, and California Polytechnic University, have offered complete courses in online searching for non-library school students.[8] These courses range from a short three- to four-week session to a quarter- or semester-long course. Courses may be offered in the School of Library

Science, be cross-listed in several departments, be sponsored by one school or department other than Library Science, be offered in a public library to the community through adult or continuing education programs. Some courses provide an introduction to a wide variety of systems after providing general information about databases and file structure. It may be easier to focus training on one system while making available an introduction to a variety of other systems. Courses are quite time consuming for the instructor with respect to planning lectures, assignments, and tests. Alternatively, sessions may be team taught to cut down on the time spent by each individual. Advantages of more in-depth course-based instruction include the abilities to introduce conceptual material, build on knowledge, and allow the user more practice. By offering academic credit, enrollment may be boosted and content may be considered more academic by the school administration, which, in turn, may increase the status of the library and librarians. Librarians teaching such courses must have a sound knowledge of course development and be skilled in giving lectures, leading discussions, and preparing course assignments.

Some libraries are able to absorb the cost of staff time and materials, and also to provide the librarian with release time. Additional costs are involved for handouts, AV materials, and online connect time. Some librarians have received additional money for teaching these courses, and departments offering the courses have shared expenses for equipment, supplies, and facilities. DIALOG and BRS both provide reduced rates for instructional programs through their *Classroom Instruction* and *Classmate* programs (DIALOG) and special *Instructor* password (BRS).

Library workbooks and computer-assisted instruction (CAI) programs are examples of programmed instruction that are particularly useful in libraries where there are few librarians and many interested end users. Workbooks are already used in some university library instruction programs to provide introductory library information. Additional sections may be inserted, or a workbook can be rewritten to incorporate computerized information sources. CAI is used in several academic, governmental, and industrial organizations to teach end users how to search.[9] Programs may be developed to simulate an online search and may be general in scope or adapted for the online searching of specific subjects. This form of instruction offers many advantages. CAI can be effective if: (1) the online system is fairly stable, requiring minimal, if any, large changes; (2) users are geographically dispersed; (3) turnover rate is high; (4) varied learning rates characterize the audience; (5) scheduling training time is difficult for users and for the library staff; or (6) teaching student progress is an important and time-consuming task. The time needed to write a CAI program as well as the expense involved may prevent libraries from using this method of instruction. Librarians need skills in developing curriculums as well as with drill and practice or simulation programs. Besides staff time, equipment costs and the costs of revisions need to be considered. Libraries may also wish to consider whether it would be more cost effective to incorporate a section on online searching within a general library program or in conjunction with online catalog training. One of the pioneering CAI programs for online searching, *Search Trainer,* was developed at George Mason University to train university faculty how to use *DIALOG, BRS* and *BRS After Dark.*[10] Texas A & M has modified *Search Trainer* for introducing *BRS After Dark* to their library users.[11] Memphis State University has designed another CAI program for end users on the Apple IIe microcomputer.[12] Several authoring systems and simulation programs are available to assist in writing computer-assisted instruction programs. Other options for computer-based instruction include a low-cost demonstration diskette for *Knowledge Index* available from DIALOG and encouraging end users to practice search techniques on databases purchased by the library on CD-ROM before attempting searches online.

Audiovisual materials such as transparencies and slide/tape and videotape programs can be used effectively to illustrate online concepts and to demonstrate search strategies and online search techniques. Audiovisuals are helpful in illustrating the search process, especially when one is dealing with large groups or if the library does not have equipment or money for an online demonstration. These materials can also be available to library users on demand and can assist in training large end-user populations in busy or understaffed libraries. The School of Medicine at the University of Maryland, for example, has developed a videotape for the *MiniMedline* system.[13] Both BRS and Wilsonline have videotapes that provide introductions to online searching specifically geared to instruction on their systems, and Learned Information markets a videotape that provides a general introduction to online searching. For online demonstrations, Kodak recently introduced *Data Show,* a projection unit that connects to a computer monitor and, along with an overhead projector, can project an online search session on a large screen. *Data Show* is very competitively priced and sells for $1200. Staff time for audiovisuals varies depending on the method used. Staff preparation time for transparencies is low when compared with that needed for other formats. In contrast, effective slide/tape and videotape programs require a great deal of preparation time and have a higher equipment cost. Costs of updating these programs need also to be considered.

Whatever training method is selected, the training program must be effectively marketed. There are a variety of ways to market training programs, including flyers, posters, newspaper articles or announcements, public service announcements on radio or television, and personal contact. Training a select group of end users before promoting the program to all library users is one way to effectively introduce end-user training. Another option is to begin with faculty members, as they often have access to microcomputers. In school libraries, selected classes or groups of students have been used. By focusing marketing on one particular group, it is also possible to assess the needs of the group and to tailor the training to accommodate a more manageable population. Another effective marketing strategy is organizing an information fair for end users. Such fairs have been successfully undertaken at Ohio State and Columbia Universities, where database vendors and producers were invited to send representatives to demonstrate search systems and software, and to distribute promotional materials. Marketing strategy will vary with the amount of staff and time available. It is critical to devote sufficient staff time to a marketing campaign. The more interest that is generated toward a library program, the greater the chances are for its continued support and growth. It is good to get more people interested than the library can serve, even if it means turning people away or scheduling additional sessions.

EVALUATION OF TRAINING

Evaluations may range from a simple questionnaire given at the sessions to pre-test and post-test assessments of the knowledge and skills of students. Evaluation serves many purposes. It contributes to an assessment of the users of a system (i.e., it helps obtain a demographic or other profile of the population reached by training). Evaluation also offers a means of getting feedback about the effectiveness of training and the extent to which training objectives were met. It gathers information required to assess the need for continued training or other forms of information. It also serves as a means of documenting the program for statistical and planning purposes. Lastly, evaluation provides needed documentation for the library administration. In this last regard, evaluation insures that data needed to modify, change, or stop the training will be systematically collected and compiled.

Broadly, the evaluation process usually assesses the end user's motivation to make use of computerized information systems, and, in addition, it assesses the attainment of basic skills required to be successful with such systems. Determining whether instruction motivates users involves ascertaining if it has enabled the end user to: (1) recognize the "material" benefits of using computerized information systems, (2) feel assured that the necessary skills can be learned, and (3) recognize that successful outcomes provide desirable personal accomplishment and esteem.

There is a core of skills needed for using any computerized information system. For example, training must enable the end user to: identify a database; divide a topic into concepts; select appropriate vocabulary; read a menu online; relate concepts using Boolean operators; input search strategies; manipulate sets; modify searches online; and print out search results. The evaluation process must show that the end user has acquired these skills and is able to use them not only with the specific system on which he or she has been trained, but also on one or more systems which have not been used before.

The evaluation process may be carried out with an experimental and with a control group. Such an extensive process is carried out at Cornell University's Mann Library. Their process is divided into three parts: a pre-test, post-test, and post-post-test. The first part serves to gather demographic data; the second is concerned with the end user's level of motivation toward using computers to retrieve information; and the third is designed to evaluate the end user's skills and his or her ability to transfer these skills to other systems and circumstances.[14]

The Systems and Procedures Exchange Center's SPEC kit on end-user searching services contains copies of evaluations and questionnaires from Cornell University, Drexel University, Memphis State University, Pennsylvania State University, Texas A & M, and the University of Ottawa. Reviewing these, and other evaluation materials, reveals the diversity of evaluation processes and instruments, and enables trainers to develop their own forms. Overall, it is important to design evaluative material that is clear to the respondent and that yields information of use to the library. It may be helpful to use different evaluation forms to separate qualitative and quantitative data by having one form for user reactions and another for data such as costs, time spent, and results.

SUMMARY

Whatever end-user training program is adopted by the library, the general tips provided below may prove useful.

1. Keep the training material as simple as possible. Use nontechnical language, and avoid unnecessary library and computer jargon.
2. Pace instruction to allow assimilation of materials, and provide some way for users to apply the training, such as by providing hands-on practice, interactive demonstration sessions, or a simulated search either through CAI or audiovisual materials.
3. If possible, provide instruction in a variety of formats to make it available to larger numbers of individuals.
4. Stress the importance of presearch planning so that users at least know what they want to search. Include a discussion of search strategy formulation related to the system to enable users to get the most from their searches.

5. Keep the expectations of end users in perspective. As trained searchers, many librarians feel that all users want and need to know all of the details of online searching, whereas most end users are satisfied with finding a few good citations.
6. Tell the user what to expect. Present a balance of information; do not downplay or overemphasize the difficulties of searching. Both extremes should be illustrated, showing lower-level phrase searching along with difficult searches that involve concepts for which synonyms and terminology may be overwhelming.[15]
7. Stress that most systems are interactive and are controlled by the user. Many users feel that if they search a topic, they will automatically be shown thousands of references. Make it clear that the search process is under the control of the searcher.
8. Try several training methods, changing or expanding them as user feedback warrants. Given the flux of technical developments, libraries have to be flexible in instructing users of new systems.

Several reports in the library literature on end-user training programs have noted the positive effects such training has on the library. Positive results may be in the form of appreciation for the work of the information specialist and for the search, thus enhancing the image of the library.[16] Academic librarians especially may find the changing role of the librarian from online search intermediary to teacher and consultant enriching and filled with new professional challenges. A major benefit of this shift is the increased assistance patrons receive from librarians during the research process, including assistance in the development of search strategies, in database selection, when equipment fails.[17] An end-user training program is a good way to introduce computer and information literacy into the library, both for end users and for library staff.[18] Bibliographic instruction programs have benefited as well. Faculty end users have been seen conveying a more positive attitude about the library's resources, which has resulted in more teachable students.[19] The introduction of an end-user search program also will allow more library users access to computer databases. Additionally, lower-cost searches are made available to more library users.[20]

Finally, the increased interest in end-user training can be seen in the large number of workshops and conference programs dealing with users and computers in libraries. Experiences gained in training users of online catalogs can serve as a basis for developing an end-user training program. In fact, some online catalog terminals, such as RLIN and OCLC, now provide gateways to online retrieval systems. Locally based systems using CD-ROM databases will provide additional training opportunities. Some libraries have developed successful programs to train their users to take advantage of computer technology for research. Others are just beginning.

APPENDIX

Library Users and Online Systems: Suggested Objectives for Library Instruction

Prepared for the Direct Patron Access to Computer-Based Reference Systems Committee, Machine-Assisted Reference Section, Reference and Adult Services Division, American Library Association, January, 1985. Approved by the RASD Board of Directors, July 1985.

Dennis Hamilton

Dennis Hamilton is associate librarian at University of California, Santa Barbara.

Janet Chisman, Sharon Cline, Nancy Crane, Carolyn Hook, James Maloney, Deborah Masters, Victoria Ann Reich, and Carol Tobin served as committee members during this project.

INTRODUCTION

The widespread use of personal computers in the home and in the office, combined with the increasing availability of various types of automated information systems in libraries, has opened up an important new area of user education. In libraries, many of these automated information systems are used directly and do not require the personal assistance of librarians as intermediaries between the library user and the information. Librarians want the users of these systems to be self-reliant and successful in accessing needed information. There is an expanding need to instruct library patrons who directly use online catalogs, online circulation systems, and other bibliographic and nonbibliographic databases. Librarians have a responsibility to develop instructional programs that will enable users to be successful with all types of online systems through the effective use of learned information-access skills. During the 1982 Annual American Library Association Conference, the Direct Patron Access to Computer-Based Reference Systems Committee undertook a project to establish learning objectives for training direct users of computer-based information systems. The members of the committee compiled a bibliography of recent journal articles and books on the topic of end-user searching of online catalogs and vendor databases. Applying their professional expertise to this new area of library instruc-

tion, the committee members developed a draft of generic learning objectives for training searchers. Comments on the draft were solicited from the RASD membership by means of an announcement placed in *RASD Update.*

SCOPE AND PURPOSE

The objectives developed are designed to facilitate library instruction where any online system is used directly by patrons. They are intended for librarians who have responsibility for devising instructional programs for online systems in school, special, public, or academic libraries. These objectives provide an outline of general topics and skills to be covered in classroom or individual instruction. They may also be used by librarians who are seeking guidance for preparing printed or online instructional aids. A selected bibliography for further reading about online searching and the training of users follows the objectives.

INSTRUCTIONAL OBJECTIVES

1.   Understanding the system
1.1   The user will know which online systems are available and what each system represents.
1.1.1.   The user will understand the relationships among the various online and manual systems provided by the library and will be able to choose the most appropriate system to satisfy a particular information need.

1.1.2. The user will be able to define the scope of each system in terms of the types of material included and the subjects and time or other periods covered, and will know which kinds of information are unique to a particular system.

1.1.3. The user will be aware of any fees incurred in using a particular system.

2. Planning the search strategy

2.1 The user will be able to analyze each information need and to develop a search strategy appropriate to the need and the system.

2.1.1. The user will be able to identify the various files that are available in the system.

2.1.2. The user will know which access points may be used within a particular file to retrieve information.

2.1.3. The user will understand the syntax and function of Boolean operators and will be able to use them to search the files in the system.

2.1.4. If the online system is under authority control, the user will understand the relationship between the authority file and other files in the system and will be able to identify and to use authoritative access points to search the system.

2.1.5. The user will understand the difference between free-text and controlled-vocabulary searching and will be able to determine which approach to use for the best search results.

2.1.6. The user will know how to select the search strategy that is the most efficient and uses the least amount of machine resources.

2.1.7. The user will understand how to narrow or broaden a search strategy.

2.1.8. The user will be aware of significant limitations of the online system.

3. Operating the system

3.1 The user will be able to operate the system in an efficient manner.

3.1.1. The user will be able to operate the terminal and any auxiliary equipment or devices.

3.1.2. If necessary, the user will be able to logon and logoff the system.

3.1.3. The user will be able to access the various files within the system.

3.1.4. The user will be able to enter search commands correctly.

3.1.5. If a choice is available, the user will be able to select the appropriate display format.

3.1.6. The user will be able to use the appropriate command(s) to page through a list of display results or to move forward or backward in the system.

3.1.7. The user will be able to comprehend and to respond appropriately to error messages and to other system prompts.

3.2. The user will be able to obtain assistance in the use of the system.

3.2.1. The user will be aware of available online help commands and will be able to use them as needed.

3.2.2. The user will be aware of any available written aids or human resources that may be consulted for assistance.

3.2.3. The user will know when it is necessary or appropriate to refer a search to a search intermediary.

4. Interpreting the search results

4.1. The user will understand how to interpret the search results and how to obtain the needed information.

4.1.1. The user will be able to identify the elements of a search display and will be able to determine which elements are relevant in retrieving the needed information.

4.1.2. When more than one item of information is retrieved in the system, the user will understand the order in which items are displayed.

4.1.3. The user will understand any instructions or procedures necessary to obtain the information or the sources of information retrieved as a result of the search.

NOTES

1. Nancy Fjallbrant and Ian Malley, *User Education in Libraries* (London: Clive Bingley, 1984).

2. Sandra N. Ward, "Course Integrated DIALOG Instruction," *Research Strategies* 3 (Spring 1985): 52–61.

3. Debra E. Kachel, "Online Bibliographic Searching: A Pilot Project," *Library Journal* 111 (May 1, 1986): 1, 28–30.

4. Dennis Hamilton, "Library Users and Online Systems: Suggested Objectives for Library Instruction," *RQ* 25 (Winter 1985): 195–97.

5. Winifred Sewell and Sandra Teitelbaum, "Observations of End-User Online Searching Behavior over Eleven Years, *"Journal of the American Society for Information Science* 37 (July 1986): 234–45.

6. Richard V. Janke, "Online After Six: End User Searching Comes of Age," *Online* 8 (Nov. 1984): 15–29.

7. Sandra N. Ward and Laura M. Osegueda, "Teaching University Student End-Users about Online Searching," *Science and Technology Libraries* 5 (Fall 1984): 17–31.

8. Mignon S. Adams and Jacqueline N. Morris, *Teaching Library Skills for Academic Credit* (Phoenix, Ariz.: Oryx Pr., 1985).

9. Dena W. Gordon, "Online Training for the End User or Information Consumer," in *Online Age: Assessment/Directions, Collected Papers Presented at the 12th American Society for Information Science Mid-Year Meeting,* comp. by Susan M. Harvey and Ellen W. Miller (Lexington: Univ. of Kentucky, 1983).

10. Clyde W. Grotophorst, "Training University Faculty as End-User Searchers: A CAI Approach," in *National Online Meeting Proceedings—1984,* comp. by Martha E. Williams and Thomas H. Hogan, 77–82 (Medford, N.J.: Learned Information, 1984).

11. Dana Smith, "CAI-BRS After Dark," *Small Computers in Libraries* 6 (Sept. 1986): 18–19.

12. Association of Research Libraries, Office of Management Studies, Systems and Procedures Exchange Center, *End-User Searching Services,* Kit 122 (Washington, D.C.: ARL, 1986).

13. Winifred Sewell and Sandra Teitelbaum, "Observations of End-User Online Searching Behavior over Eleven Years," *Journal of the American Society for Information Science* 37 (July 1986): 234–45.

14. Association of Research Libraries, Office of Management Studies, Systems and Procedures Exchange Center, *End-User Searching Services,* Kit 122 (Washington, D.C.: ARL, 1986).

15. Peter J. Vigil, "End User Training: The Systems Approach," in *National Online Meeting Proceedings—1984,* comp. by Martha E. Williams and Thomas H. Hogan, 419–24 (Medford, N.J.: Learned Information, 1984).

16. Ellen C. Brassil, "Information Management and Education: Integrating the Old with the New," *Medical Reference Services Quarterly* 4 (Spring 1985): 91–95.

17. Deborah Slingluff, Yvonne Lev, and Andrew Eisan, "An End User Search Service in an Academic Health Sciences Library," *Medical Reference Services Quarterly* 4 (Spring 1985): 11–21.

18. Janke, 15–29.

19. Susan Swords Steffen, "College Faculty Goes Online: Training Faculty End Users," *Journal of Academic Librarianship* 12 (July 1986): 147–51.

20. Michael Halperin and Ruth A. Pagell, "Free 'Do-It-Yourself' Online Searching. . . What to Expect," *Online* 9 (Mar. 1985): 82–84.

BIBLIOGRAPHY

Adams, Mignon S., and Jacquelyn M. Morris. *Teaching Library Skills for Academic Credit.* Phoenix, Ariz.: Oryx Pr., 1985.

Association of Research Libraries, Office of Management Studies, Systems and Procedures Exchange Center. *End-User Searching Services.* Kit 122. Washington, D.C.: ARL, 1986.

Beaubien, Anne K., Sharon A. Hogan, and Mary W. George. *Learning the Library.* New York: Bowker, 1982.

Borgman, Christine L. "Individual Differences in the Use of Technology: Work in Progress." In *Proceedings of the 48th ASIS Annual Meeting,* edited by Carol A. Parkhurst. White Plains, N.Y.: Knowledge Industry, 1985; "Mental Models: Ways of Looking at a System." *ASIS Bulletin* 9 (Dec. 1982): 38–39; "Psychological Research in Human-Computer Interaction." In *Annual Review of Information Science and Technology* 19 (1984): 33–64.

Brassil, Ellen C. "Information Management and Education: Integrating the Old with the New." *Medical Reference Services Quarterly* 4 (Spring 1985): 91–95.

Des Chene, Dorice. "Online Searching by End Users." *RQ* 25 (Fall 1985): 89–95.

Fjallbrant, Nancy, and Ian Malley. *User Education in Libraries.* London: Clive Bingley, 1984.

Gordon, Dena W. "Online Training for the End User or Information Consumer." In *Online Age: Assessment/Directions, Collected Papers Presented at the 12th American Society for Information Science Mid-Year Meeting,* comp. by Susan M. Harvey and Ellen W. Miller. Lexington, Ky.: Univ. of Kentucky, 1983. Microfiche.

Grotophorst, Clyde W. "Training University Faculty as End-User Searchers: A CAI Approach." In *National Online Meeting Proceedings—1984,* comp. by Martha E. Williams and Thomas H. Hogan, 77–82. Medford, N.J.: Learned Information, 1984.

Halperin, Michael, and Ruth A. Pagell. "Free 'Do-It-Yourself' Online Searching ...What to Expect." *Online* 9 (Mar. 1985): 82–84.

Hubbard, Abigail, and Barbara Wilson. "An Integrated Information Management Education Program: Defining a New Role for Librarians in Helping End-Users." *Online* 10 (Mar. 1986): 15–23.

Janke, Richard V. "Online After Six: End User Searching Comes of Age." *Online* 8 (Nov. 1984): 15–29.

Kachel, Debra E. "Online Bibliographic Searching: A Pilot Project." *Library Journal* 111 (May 1, 1986): 1C28–30.

Kobelski, Pamela, and Mary Reichel. "Conceptual Frameworks for Bibliographic Instruction." *Journal of Academic Librarianship* 7 (May 1981): 73–77.

Mancall, Jacqueline C. "Training Students to Search Online: Rationale, Process, and Implications." *Drexel Library Quarterly* 20 (Winter 1984): 64–84.

McClain, Gary R. *Lost in the Forest: Overcoming the Need to Pontificate in Course Development.* Alexandria, Va.: ERIC Document Reproduction Service, 1985. ED 261 644

Roose, Tina. "Forum on Use of Online Searching in Public Libraries." Paper read to RASD MARS Use of Machine-Assisted Reference Services in Public

Libraries Committee. American Library Association Annual Conference, New York City, 1986.

Sewell, Winifred, and Sandra Teitelbaum. "Observations of End-User Online Searching Behavior over Eleven Years." *Journal of the American Society for Information Science* 37 (July 1986): 234–45.

Slingluff, Deborah, Yvonne Lev, and Andrew Eisan. "An End User Search Service in an Academic Health Sciences Library." *Medical Reference Services Quarterly* 4 (Spring 1985): 11–21.

Smith, Dana. "CAI-BRS After Dark." *Small Computers in Libraries* 6 (Sept. 1986): 18–19.

Snelson, Pamela. "Microcomputer Centers in Academic Libraries, Part 1." *Small Computers in Libraries* 5 (June 1985): 6–9.

Steffen, Susan Swords. "College Faculty Goes Online: Training Faculty End Users." *Journal of Academic Librarianship* 12 (July 1986): 147–51.

Trzebiatowski, Elaine. "End User Study on BRS/After Dark." *RQ* 24 (Winter 1984): 446–50.

Vigil, Peter J. "End-User Training: The Systems Approach." In *National Online Meeting Proceedings—1984,* comp. by Martha E. Williams and Thomas H. Hogan, 419–24. Medford, N.J.: Learned Information, 1984.

Ward, Sandra N. "Teaching University Student End-Users about Online Searching." *Science and Technology Libraries* 5 (Fall 1984): 17–31.

Ward, Sandra N. "Course Integrated DIALOG Instruction." *Research Strategies* 3 (Spring 1985): 52–61.

Chapter 4

End-User Services Available from BRS

Stanley Nash

INTRODUCTION

Among the various search services offered by BRS Information Technologies, two are particularly appropriate for end-user searching in libraries: *BRS After Dark* and *BRS Colleague,* the latter being especially applicable to patrons interested in medicine and pharmacology. The purpose of this chapter is to provide a detailed description of *After Dark,* pointing out along the way its strengths and weaknesses relative to its potential use by library patrons. Although *Colleague* will be mentioned from time to time, for comparative purposes, the reader is advised to see Chapter 8 for a full discussion of this service. Also, a brief description of other BRS services, including *Tech Data, BRS Instructor,* and *BRS Educator* can be found at the end of this article.

During the Online '82 Conference, official word was given by both the DIALOG and BRS companies that a low-cost, "user-friendly" online search service had become available to the public for searching databases during off-peak hours. This announcement was followed by a publicity campaign through which both companies were "specifically aiming their advertising guns at the at-home and at-work self-service online market."[1] The initial target was business or "technically" oriented professionals who might have access to a personal computer. Hence, the birth of *BRS After Dark* and *DIALOG's Knowledge Index.* In 1983, BRS helped produce and market the *Colleague* search service in conjunction with W. B. Saunders, featuring reduced costs, in this case primarily for the personal use of health care professionals.

Announcement of a third service called *BRKTHRU* came in the spring of 1985. Unlike *After Dark,* which permits searching only at night or on weekends, *BRKTHRU* allowed "professional end users" to search during both day or night with a menu-driven system and a format similar to that of *After Dark.* Shortly after this announcement, BRS began to offer subscribers of the regular daytime BRS service (*BRS Search*) the option of searching a menu-driven system (*BRS MENUS*) modeled on *BRKTHRU* for a $1 surcharge in addition to the regular daytime prices. This surcharge has since been dropped.

The foregoing are all menu-driven systems, replete with a nearly comprehensive array of prompts designed to insure ease of use for those who have little or no experience with database searching. The initial emphasis on the individual home or office computer user has been shifting, or at least widening, toward institutional targets. This shift is particularly marked in the case of *After Dark,* which is clearly developing into a product that is as appropriate for end users in institutional settings, such as library patrons, as it is for home users. Undoubtedly, the positive reaction of librarians to the introduction of low-cost searching services, usable by patrons themselves, is part of this story. Richard Janke of the University of Ottawa has pointed out that within two years after the introduction of *After Dark,* "scores of universities and school libraries both in Canada and the United States...have some sort of end-user service in place or are seriously considering implementing one...." Mr. Janke attributes this wide acceptance to a variety of things, including the fact that DIALOG and BRS have "taken early criticisms to heart" and have continuously improved their end-user systems.[2] Librarians were clearly prominent among those who made an early analysis of the potential uses of *After Dark* and *Knowledge Index.*

Recently, major changes have occurred at BRS with respect to the company's end-user systems. First, BRS withdrew the *BRKTHRU* service in the summer of 1987, apparently because of its overlap with *After Dark* and with *Colleague* (which also permits daytime searching at a discount). *BRKTHRU* users have been transferred to *Colleague,* which as of early 1987 has been solely owned by BRS. Therefore, for BRS to continue *BRKTHRU* and *Colleague* would in effect be competing with themselves to some extent. Second, as of fall 1987, *After Dark* began to offer an array of new special-command features that had first been introduced exclusively by *Colleague* in late 1985. BRS has also changed the menu and replaced command listings with "Help" screens. (The new *After Dark* software is discussed in detail below.) The more powerful features of *Colleague* also appear in *BRS MENUS.* In the future, enhancements will be added to all end-user services simultaneously. In any event, in order to acquaint *After Dark* subscribers with the improved software, users will be given free time on the new practice files. One new glitch for users of *After*

Dark, however, is that prices have been increased by $2 per hour across the board.

COVERAGE

After Dark provides extensive database coverage at truly bargain rates. As of June 1987, *After Dark* offered a choice of some 80 + databases broken down into five categories: 14 databases fall under the category "Business and Finance," 15 under "Reference," 9 under "Education," 26 under "Social Sciences and Humanities," and 26 under "Sciences and Medicine." Thirteen of these databases are full-text files, including reference tools such as the *Academic American Encyclopedia* and the *Kirk-Othmer Encyclopedia of Chemical Technology*, and journals such as the *Harvard Business Review*. All of this growth is particularly impressive considering that in 1983 *After Dark* had only 22 databases available.[3] In essence, *After Dark* includes most major databases and over two-thirds of those available from the regular BRS search service.

There are several reasons why some databases are not available on *After Dark*. First, the final decision is up to the database producer, who may not wish to offer databases at cut-rate prices and, thus, lower royalties. Database producers may be concerned that lower cost availability at night may decrease usage of their files at regular prices during the day. Second, *After Dark* was designed to be a low-cost service. The addition of expensive databases would obviate that design. Finally, BRS has attempted to select databases it feels would suit its users' profile.

ACCESS AND AVAILABILITY

All BRS services can be accessed via Telenet and Tymnet for transmission at 300, 1200, or 2400 baud. (For those residing in Canada, either Telenet or Datapac must be used.) Getting connected and logging on are explained in the manuals in graphic detail. One of the positive features of logging on to these systems is that the user is prompted to specify the numbers of horizontal and vertical lines available on the user's monitor as part of the customer services option on the main menu. As a result, no display can ever scroll off the screen automatically. It had been suggested that one negative aspect of *After Dark* was the ease with which the password could be changed. In the past, to change a password, one merely had to select this option from the initial menu. For a library expecting to have a multitude of patrons using one of these systems, the ease of changing passwords could have led to security problems. This problem has been recently corrected so that now, in order to change the password, one must first select "customer services" on the main menu, and then the user must type in the original password. If a patron was already logged on and did not know the password to begin with, it could not be changed.

DOCUMENTATION AND CUSTOMER SUPPORT

After Dark offers excellent customer support services. Customer service can be called via toll-free numbers for answer to search questions or to any questions concerning services. Customer service is available from 8 a.m. every morning until 1 a.m. Monday through Friday, 5 p.m. Saturday, and 2 p.m. on Sunday. Training services vary somewhat. The *BRS Online Training Kit* includes an eleven-minute videotape that illustrates and discusses the "basics" of searching, employing examples from *BRKTHRU* and from the *BRKTHRU Training Workbook,* which includes lessons for "Getting Online," an "Introduction to Databases," an "Introduction to Searching," and "Searching Further" (nesting, command stacking, field qualification, etc.). The lessons are well written, nicely structured, and very realistic. Unfortunately, the value of the kit has diminished with the withdrawal of *BRKTHRU.* The video, moreover, is simply too short and superficial to be used as a training device by itself. For example, the film offers no explanation of Boolean logic or any details on the printing process (which has caused problems for some users). More promising is the video designed for *Colleague,* as *After Dark* and *Colleague* commands are now essentially the same. BRS also offers an instructional packet designed as a teaching aid for subscribers to *BRS Instructor* passwords. The packet includes diagrams, sample searches, and instructional text on topics such as getting online, creating a database, the search process, logical operators, truncation, printing, paragraph qualification, and controlled vocabulary. Although at present BRS does not offer computer-assisted instruction (CAI) programs for end users, some have been developed at colleges and universities, such as the CAI package written by Clyde W. Grotophorst of George Mason University for their "*After Dark* End-User Program."[4] Libraries involved in end-user programs should be on the lookout in the library literature for reports on such programs, since it may be possible to obtain copies of programs. Software also is available, making it easy for librarians to design their own CAI packages.[5]

BRS provides *After Dark* subscribers with a user's manual. *After Dark's* 1984 manual included 24 pages of instructional text followed by four appendixes and a one-page glossary. Several critics had remarked on the briefness of this document, particularly with respect to the paucity of space devoted to describing most of the databases.[6] Other drawbacks noted were the lack of an index and the small amount of detail given to "search techniques, such as paragraph qualification."[7] A new, vastly improved manual appeared in August 1986, which, at some 40 pages, was nearly twice the length of the first. *After Dark*'s newest manual is by far the best one issued to date. It explains the new search features and menu in detail, spending considerable time discussing searching techniques and strategy under the rubric "Nine Basic Steps of Searching." Appendixes include information about logging on, a summary of commands, language codes, and the "BRS Aid Pages." However, the manual still needs improvement in two areas. First, the index needs cross-references and more user-friendly language (e.g., the purge command is under "PG"). Second, more detail and clarity are needed in the brief section on full-text searching.

Documentation is also now available online in the "How to Use *After Dark* Service," an option on the *After Dark* main menu. Additionally, a number of practice databases are available, and suggested sample searches will be added shortly to assist novice searchers.

To update system features, BRS puts out a newsletter-type publication. Since the beginning of 1985, the bimonthly *Newsbrk* has been published, serving both *After Dark* and *BRKTHRU* users. Subscribers receive the newsletter along with the *BRS Bulletin*. Newsbrk offers information on new databases, search techniques, and search strategies, and instruction on using services or new databases. It also announces forthcoming services and numerous free user aids from database producers.

For all BRS customers there are, of course, a variety of formal training sessions ranging from the introductory level to specific instruction using databases such as *Medline,* the education databases, the business databases, and the biomedical databases. There is also a session for full-text searching. Although these sessions are geared to the regular service customer, they also have obvious value for those interested in developing advanced searching skills. In the case of *BRS Instructor* (see below), an introductory training session is offered for free to online teachers. Applicable to certain searchers, regardless of the service they have contracted for, are a number of publications sold by BRS. These publications include training manuals for the business, education, medical, and biomedical databases, as well as one for full-text searching.

EASE OF USE

After Dark is designed to be user friendly and uses menus with many prompts and directions that guide the user from logon to logoff. In regard to command structure and system features, *After Dark* and *Colleague* are now very similar. As mentioned earlier, *After Dark* now includes *Colleague*'s sophisticated commands and special features.

After logon, prompts appear that ask if the user wishes to see a broadcast message. Following this prompt, the main menu's choices appear. Each choice is numbered, and the user is instructed merely to type in the number or "H" for help and then press "return." The menu includes options for the search service, "BRS *After Dark* Update," "How to Use BRS *After Dark*," and "Customer Services." The "*After Dark* Update" option tells subscribers about new service features and databases; the "How to Use *After Dark*" option describes current services and features; and the "Customer Services" option is the vehicle for changing passwords, changing screen displays, and identifying to the system the user's communication software.

After a selection has been made for the search service, the next menu appears, which is a list of the database categories that BRS calls "libraries." There is also a category for practice databases that are offered to *After Dark* subscribers to help them learn the newest system commands and features. After the user chooses one of the database categories by typing in the four-letter label of a library (e.g., "SCME" for "Science and Medicine" databases), a list of databases along with their four-letter labels appears on the screen, (e.g., "INFO" for "*ABI/Inform*"). Once a database has been chosen, a prompt appears that asks the user to "enter search terms, command, or 'H' for help." This last prompt is the most profound of the changes in the *After Dark* system. Up until fall of 1987, the user would be offered a choice of either a brief list of commands or an annotated list of commands. One list or the other would be repeated after each command issued by the user. The new *After Dark/Colleague* software, however, lists commands and explanations of commands only when a help (H) command is entered. Although some studies seemed to indicate that many end users either liked the original *After Dark* menu or at least had no objection to it,[8] BRS feels that users will eventually enjoy the streamlining of the new system. Also, since the *After Dark* manual includes a "Quick Reference Guide," users can simply keep this card handy while searching.

The basic commands and features are straightforward and easy to master. Searching is accomplished by responding to the automatic prompt "Search 1 >>" by typing in the term or terms the user wishes to search; however, the command "S" must be entered to return to search mode after printing or displaying a document. Terms also can be entered (typed) as phrases, such as "computer searching." This phrase is taken by the system to imply adjacency (the equivalent in BRS's regular search system would be "computer ADJ searching"). After the user enters a search term, or terms, the system replies with "Answer 1 >>" (1 being the first set created), followed by the number of documents found (e.g., "Answer 1 >> 7" documents found). The system permits the use of Boolean operators, nesting with parentheses, and field or paragraph qualification. Field or paragraph qualification is achieved just as it is in the standard BRS search service. For example, one can enter "end user.ti." to restrict the term "end user" to the title field. Similar operations can be performed for the descriptor (.de), author (.au), abstract fields (.ab.), and others. Although limiting is not available, for most databases language and year of publication can be searched directly, e.g., "82.yr." will search all documents published in 1982. Similarly, a search command of "en.lg." will search for all publications in the English language. The exact format for searching year of publication will vary with the database being searched. For language of publication searches, there is a standard two-letter code for most of the prominent languages in the world. Over 80 language codes are listed in Appendix C of the *After Dark* manual, including "TM" for "Tamil" and "PU" for "Pashto." One can also search a term or terms by excluding fields to be searched, e.g., "money machine...ti." looks for "money machine" every place in the basic index but the title field.

Truncation is the same as for BRS's regular daytime service, i.e., the dollar sign ($), optionally followed by a number to restrict the number of characters to follow, e.g., "smok$3" (left-handed truncation is possible on some databases as well). All of BRS's proximity operators ("SAME," "WITH," and "ADJ") may be used, although, again, "ADJ" is implied when searching more than one term as a phrase. Proximity and Boolean operators are termed "connectors" in BRS documentation. Terms or names also can be expanded on *After Dark* through the "Stem" command (ST). To expand terms, the user would type in "ST" at a prompt such as "Search 1 〉〉." The system would then ask the user to type in the term to be expanded. The result would be an alphabetical list of terms included in the system's online dictionary that begin with the search-term string. Sets can then be created by selecting one or more of these terms by the numbers appearing to the left of each term. For example, if one were unsure of the spelling of an author's name, the name could be expanded, and if variant spellings were found, one complete set could be created for that author.

To print or display a given set online (*Colleague* permits offline printing; *After Dark* does not), the user types "D" at a prompt. The system then asks the user to type in the number of the search answer he or she wishes to have displayed and printed (e.g., to print documents in set "Answer 2," the user would type "2"). The user is then prompted to indicate the format on which the documents should be printed. Replies for bibliographic databases would be "S" for "short," which includes author, title, source, and publication date, "M" for "medium," which is the same as "short" with the descriptors added, and "L" for "long," which prints the full record with all fields. As a result of user demand, BRS is also including the options of specifying "TI" to display only titles for browsing purposes and "TD" for tailored display," which permits the user to specify particular fields to be displayed. Replies for full-text databases are "S," which yields the same result as it does with bibliographic databases (citation only); "M," which includes everything in "S," as well as the abstracts plus hits, (i.e., the paragraphs that include the search term); and "L" for the complete document. At the prompt, the user can type a range of numbers (e.g., 1–10), a specific number for one document, "all," or simply "carriage return," which would display the first document (pressing "carriage return" again would display the next document). Once you understand the system, this process can be streamlined by command stacking. When one uses the command stacking symbol (the semicolon), the routine described above for printing from bibliographic databases requires the user to type in something like the following: "D"; "2, S"; "1–10" ("D" for "display," "2" for "Answer 2," "S" for the short format, and "1–10" for the first ten documents in answer set 2). Command stacking can be used for searching to bypass several menu options as well, e.g., in changing from one database to another.

There are several other command options: "PG" for "purge," which allows the user to "erase" specific search statements and answers; "C" for changing databases without returning to the main menu; "M" for returning to the main menu, "L" to see a list of libraries; "R" to review previous search statements; and "O" for "off," to end the search and exit the system.

A number of special features previously available only on *Colleague* are now also available on *After Dark*. What follows is but a brief summary of these features. The command "H" for "help" can be typed in at any prompt and will produce a help menu with six types of help to choose from: basic commands, search terms, connectors, truncation, searching specific fields, and advanced commands (over 200 "helps" screens are included!). There is a tradeoff here, however. The "Help" command is also a substitute for the option of having continuous command displays. (The list of all commands would now be too cumbersome to display at each prompt.) Thus, as mentioned before, for a review of commands at any given time, a "Help" command *must* be executed. The PC command for "print continuously" allows for uninterrupted printing of documents to disk or printer without having to press "enter" each time to go to the next screen display. The "OC" command for "off continue" permits signing off without losing a search strategy and results. In effect, using "OC" produces an automatic "SAVE," which can be accessed when logging on later that day or up until 4 a.m. EST the next day. Several of the new features allow for more control over browsing through documents. Typing in "E" (for "expand") and the number of a specific document while scanning in the short or medium format causes the specified document to be displayed in the long format. A variation of this is the command "K" (for "key words") in full-text databases. This command produces a display of paragraphs that include the user's search words from a short-format listing. This display is achieved by expanding a given document, as just described, then typing "K." Yet another related option for full-text files is the "Z" command for "zoom." Zooming allows the user direct access to cited references when scanning a full-text document. To use this function, the user would type "Z" and the number of the reference desired, while displaying a document. "RD" for "resume display" brings the user back to where he or she was before entering "E," "K," or "Z." Features available on *Colleague* but not on *After Dark* include search saves, offline printing, and SDIs.

PRICING

After Dark is offered at reduced cost compared with BRS's regular online search charges. The tradeoff is that, as the name implies, *After Dark* online searching may be done only in the evenings or on weekends. Subscribers to *After Dark* may search from 6 p.m. (local time) to 4 a.m. Monday through Friday; 6 a.m. (eastern time) to 2 a.m. on Saturdays; and, as of recently, 9 a.m. (eastern time) to 4 a.m. on Sundays. After an initial start-up fee of $75 and a monthly minimum of two hours use of $12, cost consists mostly of actual searching time, including telecommunications charges. With few exceptions, printing online is usually inexpensive, ranging from 3 cents to 13 cents per citation for most databases—indeed, you can print only online. Online connect charges vary from database to database but can be as low as $8 per hour for *ERIC*. As of September 1987, all databases increased in price by $2 per hour. Most databases still fall into the range of $10 to $20 per connect hour. Some criticism has been made concerning the accounting methodology. Currently, there is no way of estimating the cost of a given search until billing is received from BRS, since no cost is given online. As a result, libraries implementing an end-user service could run into billing problems.[9] According to BRS, a cost estimator is now under development. BRS has also been praised in regard to billing, for unlike *Knowledge Index*, *After Dark* customers can establish deposit accounts. In fact, this option and the very low rates were among several reasons why one University chose *After Dark* over *Knowledge Index* for its end-user service.[10] It should be mentioned that a library using *After Dark* can take advantage of the discount available for additional passwords ($35 for each password after the initial one at $75).

Based on end-user studies conducted at various college libraries, *After Dark* has indeed proved highly cost effective. At Pennsylvania State

University, for instance, the average cost for thirty minutes online was $4.80. In addition, of those studied, the most expensive search cost $12.51, prompting one of the librarians involved with the project to remark that if one were to judge from these results, online searching "could be within the means of even the most impoverished graduate student."[11] Similar cost figures discovered through several other studies.[12] Given recent price changes and the fact that these studies were done before comprehensive print charges were imposed, the reader should adjust any projected cost estimates accordingly.

END-USER RESPONSE

Having discussed *After Dark,* we should now ask whether it has met the demands of the end user. Several end-user studies, conducted at college and university libraries using *After Dark,* affirm that essentially, novice end-users are very satisfied with the service. A study done at the University of Wisconsin-Stout in 1983 reported that participants (20 in all, consisting of a mixture of faculty and students with no prior search experience) were "personally satisfied" and indicated a great deal of enthusiasm" for the system. 60 percent said that the searching process was "easier than expected"; (30 percent said it was "extremely easy." Moreover, 85 percent thought that their search results were good to excellent, and none considered the results poor.[13] Similar reactions and results were reported from studies done at the University of Ottawa, where the 22 end-user participants included faculty, graduate students, undergraduates, and special part-time and external students;[14] and at Pennsylvania State University, where 18 graduate education students performed searches for the study.[15] For all the confidence the users demonstrated, it is interesting that the majority—in all three studies—wanted an experienced librarian searcher to be available "to help out, if need be."[16] Moreover, in the study done at Wisconsin "only three searchers performed their entire searches without seeking help during the search."[17] Two problems that stood out as seriously recurrent for end users were the use of truncation and the printing process. In the study at Wisconsin, 23 searchers used truncation, but only three used it "correctly."[18] This problem should be mitigated by the new "help" screen for truncation. As to the steps involved in printing a document, Linda Friend at Pennsylvania State University has commented that the "online explanation of how to choose which documents to print is unclear and confused the majority."[19] This fact has also been echoed by those involved in the other studies mentioned above, as well as by those in a study done at Memphis State in 1984.[20] It should be pointed out, however, that printing steps and prompts would be technically very difficult to modify.

Librarians responsible for end-user services using *After Dark* and other systems have found that end users experience difficulty with advanced searching techniques and concepts that are part and parcel of the online searching process, regardless of the system used. Richard Janke of the University of Ottawa, referring to his own experience with end users, has commented that "unquestionably the most frequently heard complaint was this: end users all too often are not fully aware of the application of Boolean logic in formulating an effective online search strategy."[21] Similarly, Elaine Trzebiatowski, assessing the aforementioned study done at the University of Wisconsin, points out that in that study, the "AND" concept was not fully comprehended, even though everyone used it; and "OR" was used only by a handful of participants.[22] The addition of numerous "help" screens should render *After Dark* more user friendly. However, its new sophistication (i.e., special features) should be a caveat that user education is still called for.

OTHER SERVICES

Finally, although the most attention has been paid to *After Dark* because of its obvious appropriateness for library patrons, a few words should be addressed to other BRS end-user services. *Tech Data,* a joint product of BRS and Information Handling Services, is a menu-driven system designed for use by engineers. Including databases such as *Compendex* and the full text of the *Kirk-Othmer Encyclopedia of Chemical Technology, Tech Data* is most suitable for a corporate budget. After a registration fee of $50 to $100, *Tech Data* can be searched at a flat rate of $90 per hour for "open access," with slightly lower rates for prepaid subscriptions. *Tech Data*'s subscribers can search during the same hours as BRS's regular search customers. *BRS Educator* is a service for educational "personnel" working in elementary or secondary education. This group includes teachers, school librarians, administrators, and media center coordinators. The system is command- or menu-driven, whichever the user chooses at sign-on. The one-time registration fee of $75 includes up to five passwords and $25 worth of free search time. The search rate is $18 per hour plus royalties and telecommunications charges. There is no monthly minimum. Nearly all BRS databases are available for searching on this system.

BRS Instructor is available to any institution giving "format instruction" in online searching. As is true with the regular BRS service, users now can select between menu-driven or command-driven searching. There is no registration fee for up to 12 passwords, which also includes a free user's workbook. As with *Educator,* additional passwords are $20 each. Charges are confined to a flat rate of $15 per hour, including telecommunications costs. The software for both *Educator* and *Instructor*'s menu-driven options is the same as for *After Dark* and *Colleague*.

With regard to libraries teaching patrons to search, it should be pointed out that an important by-product of *Instructor* has been the educational materials developed by BRS that can be used to support end-user training programs. Based on suggestions from a questionnaire BRS sent to *Instructor* password users, which included requests for CAI tutorials, videotapes, and transparencies, librarians can expect new and advanced instructional materials to be forthcoming from BRS.[23] The *BRS Instructor Directory*, which includes colleges and universities, special libraries, library schools, and even several high schools, was a result of this same survey and should prove a useful foundation for information sharing on teaching methods employed throughout the country.

Recently BRS instituted a new service, *BRS On Site*, whereby BRS will sell its search software to libraries along with leased tapes of major BRS databases. *BRS On Site* allows libraries to offer fixed-cost unlimited online searching throughout a campus or other institution. *On Site* is available for IBM mainframes and several minicomputer systems. Prices begin at $25,000 for one database, and $15,000 for each additional database plus database producer fees.

Last, but not least, BRS has, as of summer of 1987, entered the CD-ROM market under the name *BRS Colleague Disc*. The first product, *Medline*, covers the years from January 1986 to June 1987 on two discs, with an update in December 1987 covering the entire 1987 year. The *Medline* CD-ROM contains only English-language citations and is searched using *Colleague* software.

NOTES

1. Richard V. Janke, "BRS/After Dark: The Birth of Online Self-Service," *Online* 7 (Sept. 1983): 12.

2. _____, "Online After Six: End User Searching Comes of Age," *Online* 8 (Nov. 1984): 15–16.

3. Elaine Trzebiatowski, "End User Study on BRS/After Dark," *RQ* 23 (Summer 1984): 446.

4. A free copy of this program may be obtained by writing to Clyde W. Grotophorst, George Mason University Libraries, Fairfax, VA 22030. Be sure to include a blank floppy disk and postage along with your request.

5. *See*, for example, Keith J. Stanger, "Dan Bricklin's Demo Program," *College and Research Libraries News* 47 (Oct. 1986): 582–85.

6. Linda Friend, "Independence at the Terminal: Training Student End Users to Do Online Literature Searching," *Journal of Academic Librarianship* 11 (July 1985): 140; Sharon Mader and Elizabeth Park, "BRS/After Dark: A Review," *RSR* 13 (Spring 1985): 27.

7. Mader, 27; Friend, 140.

8. Friend, 139; Janke, "BRS/After Dark," 15.
9. Mader, 27.
10. Friend, 137.
11. Ibid.
12. *See,* for example, Elaine Trzebiatowski, 449, where the end-user study at the University of Wisconsin-Stout resulted in a mean cost per search of $4.62 and the range for 20 searches was between $1.93 and $12.92. *See also* Mader, 27, where the average cost per search for the study done at Memphis State University was $11.25 per hour!
13. Trzebiatowski, 447–48.
14. Janke, "BRS/After Dark," 16.
15. Friend, 137–39.
16. Janke, "BRS/After Dark," 16; Trzebiatowski, 449; Friend, 139.
17. Trzebiatowski, 448.
18. Ibid.
19. Friend, 140.
20. *See* Janke, "BRS/After Dark," 16; Trzebiatowski, 448; Mader, 26.
21. Janke, "Online After Six," 21.
22. Trzebiatowski, 448.
23. *BRS Bulletin* 10 (1986): 35.

BIBLIOGRAPHY

Dodd, Jane, et al. *Texas A & M University Library. A Final Report from the Public Service Research Projects. A Comparison of Two End User Operated Search Systems....* College Station: Texas A & M Univ. Library, 1985. ERIC ED 255 224

Dolan, D. R. "Non-Technical Literature: Getting It Out of Data Bases: BRS/After Dark." *Database* 7 (Aug. 1984): 94–103.

Friend, Linda. "Independence at the Terminal: Training Student End Users to Do Online Literature Searching." *Journal of Academic Librarianship* 11 (July 1985): 140 + .

Halperin, M., and R. A. Pagell. "Free Do-It-Yourself Online Searching...What to Expect." *Online* 9 (Mar. 1985): 82–84.

Janke, Richard V. "BRS/After Dark: The Birth of Online Self-Service." *Online* 7 (Sept. 1983): 12–29.

_____. "Online After Six: End User Searching Comes of Age." *Online* 8 (Nov. 1984): 15 + .

Kesselman, Martin. "Online Update (After Dark)." *Wilson Library Bulletin* 58 (May 1984): 652–53.

Mader, Sharon, and Elizabeth Park. "BRS/After Dark: A Review." *RSR* 13 (Spring 1985): 27 + .

Ojala, M. "Knowledge Index: A Review." *Online* 7 (Sept. 1983): 31–34.

Smith, Dana. "CAI-BRS After Dark." *Small Computers in Libraries* 6 (Sept. 1986): 18 +

Tenopir, Carol. "Dialog's Knowledge Index and BRS/After Dark: Database Searching on Personal Computers." *Library Journal* 108 (Mar. 1, 1983): 471–74.

Trzebiatowski, Elaine. "End User Study on BRS/After Dark." *RQ* 23 (Summer 1984): 446–50.

Chapter 5

End-User Services Available from DIALOG

Sarah B. Watstein

INTRODUCTION

Any discussion of the birth of online self-service and the personal microcomputer owner must take into account DIALOG as one of the moving forces behind the online generation. Even a cursory review of the literature of end-user searching in libraries reveals discussion of developments at DIALOG, as well as discussion of the design, implementation, evolution, and evaluation of systems that have influenced and that continue to influence the shape of end-user searching. Before proceeding, it is important to begin with the basic facts about DIALOG and with a review of the fundamental characteristics of the search systems of DIALOG. DIALOG Information Services, Inc., a wholly owned subsidiary of Lockheed Corporation, is headquartered in Palo Alto, California, with offices in Boston, Chicago, Houston, Los Angeles, New York, Philadelphia, and Washington D.C. DIALOG representatives are located in Canada, Europe, Japan, Korea, and Australia, serving DIALOG customers in 76 countries. DIALOG has offered online access to references, abstracts, and complete texts of published literature since 1972.

DIALOG provides the DIALOG Information Retrieval Service, the world's largest and most comprehensive online databank, with more than 280 databases covering virtually any topic used by 80,000 customers in 76 countries. DIALOG also offers *Banknews; Cendata; Classmate,* an instructional package that extends its *Classroom Instruction Program,* a service that has offered online searching at reduced rates to schools, colleges, and universities since 1976; *DIALOG Business Connection,* an applications-oriented service for the business market, as well as a new instructional program for academic institutions; *Dialmail; DIALOG on-Disc;* and *Knowledge Index,* a reduced-rate evening and weekend service.

DIALOG was initially started from the point of view of the intermediary with training or experience, i.e., as a complex command-driven system. The emphasis had been on reference information rather than primary information, and on databases rather than data. In effect, these features made DIALOG unapproachable to the end user.

DIALOG has historically tried to make its regular service more accessible by providing several *On Tap* databases (online training and practice) and a classroom instruction plan. Several subsets of heavily searched databases are available as *On Tap* files and can be searched at the low price of $15 per hour including telecommunications costs. New searchers, or searchers unfamiliar with a particular database, can practice various search techniques before attempting a search on a file at full-connect hourly rates. *On Tap* database chapters include sample questions on which to practice. The *Classroom Instruction Password* (CIP) account allows almost all DIALOG's databases to be searched at a flat rate of $15 per hour including telecommunications charges. CIP is available only for course-based instruction, and some academic libraries and departments have made use of it in teaching classes on online searching. The CIP program is also used by most library schools in training future librarians on the DIALOG system.

In an attempt to make its system more accessible to end users, DIALOG has introduced some new services. With these services, DIALOG has removed several of the obstacles confronting end users by providing easy-to-use command languages that require minimal training. In particular, three of these systems are considered in this chapter. *Knowledge Index, Classmate,* and *DIALOG onDisc;* the new *DIALOG Business Connection* is discussed in Chapter 7. *DIALOG Business CIP* (Classroom Instruction Program), announced in spring 1987, introduces undergraduate and business students to business applications. This educational program is not discussed in this chapter. Also not discussed is the *DIALOG Medical Connection,* announced in summer 1987. *DIALOG onDisc,* DIALOG's foray into database publishing on CD-ROM, is a recent introduction and will be only briefly discussed.

KNOWLEDGE INDEX AND CLASSMATE

Background

The date is November 1982, and the event is the launching of *Knowledge Index* in the United States. In November 1983, North American service is extended as the service is launched in Canada, and in 1984, the service is launched in Europe. *Knowledge Index* is DIALOG's "attempt to capture a sizeable share of the home-based telecomputing market."[1] *Knowledge Index* is characterized as a "low-cost, after-hours information service aimed at home owners of personal computers."[2] Its target customers consist of microcomputer users, students, educators, physicians, engineers and scientists, lawyers, and just about everyone in the family. In other words, its market embraces a wide range of people in the home, business, and professional environments. The two slogans on the cover of *Knowledge Index*'s 1986 brochure illustrate the company's market strategy and indirectly profile a target end user: "Information—Online All Night" and "How to Get into the Library at 3 a.m." The inside cover and title page portray a library colored bright red, with a wild assortment of researchers trying to get in. Try they do—on stilts, high wires, ladders, unicycles, and via balloon, stork, parachute, kite, skateboard, human ladder...Police and fire officials are also present, and the moon is out, to reinforce the message that this service is for those who can't squeeze their research into a regular nine-to-five day.

On September 25, 1986, at the American Association of School Librarians Conference in Minneapolis, DIALOG announced *Classmate* as an aid for educators seeking to "incorporate online information retrieval into their curriculum."[3] *Classmate* was characterized as a "complete instructional package for introducing online information retrieval to high school students."[4] *Classmate* is specifically designed for the middle school through the undergraduate level. The simplified commands are user friendly, and easy-to-learn search functions, as well as smaller families of databases, are features of this program that make it particularly appropriate for this audience.

Coverage

Both *Knowledge Index* and *Classmate* currently feature access to more than sixty popular, general interest DIALOG databases in the areas of agriculture, books, business information, chemistry, computers and electronics, education, engineering, government publications, law, magazines, mathematics, medicine, news, psychology, and reference. Each category contains at least one database. These databases are "identical to their DIALOG counterparts in terms of content, coverage, and regularity of updates, although exceptions in "ENGI 1" (Engineering Index) and "MAGA 1" (Magazine Index) coverage should be noted."[5] Each database contains "citations" or "references" that point to articles or books within one broad subject or from a group of publications. Citations are often accompanied by abstracts summarizing the original documents. Some databases also contain full-text articles. Database briefs include more detailed information on each database, and are located in the *User's Workbook*.

For example, the Business and Information Section database briefs cover the *ABI/Inform, Trade and Industry Index,* and *Harvard Business Review* databases. For each database, information provided includes an overview, list of subject areas covered, scope, sample citation, tips for searching subject and non-subject concepts, and material on displaying results. A search example is also contained in the brief.

The *Knowledge Index* Document Ordering Service can be used to obtain copies of articles and other documents not conveniently available at user's libraries. Orders are electronically transmitted to the document supplier, who locates the article and mails a copy of it to users. The charges for ordering documents are stated in the *Knowledge Index* price list. Orders can be billed by the document supplier to credit cards. The *User's Workbook* discusses using the online ordering feature in detail.

Access and Availability

Users can access any of DIALOG's services through one of three communications networks. DIALOG recommends using Dialnet, its own private network, which is the least expensive option. One of the public networks, Tymnet or Telenet, can be used as well. Local telephone numbers for these networks are given in the appendixes to all of DIALOG's user manuals, and detailed network logon and logoff procedure instructions are given as well. The regular DIALOG service is now available through a gateway from RLIN and OCLC.

Virtually any personal computer can act as a terminal to communicate with DIALOG if equipped with the proper hardware and software attachments. A serial interface and modem must be used to connect the user's computer to the phone lines for communicating with DIALOG. DIALOG offers its own communications software package, *DIALOGlink,* for the IBM-PC, which provides for storing logon procedures, uploading stored search strategies, typing ahead of DIALOG responses, and downloading. *DIALOGlink* also contains several accounting functions, which keep track of a library's search accounts, searcher volume, and bill preparation. Recommendations for selecting other communications software are noted in "Making the DIALOG Connection...," a one-page instructional flyer (1986) from DIALOG Information Services. This flyer also addresses how to make the DIALOG connection using other terminals; lists specifications that a terminal, personal computer, word processor, microcomputer, and accompanying modem must meet in order to access DIALOG services; and discusses *DIALOGlink* in detail.

To sign up for *Knowledge Index,* customers must complete a customer agreement. The agreement is fairly standard, asking for name and address, telephone number, credit card information, and authorized signature. Customers are asked to answer several questions as well regarding occupation, affiliation, how they plan to use the system, which databases they are interested in, how they learned about the system, and which equipment and communications or search software will be used to access the system. After the customer agreement is returned to DIALOG, an order confirmation sheet is sent to the customer, including a *Knowledge Index* account number and password.

To initiate service for *Classmate,* the library or school must complete an order form and questionnaire. For *Classmate,* the order form includes a description of the *Classsroom Instruction Program* and terms and conditions. *Classmate* has the same restrictions as the *Classroom Instruction Program* for the regular DIALOG service in that it must be used for course-based instruction. The questionnaire asks for the level of instruction for which the proposed program will be used; names and numbers of the courses in which the account will be used, as well as the names of the responsible instructors; subject area(s) in which instruction will take place; number of students expected to participate in the program per year; time of year when the school or library expects to make the heaviest use of passwords; terminal and modem speeds to be used; type of equipment to be used; number of students to be online simultaneously; and number of passwords requested. An authorized signature must accompany each order form. Up to ten passwords can be requested at no extra charge. Additional passwords can be obtained for a surcharge of $25 per password.

Classmate, as it is used by classes, is available during regular hours of DIALOG operations. *Knowledge Index* is available as a nighttime end-user search service, Monday through Thursday, 6 p.m. to 5 a.m. the next morning; Friday 6 p.m. to midnight; Saturday 8 a.m. to midnight; and Sunday 2 p.m. to 5 a.m. on Monday.

Documentation and Customer Support

Documentation for *Knowledge Index* includes a *User's Workbook,* a self-instructional manual containing all the necessary information for effective use of the system, and a demonstration disc. The *User's Workbook* is arranged in five parts: "Logging On," "Search Basics," "More on Searching," "Ordering Documents," and "Advanced Searching." In addition, there are appendixes, an index, and "Database Briefs." The demonstration disc offers a general introduction to the service, interactive instruction on the three main commands, and a small searchable database (54 abstracts from *ABI/Inform* on computer and telecommunications topics). The disc is available for the IBM-PC and compatible computers. It requires at least 256K of RAM, DOS 2.0 or a later version, and at least one floppy-disk drive. The program runs in color but can also be viewed with monochrome monitors. A quarterly newsletter, *Knowl-*

edge Index News (ISSN 0740–4913), produced by the *Knowledge Index* service contains announcements of new databases, technical tips, staff news, advertisements, and letters from users.

Complete curriculum materials accompany *Classmate* so that online searching can be easily incorporated into any course. Documentation that accompanies *Classmate* consists of a self-instructional user's manual, service newsletter, *Classmate Student Workbook,* and *Teaching Guide.* The *Classmate Student Workbook* and *Teaching Guide* are identical, but the latter contains materials printed on yellow paper solely for the instructor, masters for creating instructional overhead transparencies, a curriculum of in-class activities, readings and lectures from text material, assignments, tests, and discussion sections. The workbook unit is presented in two segments, each lasting five days. The first segment deals with the preliminaries of online searching, and the second with more advanced techniques. Basic topics covered in the first segment include equipment, logging on, planning a search, the importance of synonyms and truncation, Boolean logic connectors, choosing the right database, *Knowledge Index* search commands, and sample practice questions. Advanced techniques covered concern author name, journal name, and company name searching. Students have the opportunity to perform both a simple search locating information about a suggested topic and search on a topic they have chosen. *Knowledge Index* is used as the system of reference, and the *Knowledge Index User's Manual* is recommended for additional background information on and documentation of the system's capabilities and databases. The new *Knowledge Index Slide Show* is suggested as an optional component of the first segment of the unit. In addition, the *Classmate Starter Package* is available, which includes the *Classmate Teaching Guide* and the *Knowledge Index User's Workbook.*

Whenever help is needed while the system is connected to *Knowledge Index* or *Classmate,* the question mark (?) can be entered for a list of the options available. Such options include "Help Sections" (for a list of sections and databases), "Help Commands" (for a description of all commands), and "Help Help" (for a list of all "Help" commands). When the word "Help" is entered followed by the appropriate section, command, operating category, etc., additional information about that item will appear. Personal assistance from DIALOG staff in the United States is also available through a toll-free number. Phone numbers and hours are listed in the users' workbooks.

Ease of Use

The basics of searching *Knowledge Index* and *Classmate* consist of planning the search (i.e., writing down the search topic, and identifying main concepts), choosing a section, beginning in a section online, finding information on the topic, using synonyms for main concept words, and modifying searches in progress.

Once a topic and its main concepts are identified, users select a section in which to search. If there is only one database in the section, the search will be connected to that database. Sections that have more than one database give users a menu of the databases from which to choose. A subject index of topics at the back of the *User's Workbook* assists in the selection of a database in which to search. Users are advised to try more than one section when looking for information on a subject because of the interdisciplinary, or interrelated, character of most subjects. Users are also advised that sections may cover more subjects than their names imply.

Having written down their search topics, identified main concepts, and chosen a section, users tell the system which section to search by using the command "Begin" (abbreviated "b") followed by the section name. Appropriate databases are indicated by using the database abbreviation. "Begin" can also be used to move from one database to another. The question mark (?) prompt signals that the system is ready to receive commands. The command "Find" (abbreviated "f"), similar to DIA-LOG's "Select" command, instructs the computer to locate citations containing the main concept words identified. The "Find" command determines the number of records in the database that contain the search word(s), and stores them in a set. To locate citations containing the terms selected, users simply type "Find," followed by the terms connected by the appropriate Boolean logic operators. Three logical connectors are used in online searching—"OR," "AND," and "NOT." "Recap," another command, is used to view the name of the database and to list all the sets created so far in the search. The "Display" command (abbreviated "d") allows users to see the references, and "logoff" is used to disconnect from the system.

The databases on *Knowledge Index* and *Classmate* contain citations or references that point to articles within one broad subject or that come from a group of publications. Because each database is an individual product (i.e., produced by different companies) aimed to answer specific types of information needs, occasionally, special searching capabilities are needed. Reading the "Database Briefs" in the *User's Workbook* keeps users aware of such capabilities.

Once users have been through the basics of locating information and displaying it, the system makes it possible to conduct more sophisticated searches. Some of these searching techniques include qualifying the "Display" command statement; using the wildcard character "?" for truncation, to search on word stems or variant spellings; using "Find" to do non-subject searching; using the "Expand" command to help with the selection of author names; and using "Find" to search for journal names.

Locating a specific author, publication, or other pertinent information (e.g., company names, people such as actors or actresses, published computer programs, or publication dates is a straightforward process. Non-subject searching is possible by using "Find" and the name of a person in order to retrieve articles about that person, or by using "Find" and the author code to locate citations for articles written by a particular person.

The "Expand" command is useful for looking into the database dictionary to see a listing of alphabetically similar terms in the file. The "Expand" command is thus a window into the database. After viewing the various choices, the user can then select pertinent information. The "Expand" command together with the appropriate prefix code (e.g., "Au = " for "author") can also be used with subjects, publications, company names, and published computer programs. In order to restrict a search to a particular span of time, the user can employ the date of publication in the search strategy. This date is indicated in one of two ways, by year or by the complete date.

The results of a search can be displayed in either short, medium, or long formats. The short version usually consists of the title, plus an accession number in the database. Medium displays usually contain just the bibliographic citation, and long displays contain the entire item record, including the citation, abstract, and descriptors. Each qualifier can be abbreviated by "s" for "short," "m" for "medium" and "l" for "long."

Enhancements to the *Knowledge Index* were made in spring of 1987, when the new *Knowledge Index* search software became a reality. Designed to get a faster response from the computer, the search software offers several new features, including a more sophisticated "Find" command, a "Type" command for continuous output, new ways to restrict searches with the "Limit" capability, and the availability of the "Keep" command to set aside records to order through the "Dialorder" document delivery service. The new search software is almost completely compatible with the earlier version of *Knowledge Index,* so users don't have to change the way they search at all, unless they want to try some of the enhancements.

Pricing

Knowledge Index is charged at the flat rate of $24 per hour. A one-time fee of $35, chargeable to a credit card, entitles customers to a *User's Workbook* and two free hours. New users are given one month to use this $48 credit after they first logon. The cost of access to *Knowledge Index* is based on the amount of time the user is connected to DIALOG, and includes all network telecommunications costs. Users can check how much a search session is costing by entering the command "Cost" at any time while searching. Unlike *BRS After Dark,* there are no minimum fees or monthly handling charges. Other charges that might be incurred for *Dial-mail,* DIALOG's electronic mail service, are a $12 per hour connect charge, a per night charge for conference and bulletin board hosts, a per page charge for offline printing of messages, and a per night charge for online storage of messages. In addition, on *Knowledge Index*, charges are incurred for purchasing the full text of documents and articles while online.

The *Classmate* program geared for high school instruction features a low online connect rate of $15 per hour, including telecommunications costs. There are no type or display charges, monthly minimums, or subscription fees. The *Knowledge Index/Classmate User's Manual,* along with a subscription to the service's newsletter, can be ordered for $30. The *Student Workbook* is $8—$5 each for ten or more copies. The *Teaching Guide* is $20—$15 each for ten or more copies. A *Classmate Starter Kit,* available for $45, contains the *Teaching Guide* and a *Knowledge Index/Classmate User's Manual.*

End-User Response

Articles evaluating the *Knowledge Index/Classmate* interface are numerous. The *Classmate* curriculum has been successfully tested in schools throughout the country; however, as of this writing, end-user response has not been reported in the literature. The following discussion notes those articles that compare *Knowledge Index* with its parent system, DIALOG, and with *BRS After Dark.* Glossbrenner and Kaplan compare the system with the DIALOG search software, which is discussed first.

Glossbrenner's 1984 article reviews differences between the access hours, rates, coverage, and search language and techniques of *Knowledge Index* and *DIALOG.* He finds the off-hours access attractive, the rates reasonable, coverage adequate, and the commands easy to understand and use. Glossbrenner offers two caveats pertaining to *Knowledge Index*—the variability of the currency of the information in the different files, and the importance of reading the manual.[6]

Kaplan's 1985 article considers the system's goals, market, costs, availability, coverage, protocols, and ease of use. Some advantages noted are *Knowledge Index*'s low cost, after-hours service, limited number of files, easier nomenclature, and records that are indistinguishable from their DIALOG counterparts in full format and that contain the same elements. Disadvantages noted are an abbreviated and simplified structure that frustrates sophisticated searchers; file limitations; format restrictions; and lack of certain features, such as SDIs, storing strategies, and offline printing, which do not recommend it for complex or comprehensive searches; another disadvantage is the *Knowledge Index* option of three record-formats, compared with DIALOG's eight or nine. In general, Kaplan rates *Knowledge Index* as a high-quality, reliable, responsive system, which, although it lacks its parent system's flexibility and power, has much to commend it. Comparisons with consumer-oriented utilities, such as CompuServe, note similarities and differences in cost and coverage.[7]

The Janke and Ojala articles, in contrast to the above-mentioned reviews, offer evaluations of *Knowledge Index* and comparisons with *BRS After Dark*. Janke's 1983 article discusses the systems' coverage, ease of use, commands, hours of access, and cost. Janke notes that: (1) *BRS After Dark* offers access to more databases; (2) both systems are easy to use—from a librarian's point of view; (3) *BRS After Dark*'s commands are a little more cryptic than its counterpart's, and BRS has weakened itself by doing away with the online printing of many of the less significant fields for each of the databases; (4) *Knowledge Index* is less familiar in its database access, command, and online printing protocols; (5) hours of availability are comparable; and (6) *BRS After Dark* has the clear advantage when it comes to per hour online connect rate. Overall, Janke is almost equally enthusiastic about these two systems.[8]

Ojala's 1983 review of *Knowledge Index* considers the following: market, coverage, organization, power, flexibility, ease of use, documentation, conception and execution, and software. A summary of her reviews of *BRS After Dark* and of *Knowledge Index* follows, enabling librarians to better determine which system is appropriate for experienced and which for inexperienced online searchers. In general, Ojala prefers *Knowledge Index* over *BRS After Dark*. She notes partial overlap in coverage between the two systems, and differences in system organization in that *Knowledge Index* is command driven, while *BRS After Dark* is menu driven. Differences in the systems' power, flexibility, and ease of use, given the many difficulties inherent in menu-driven systems, are also discussed. Ojala also contrasts the two systems' documentation—the *Knowledge Index Workbook* is rated highly as a "crash course" in online searching, while its counterpart's *User's Manual,* concerned more with logon procedures and rudimentary search requests, contains short database descriptions that give "less of a flavor of the database idiosyncracies than does *Knowledge Index*."[9]

Summary

Both *Classmate* and *Knowledge Index* allow for elementary, intermediate, and advanced searching. In sum, there are "just 12 simple commands, only five of which are used regularly for most searches," and searching "features simplified search commands that are easy to learn and use."[10] The *User's Workbook* provides search examples and worksheets on which to practice and reinforce what has been learned, thus taking users through *Knowledge Index* and *Classmate* step by step.

DIALOG onDisc

This chapter concludes with a brief discussion of the *DIALOG on-Disc* family, a series of CD-ROM products based on popular databases available from DIALOG. These CD-ROM databases can be searched with the same online commands as *DIALOG2* or through a series of easy-to-follow menus.

DIALOG onDisc is aimed at students, faculty, researchers, and others with access to personal computer workstations in libraries, businesses, and academic institutions worldwide. *DIALOG onDisc* is also targeted at librarians, who like the following facts: (1) the ease of use for *DIALOG onDisc* products makes it far less staff intensive than most online services in libraries today; (2) the products require no additional staffing; and (3) with unlimited searching being available at a fixed cost, librarians can budget accurately.

DIALOG onDisc products come on one or more CD-ROMs, with retrieval software, documentation, and support. Regular update discs are shipped as more current information becomes available. Any combination of databases, with optional PC workstation hardware, can be leased. The advantages of these products are their comprehensive search capability; the power they can provide when teamed with searching DIALOG online; the availability of unlimited searching; and convenience for unlimited users. *DIALOG onDisc* is the first CD-ROM product to include search software that equals the full power of a major online retrieval system. Search capabilities include defining record formats for display or printing, sorting the information before printing it, and downloading search results for further manipulation and analysis. When finished with a search on the CD-ROM database, users can switch easily to an online search with DIALOG's *DIALOGlink* communications software in order to obtain more recent information. Besides providing convenient unlimited search time, *DIALOG onDisc* enables users to browse through references while they develop and refine search strategies. These refined strategies can then be saved and executed online on DIALOG without the costs that would normally be incurred for strategy development.

The DIALOG command language and "Easy Menu" constitute the two search options for *DIALOG onDisc*. The "Easy Menu" option makes it easy to demonstrate *DIALOG onDisc* products to beginners, and it also makes searching by novices a simple and rewarding process.

After logon, a "Select 'Search Mode'" screen appears. Users select from "DIALOG Command Search," "Easy Menu Search," "Online

Search," or "Return to DOS." "DIALOG Command Search" is essentially traditional DIALOG, and as such, it is characterized by a clear and logical command language. DIALOG searching techniques are the same, and users can learn about searching *DIALOG onDisc* at standard DIALOG training seminars. Practicing on CD-ROM at seminars held in the DIALOG offices is a regular component of these seminars. The "Easy Menu Search" offers users the options of searching by subject descriptors, title, author name, journal name, publication year, or additional fields such as identifier, abstract, corporate source, language, or document type. When a subject search is initiated, and terms entered, the system responds by highlighting that term in a rotated alphabetical display, and by indicating records retrieved for each term in the display. Users may then elect to display, print, sort, or transfer (download) the records found; modify the current search with additional criteria; begin a new search; or quit the "Easy Menu" mode. Each of these activities— "Display," "Print," "Modify," "Begin," or "Quit"—constitute easily understood and self-explanatory commands that can be entered in full or abbreviated format.

Cost varies with the database(s) purchased on CD-ROM. *ERIC* is the first database available on CD-ROM from DIALOG. *DIALOG onDisc ERIC* contains the complete thesaurus of *ERIC* descriptors for searching. Two discs are available: current *ERIC* information from 1981 to the present, or the complete *ERIC* file. *DIALOG onDisc ERIC* leases for $950 per year as a prepaid license fee for the current file (1981–present), or $1650 per year for the complete *DIALOG onDisc ERIC* subscription. This service includes disc(s), quarterly CD-ROM updates, *DIALOG onDisc Manager Search* software and telecommunications software, documentation, searching assistance from a telephone hotline, and shipping. Prices for quantity orders vary.

In May 1987, *Medline* and NTIS were introduced to *DIALOG's onDisc* product line. *OnDisc Medline* is now in a two-disc format, containing current records and a one-year backfile. The two discs are available through June 1988 for $1250. After June, the cost will be $1450. Backfile discs will become available during the first half of 1988. The complete version will consist of five discs going back to 1984. This version may be ordered through June 1988 for $2250. After June, the annual cost will be $2450.

OnDisc NTIS consists of a single disc covering 1984 through 1988. A two-disc version of *OnDisc NTIS* will become available during the first half of 1988, and will cover the years 1980 to 1988. Through June 1988, the single disc is available at an annual subscription fee of $2350. This fee includes the initial disc and quarterly updates. Beginning in July 1988, the annual fee will be $2750.

DIALOG onDisc products require access to the following equipment: an IBM-PC or compatible with DOS 2.0 or a higher version; 384K RAM minimum (640K recommended); a hard disk with at least one megabyte of free space; a Philips CM 100 or a Hitachi CDR-1502S CD-ROM drive with controller card, both industry standard brands; and a Hayes or compatible modem. A special DIALOG/Philips arrangement helps with the purchase of a Philips CD-ROM drive, or users can lease the entire personal computer workstation through special arrangements DIALOG has made with equipment vendors.

Toll-free telephone hotline support for searching assistance is available 24 hours a day, five days a week, and on Saturdays from 10:00 a.m. to 6:00 p.m. EST. Documentation for *DIALOG onDisc* products is minimal at this writing. A brochure, *"DIALOG onDisc:* Information for Everyone," is available from DIALOG for users desiring more information. A special floppy diskette designed to view the *DIALOG onDisc* product line allows users to learn the main benefits and capabilities of *DIALOG onDisc*, get a realistic impression of product performance, and acquire a general understanding of how *DIALOG onDisc* works. *ERIC, Medline,* and *NTIS* are discussed within the diskette.

Given the promises of this resource—special benefits when the system is purchased from DIALOG; the best of both worlds for DIALOG online subscribers; unlimited searching and convenience for unlimited users; two search options; comprehensive search capabilities; the packaging of a mountain of information; and proven technology—and its potential, positive reviews of *DIALOG onDisc* products are beginning to appear in the library literature. In looking at these products, one must consider the pluses and minuses of such systems, as well as their impact on collection development and resource sharing decisions. Looking ahead, and to relate this discussion back to earlier discussions of online searching in schools, it is clear that CD-ROM-based search systems will be studied closely by school librarians and media specialists. *DIALOG onDisc* products and other CD-ROM databases promise to change the means and pace of implementing end-user online searching.

NOTES

1. Robin Kaplan, "Knowledge Index: A Review," *Database* 8 (June 1985): 122.

2. Ibid.

3. *Prepare Students to Meet the Information Challenge* (brochure). Palo Alto, Calif.: Dialog, n.d.

4. Ibid.

5. Kaplan, "Knowledge Index," 123.

6. A. Glossbrenner, "Looking It Up on Knowledge Index," *PC* 3 (July 24, 1984): 369, 372.

7. Kaplan, "Knowledge Index," 122–28.
8. Richard V. Janke, "Online After Six: End User Searching Comes of Age," *Online* 8 (Nov. 1984): 15–29.
9. M. Ojala, "Knowledge Index: A Review," *Online* 7 (Sept. 1983): 31–34.
10. Martin Kesselman, "Online Update," *Wilson Library Bulletin* 61 (June 1987): 53.

BIBLIOGRAPHY

Aversa, Elizabeth Smith, and Jacqueline C. Mancall. "Planting the Seed...Online in the Schools." *Online* 11 (May 1987): 15–19.

"Dialog Introduces New Service for Business Users." *IDP Report* 7 (Apr. 11, 1986): 1–3.

"Dialog Launches Knowledge Index in Europe." *Online Review* 8 (Aug. 1984): 288–89.

Fiebert, Elyse Evans. "Online at Radnos High: A Pattern of Change." *Online* 11 (May 1987): 19–21.

Glossbrenner, A. "Looking It Up on Knowledge Index." *PC* 3 (July 24, 1984): 369, 372.

Janke, R. V. "Online After Six: End User Searching Comes of Age." *Online* 8 (Nov. 1984): 15–29.

Kaplan, Robin. "Knowledge Index: A Review." *Database* 8 (June 1985): 122–28.

Kesselman, Martin. "Online Update." *Wilson Library Bulletin* 61 (June 1987): 53–54.

Latamore, G. B. "On-Line Services: The Business Connection." *Popular Computing* 4 (Mar. 1985): 75–78, 80.

Lodish, Erica K. "Classmate to 2100: Dialog at Montgomery Blair." *Online* 11 (May 1987): 27–31.

Lynch, Eugene A. "Online at East Lyme (CT): Dow Jones Gets High Marks." *Online* 11 (May 1987): 21–24.

Newman, Donald. "Dialogue on Dialog: Interview with Roger Summit." *Wilson Library Bulletin* 61 (Jan. 1986): 21–25.

Ojala, M. "Knowledge Index: A Review." *Online* 7 (Sept. 1983): 31–34.

Rodgers, R. T. "The Wide World of Dialog and the Knowledge Index Alternative." *Lawyer's PC* 1 (May 15, 1984): 1–7.

Smith, Bev. "DIALOG—Patriarch of the Online Generation Holds Industry Lead." *Information Today* (May 1984): 11–13.

Tenopir, Carol. "Dialog's Knowledge Index and BRS/After Dark: Database Searching on Personal Computers." *Library Journal* 108 (Mar. 1, 1983): 471–74.

Tootill, Peter. "Knowledge Index." *Personal Computer World* 8 (Sept. 1985): 134.

Vollaro, Alice J., and Donald T. Hawkins. "End-User Searching in Large Library Network: A Case Study of Patent Attorneys." *Online* 10 (July 1986): 67.

Wilburn, G., and M. Wilburn. "Knowledge Index: A New Service Offering the Professional Databases of DIALOG." *InfoAge* 2 (Dec./Jan. 1983–84): 36–37.

Walcott, J. Andrew. "The Rutgers Prep Experience." *Online* 11 (May 1987): 24.

Chapter 6

End-User Services Available from H. W. Wilson and the Information Access Company

Rosemarie Riechel

The end-user products available from H. W. Wilson and from the Information Access Company (IAC) provide access to very current databases covering a broad range of topics via systems with attractive searching features. An examination of the automated services of the two companies seems to indicate that they are complementary, not competitive. Wilson, the youngest of the online vendors, offers more databases than IAC, but IAC's databases contain more retrospective material (i.e., the *Magazine Index* goes back to 1959, and the *National Newspaper Index* starts with 1979).

Although the aim is the same, each service offers unique features as well as some drawbacks. The records in the databases of one service are not altogether the same as those in the other. Are the products of one company to be preferred over those of the other? The answer to this question depends on individual assessment of the products, determination of user needs, and the availability of funding. Access to both services is, of course, the ideal, since what cannot be found via the Wilson indexes might be located through *Search Helper* or *InfoTrac*. Further qualitative and quantitative study is needed in order to draw accurate conclusions.

The following examination of the automated services of the two companies considers their background, access, and availability, including equipment requirements, and describes their services with respect to coverage, pricing, documentation, and customer support, and their actual or potential use with end users.

H. W. WILSON SERVICES

Background

The H. W. Wilson Company's print publications have appealed to the library market since 1898, with the introduction of the *Cumulative Book Index,* followed by the *Readers' Guide to Periodical Literature* in 1901. When Wilson entered the online marketplace, the tradition of controlling all operations to ensure the quality and timeliness of its publications was continued. Wilson was entering a competitive market occupied by established vendors, particularly DIALOG and its impressive collection of databases. The quality of the widely known Wilson printed indexes called attention to a new online service (*Wilsonline*) that offered access to unique databases. *Wilsonline* was introduced in November 1984 after two years of in-house testing, followed by extensive on-site testing and evaluation by public, academic, and school libraries. *Wilsonline* was designed primarily for intermediaries. More recently, access for end users has been provided to *Wilsonline* through the introductions of *Wilsearch,* a front-end software package, and *Wilsondisc,* which includes *Wilsonline* databases on CD-ROM.

Wilsearch was developed as a result of Wilson's efforts to market its online databases as widely as possible by providing a package that would offer simplified online searching to anyone. *Wilsearch* was introduced in July 1985 as a menu-driven front-end software package for end-user searching. It also serves as a communications software package, because the librarian or other intermediary with a *Wilsonline* password can also use it to access *Wilsonline* directly.

Wilsearch was designed to allow quick access to all Wilson databases with minimal assistance. It offers inexpensive searching and is excellent for ready reference, such as verifying bibliographic citations and creating quick bibliographies.

Wilson's look at CD-ROM technology for the storage of extensive databases (e.g., a year's worth of *Readers' Guide* and other retrospective databases) resulted in the announcement of *Wilsondisc,* a CD-ROM search system previewed at the 1986 American Library Association annual conference in New York and introduced at the 1987 midwinter conference in Chicago.

Coverage

Like the printed indexes, coverage for *Wilsonline* ranges from general to specialized subjects and technical information of fairly recent vintage. The databases available through Wilsonline include:

Applied Science and Technology Index, 1983–present
Art Index, Oct. 1984–present

Bibliographic Index, Nov. 1984–present
Biography Index, July 1984–present
Biological and Agricultural Index, July 1983–present
Business Periodicals Index, June 1982–present
Cumulative Book Index, Jan. 1982–present
Education Index, Sept. 1983–present
Essay and General Literature Index, Jan. 1986–present
General Science Index, May 1984–present
Humanities Index, Feb. 1984–present
Index to Legal Periodicals, Feb. 1984–present
LC MARC Database, Jan. 1977–present
Readers' Guide to Periodical Literature, Jan. 1983–present
Social Science Index, Feb. 1984–present
Vertical File Index, Dec. 1985–present

In addition, three databases were developed to maintain authority control over the journals, names, and publishers included in all the bibliographic databases: *Publishers Directory, Journal Directory,* and *Name Authority File.* These databases can be searched for information and verification.

Wilsearch includes access to all *Wilsonline* databases. For *Wilsondisc,* the databases currently available in CD-ROM include *Applied Science and Technology Index, Art Index, Biography Index, Business Periodicals Index, Cumulative Book Index, Education Index, General Science Index, Humanities Index, Index to Legal Periodicals, Library Literature,* and *Social Sciences Index.*

Access and Availability

If online searching is already being done, new equipment will not likely be needed to access *Wilsonline.* Any standard ASCII computer terminal (CRT or print) can be used, as well as most microcomputers. For access via a microcomputer, one needs a telephone line, serial interface, modem, and communications software. Wilson's commitment to currency of information is evident, since the databases are updated continuously, at least twice per week.

Wilsearch can be used with the IBM-PC, -XT, -AT, -PC jr., and IBM-compatibles and a Hayes modem (128K of memory is required; 256K is necessary for the PC jr.), or with an Apple IIe with 128K of memory, a floppy disk drive (two for faster searching), a Hayes 1200-baud modem, and a super serial card. Security problems, particularly with regard to the software, seem likely. For instance, a patron might remove the *Wilsearch* program diskette and replace it with a personal one and tie up the computer. Then, too, it seems rather easy to tamper with the set-up portion of the program, causing problems for staff as well as for other end users.

Because of *Wilsondisc,* Wilson became a value-added dealer of IBM-PCs and peripherals. The company offers a workstation package that includes both the software and the hardware now based in the IBM PS/2. The $4995 price includes installation and one day of training. At present, a workstation is needed for each database purchased unless a library is willing to swap discs. Wilson is committed to incorporating jukebox technology as soon as it is available, allowing access to multiple databases from the same station.

Documentation and Customer Support

The *Wilsonline Guide and Documentation* clearly describes system commands; gives information for efficient searching; and includes a tutorial, a description of each database, searchable fields, etc. A quick reference guide includes a list of databases, logon and logoff procedures, system commands, search/print qualifiers, and system messages. A subscription to *Wilsearch* includes a quick reference card, a guide to the system, and a *Wilsonline Guide.* Online "help" screens on *Wilsonline* also provide immediate information. A toll-free number is available Monday through Friday from 9 a.m. to 8 p.m. EST, and Saturday from 9 a.m. to 5 p.m. EST for assistance with any of the *Wilsonline* services.

One-day training sessions on *Wilsonline* are offered for $60 per person; and a half-day seminar, focusing on searching in various subject areas, is available for $30. Free update sessions were begun to introduce new system features to *Wilsonline* users.

Online Searching: An Introduction to Wilsonline, a 28-minute video, can be purchased for $89. The video introduces *Wilsonline* and *Wilsearch,* and discusses online information retrieval in general, as well as the advantages of *Wilsonline.* The use of various commands, features, and sample search strategies are shown in order to demonstrate the system's capabilities. The videotape is also available as part of a special training package that includes *Wilsonline* training, two hours of free search time, search manuals, and a *Wilsearch* demonstration diskette for $159 ($119 without the training and search time).

Ease of Use

Wilsonline was designed for ease of use by inexperienced and experienced searchers (who might be discouraged by the thought of learning yet another search protocol). After logon (via Telenet or Tymnet), the searcher can choose from three file commands: the "Files" command alone lists all available databases; the "File" with database mnemonic(s) is used to enter a particular file or to conduct a multi-file search; and "File ?" is entered if the user does not remember which file was being searched.

Files on *Wilsonline* can be searched using controlled vocabulary or free text, and the terms entered can be combined using the three Boolean operators "AND," "OR," and "NOT." Various qualifiers, an online thesaurus, and automatic switching from the "see" reference to the preferred term are available as additional attractive features.

In response to user comments, Wilson added several system enhancements in November 1986. Searching on *Wilsonline* has been improved by the addition of proximity searching, nested Boolean logic using parentheses, changes to the "print" and "neighbor" commands, and a new "explain" command.

On *Wilsearch*, the main menu has seven options that allow the searcher to go to *Wilsearch*, to look at an overview of the *Wilsonline* system, to review the results of the last search, to go directly into *Wilsonline*, to go into the set-up menu (designed to enter the Telenet and Tymnet phone numbers and to enter the *Wilsearch* and *Wilsonline* user ID and password), or to exit to DOS.

The database selection menu lists the various subject areas; and, once a selection is made, *Wilsearch* will select the appropriate databases. The database selection screen also gives the searcher the option of choosing up to two databases him- or herself and having them searched simultaneously.

The search strategy screen lists the search access points and instructs the user in the development of the search. The Boolean "AND" is assumed, but terms can also be "OR"d together by keying in the word "any." After the search has been formulated, *Wilsearch* automatically logs on to *Wilsonline*, performs the search, downloads up to ten citations, and automatically logs off.

The "search results" screen allows the user to review the results and to print them. *Wilsearch* asks the user if each citation is relevant. For those so designated as relevant, *Wilsearch* displays the subject headings, which may be used in researching the same topic in order to possibly improve retrieval.

With the set-up menu on *Wilsearch*, the library can prevent abuse of the service by specifying the number of searches a patron can run and by limiting the number of references that can be downloaded. This feature makes charging the patron easy, if fees are desired.

It was decided with *Wilsondisc* that total access to *Wilsonline*, *Wilsearch*, and the CD-ROM Wilson database would be provided in a single integrated search system. The ability to switch from searching the CD-ROM database to online using the same search strategy is an exciting feature. The idea is to search the disc for retrospective information (with no online charge involved) and then change to *Wilsonline* directly, or via *Wilsearch*, for current data (the only charge is for telecommunications costs.) There are four search modes to accommodate all searchers, ranging from the novice to the experienced user, including BROWSE, WILSEARCH, WILSONLINE, and EXPERT WILSONLINE. BROWSE, the easiest mode, is designed to give the new user a taste of online searching by providing quick and simple access to subject headings and to "see" and "see also" references. When a subject is typed in, an alphabetical list of related terms plus postings is displayed. If no postings are found for the subject sought, one can view "see also" terms or display other related terms. The WILSEARCH mode (also aimed at inexperienced users) guides the user through the search process with the help of menus, as with the *Wilsearch* front-end software. The WILSONLINE mode offers the same search capabilities that are available through *Wilsonline*, including truncation, nested Boolean logic, and print commands. EXPERT WILSONLINE is designed for the experienced searcher and uses *Wilsonline*, plus it includes continuous viewing of the search strategy, expanded screen handling, and windowing functions.

Pricing

Annual subscription rates for *Wilsonline* range from $300 to $2400, and hourly connect-time rates vary for each database. The pricing schedule was designed to make *Wilsonline* affordable to most libraries, particularly the new market of small- and medium-sized libraries lacking online access because of budget limitations. There are no sign-up costs, no charges for online prints, no charges for saved searches, lower rates if the library subscribes to Wilson printed index(es), and lower fees for deposit accounts. A package can be tailored to suit individual subscribers.

Wilsearch pricing is exceedingly attractive. There is an annual licensing fee of $150 for the software, consisting of a copy-protected diskette plus a back-up diskette, with updated versions of the software being sent when available. A search (defined as the downloading of ten references per logon) can cost as little as $1. Various payment options are offered. Prepaid options include $750 for 250 searches at $3 per search, $1000 for 500 searches at $2 per search, and $2000 for 2000 searches at $1 per search. The non-prepaid option costs $5 per search, and customers are billed monthly for searches actually made. There is no charge if nothing is found (i.e., no results or zero postings), and there is no hourly charge for computer time. A special demonstration diskette of *Wilsearch* is available at a special rate of $20 for 20 searches.

Wilsondisc databases on CD-ROM vary from $1095 to $1495 per year. *Wilsondisc*'s pricing is very attractive when a library considers that it includes unlimited access both to the CD-ROM database and to searching that database online. Discs are updated on a quarterly basis and are mastered in March, June, September, and December. A demonstration disc is available for $99 that includes coverage from April through September

1986 for each of the Wilson indexes. The $99 is then applied to the first invoice if the decision to subscribe to any of the *Wilsondisc* databases is made.

End-User Response

A search of the library literature revealed that little on-site use of *Wilsearch* in libraries has been studied in any depth. One evaluation done at the University of Maryland is quite critical of *Wilsearch*. Drawbacks noted in the review include the following comments: (1) the option of "main menu," which provides direct access to *Wilsonline*, should not be included, as this option demands expertise that the end user probably does not have; (2) the set-up and exit to DOS options should not be available to patrons; (3) the selection and database selection menus are unclear as to separate choices; (4) certain keys and screens are confusing, e.g., the difference between subject headings and subject words; (5) the use of the Boolean operators "AND" and "OR," and the method of entering them is unclear; and (6) receiving one reference at a time rather than being able to print them all in one step is time consuming.[1] This reviewer, however, did note that the price is right and that the product is generally a good one. Although he felt that *Wilsearch* would be difficult to use without staff assistance, the purchase of the demonstration diskette is recommended as an economical way of assessing the product. Other reviews find that *Wilsearch*'s features are quite self explanatory, that the "help" screens are good, and that the database is efficient and inexpensive. They give *Wilsearch* good marks, but like the review noted above, many do not view it as a system that can be run and fully understood by the end user. Some assistance and modification is needed before the end user can search independently and without the level of training that is currently necessary. The need for training and assistance might also have an impact on staff by taking time away from reference desk service. For some libraries, it might be necessary to limit hours of access to *Wilsearch*, depending on the availability of librarians. In a recent review in *Online,* libraries were urged to carefully weigh the pros and cons of the product before making the commitment to purchase *Wilsearch*. Indeed, for many, the Wilson hard copy indexes may be more user friendly than *Wilsearch*, albeit they do lack Boolean and proximity search capabilities.

Summary

Wilson has responded to the anticipated and expressed needs of its users and potential subscribers by adding enhancements, by maintaining editorial control and currency of data, and by creating an easy-to-use and economical system. *Wilsonline* is an excellent online reference tool, providing quick access to bibliographic information. With the additions of *Wilsearch* and *Wilsondisc,* Wilson is now able to offer access to its indexes and databases in a variety of electronic formats. Whether *Wilsondisc* is a success or not depends on user preference.

INFORMATION ACCESS COMPANY

Background

The Information Access Company (IAC), the developer of an impressive list of automated products, was begun in 1976 and acquired by Ziff-Davis (a major U.S. magazine publisher) in 1980. Committed to providing comprehensive coverage of current as well as retrospective information, IAC caught the attention of libraries with its creation of an online guide to general interest periodical literature, the *Magazine Index,* which provides bibliographic information for articles published in more than 400 popular magazines (dating from 1959 to the present, with a small gap from 1970 to 1973). Subsequent databases increased the number of publications that could be quickly accessed to retrieve information on a variety of subjects, i.e., business, national and international events, consumer products and services, government regulations and policies, people, places, dates, legal facts, and industry and computer news.

IAC saw the potential inherent in a product that uses the microcomputer to extend the accessibility of the company's online databases to a wide range of users and that attracts many potential users wanting to conduct their own searches with the aid of a front-end package requiring no training or knowledge of online searching. The introduction of *Search Helper* in 1982 was timely, since it coincided with the increased use of microcomputers in homes, offices, and libraries, and with the resulting search for new and innovative applications. Do-it-yourself online searching was an attractive concept, and with *Search Helper,* IAC offered a system that promised ease of use, predictability, and impressive cost savings. *Search Helper* was discontinued December 31, 1987. According to IAC, this discontinuance was due to DIALOG's system enhancements and subsequent interface problems with the *Search Helper* program, and with the expense of either maintaining compatibility or changing vendors.

InfoTrac was introduced in January 1985 to provide efficient, low-cost access to current bibliographic information by combining computer access with optical disc storage. *InfoTrac* includes citations from about 900 publications indexed in the *Magazine Index,* the *Business Index,* and the *Legal Resource Index.* It was not designed to replace the IAC microfilm indexes and does not replace online searching via *Search Helper* or via the major online vendors. Rather, the aim was to appeal to an identified market for unassisted public access to general reference periodicals and business information in large public or academic libraries by offering a product with a fixed, predictable cost. Additional videodisc products announced include *LegalTrac,* which contains indexes to more than 700 law publications, the *Government Publications Index,* and eight-year cumulation of the *GPO Monthly Catalog,* and the full text of the *Wall Street Journal.* Additional enhancements to *InfoTrac* announced by IAC include dial-out capabilities from the *InfoTrac* workstation to online databases, and downloading capabilities from both *InfoTrac* and online services.

InfoTrac is attractive because it is designed for ease of use and is strictly for the end user while offering features superior to the single-topic linear searching of the microfilm indexes. A number of online searching capabilities are available, including the ability to browse through an online thesaurus while constructing a search strategy, to locate precise subject headings in order to retrieve relevant citations, to rapidly retrieve data that is generally difficult to gather manually, and to search for material drawn from different databases, thereby eliminating multiple look-ups in a number of indexes. Another advantage of *InfoTrac* is derived from the large storage capacity of videodiscs—extensive access to current information at a fixed cost.

IAC introduced its newest laser-disc product, *InfoTrac II,* at the 1987 ALA midwinter conference in Chicago. Also known as *Magazine Index Plus, InfoTrac II* includes the four most current years of the *Magazine Index* database, plus three months of current citations from the *New York Times.* Unlike *InfoTrac I,* this latest product is a single-user station with the disc player contained within the microcomputer. And this year, a special academic version of *InfoTrac* in CD-ROM, suitable for undergraduate research, was brought to market.

IAC announced yet another innovative product at the National Online Meeting in May 1987. This development includes a single workstation that allows access to any of the *InfoTrac* databases on videodisc as well as DIALOG's *DIALOG onDisc* CD-ROM databases such as *ERIC.* The idea is to allay fears of product obsolescence by making an existing product even more attractive. Enhanced *InfoTrac* is an intriguing marriage of technologies that bears watching.

Coverage

Databases available from the Information Access Company include the *Magazine Index* and the *Magazine ASAP,* which indexes articles in popular magazines with the ASAP file, including the full text of articles from more than 80 of these magazines; the *Trade and Industry Index* and the *Trade and Industry ASAP,* which index business journals emphasizing trade, industry, commerce, and technological developments, and include the *Wall Street Journal, New York Times Business Section,* and *PR Newswire;* the *National Newspaper Index,* which indexes the *New York Times, Wall Street Journal, Christian Science Monitor,* and national and international news items published in the *Washington Post* and *Los Angeles Times;* and *Newsearch,* which contains the current month's news only and provides a daily update of the publications covered in other IAC databases. More specialized IAC databases include the *Legal Resource Index, Management Contents, the Computer Database,* and *Industry Data Sources.*

All of these databases are available online via *DIALOG* and *BRS,* while *Magazine Index ASAP* and *Trade and Industry ASAP* are accessible through Mead Data Central's *NEXIS* as well. All but two of the databases are updated monthly. *The Computer Database,* covering a rapidly changing technology, is updated biweekly. *Newsearch,* updated daily, makes it possible to conduct online searches in a number of IAC databases for information or articles that appeared in the last 24 hours or within the month in any of more than 2500 publications indexed. The currency of the *Newsearch* database reaffirms IAC's commitment to providing access to current and timely information.

InfoTrac databases include the *InfoTrac* core database, which includes three years' worth of indexing from approximately 900 periodicals taken from the *Magazine Index* and from the *Trade and Industry Index,* as well as from the *New York Times* and the *Wall Street Journal; LegalTrac* covers approximately 750 legal publications dating from 1980 to the present; the *Wall Street Journal Database InfoTrac* includes the full text of the journal for the past twelve months; and the *Government Publications Index* contains the last eight years' worth of the *Monthly Catalog.*

Access and Availability

For *InfoTrac*, multiple stations (up to four) allow end users to simultaneously search for citations without any effect on response time. Each access station consists of an IBM-PC with 256K of memory, one floppy disk drive for the program disk, a monitor, and an HP-Thinkjet printer. IAC provides security enclosures for the hardware the company supplies in order to keep the system fixed and tamper-proof. A central control unit (also secreted) consists of one controller, a multihost interface, a videodisc player, and interface cards and cables that are attached to the microcomputers. *InfoTrac* is updated on a monthly basis. After sixty months of continuous subscription, the hardware becomes the property of the subscriber. If a library owns the necessary hardware, subscriptions for the videodisc alone are also available. Unlike *InfoTrac, InfoTrac II*

(*Magazine Index Plus*) is a single-user station with the disc player contained within the microcomputer.

Documentation and Customer Support

Since Library of Congress Subject Headings are used with IAC databases, the *Subject Guide to IAC Databases* is helpful for users in choosing precise terms when formulating a search. IAC has a toll-free number for customer service, which should be called by the staff in charge and not the end user.

Subscriptions to *InfoTrac* include a manual that adequately explains the system and answers questions about its operation for the staff responsible for the service. For users, there are color-coded function keys on the IBM keyboard, along with a corresponding coded instruction card. On-screen program prompts are easy to understand, and the appropriate subject headings and "see" references are highlighted. A "help" key that displays a menu of online "help" screens is also available.

Ease of Use

Although *Search Helper* has been discontinued, its interface and use within libraries are of interest in demonstrating the potential front-end software holds for end users. *Search Helper* was created by IAC to provide the following advantages to libraries and end users. First, the use of *Search Helper* saved professional staff time, since patrons needed no intermediary. Second, bibliographic data could be retrieved quickly and economically, and patrons were able to compile and update their own bibliographies. Third, *Search Helper* enhanced the existing reference and information services, particularly by providing quick access to current information. Fourth, the database offered predictable online searching costs. Fifth, it could be used to introduce online searching to librarians lacking prior knowledge.

The menu screens on *Search Helper* were clear and easily understood by the end user and, if followed correctly, resulted in successful searches. Before a search could be executed on *Search Helper*, the software ran through some diagnostic telecommunications tests. The *Search Helper* introductory screen welcomed the searcher and indicated that the "return" key had to be pressed to continue with the program. The next menu screen to appear was the database selection screen. A brief on-screen description was provided for each database. A topic definition screen asked the searcher to indicate whether information about a person or a subject was wanted. At this step, the searcher was provided with concise instructions and examples on entering terms. Terms and phrases could be added by following the same topic definition screens in order to modify the search, or the search could be executed. *Search Helper* then logged on, connected to the chosen database, executed the search, downloaded the first 20 references into the microcomputer, and logged off. Without any time or cost restrictions, the searcher could display or print either all 20 or only selected references. If the next 20 references were requested, *Search Helper* again logged on to the database and downloaded them for browsing and printing, but this second request constituted an additional search.

After logging on to the database, terms were "AND"ed, the only Boolean operator that was available via *Search Helper*. A person's name was retrieved when the first name and last name appeared in the same field, regardless of sequence. When a subject was specified, references were retrieved when they occurred within two words of each other (the DIALOG 2W proximity operator was added automatically) in the sequence entered.

With *InfoTrac*, the searcher can easily browse a thesaurus for relevant terms or examine cross-references in order to locate more appropriate or related concepts; he or she then can quickly move to any term to view and print relevant citations.

Color-coded function keys with a corresponding instruction card affixed (with velcro strips) to the front of the IBM-PC, concealing the disk drive, easily guide the user through the search, retrieval, and printing steps. Subject headings or names occur in a single alphabetical listing using Library of Congress headings. "See" and "see also" references appear after the subject headings. If no exact match for the term entered is found, the system displays the subject guide at the point of closest match.

The bibliographic data provided for each citation includes an article accession code for the full text available in IAC's *Magazine Collection* or *Business Collection* (microfilm libraries that contain the complete issues of several popular and business magazines). Demand for periodicals not held but frequently requested may be filled by subscribing to particular periodicals, via interlibrary loan, or by subscribing to yet another IAC product, such as these microfilm collections.

In the February 1987 issue of *Database,* Hall and Talan of San Francisco State University, and Pease of California State University at Chico identified the following problems with using *InfoTrac*: (1) if the quality of the answer is to be high, undergraduates cannot search efficiently without some training and assistance, since they do not understand subject limitations and tend to use incorrect search strategy; (2) the majority of the periodicals indexed are business or trade and industry oriented, resulting in a paucity of general interest, scholarly, and research journals; (3) authority control is inadequate, and there is a greater-than-average error rate in the indexing; and (4) with IAC's emphasis on speed and convenience, rather than on building search strategy skills, *InfoTrac* cannot be called a learning tool; the system creates the illusion that the student need go no further to complete research.

Pricing

The annual subscription rate for *InfoTrac* (as of January 1986), including all hardware and maintenance, is $13,000 for one access station, plus $1000 for each addition access station up to four. If other databases are included, the initial cost is even greater. The price is reduced to $7500 plus the cost of the database(s) if the library owns the access stations, and to $4000 plus database(s) subscription(s) if both the access stations and the control unit are library owned. The annual subscription rates (including monthly updates) for the databases currently available on the *Info-Trac* system are $4500 for either the *InfoTrac* or the *LegalTrac* databases, $3500 for the *Government Publications Index,* and $5500 for the *Wall Street Journal* database. Discounts are available for multiple system and database subscriptions. The *InfoTrac* system is also available on a free trial basis. *InfoTrac II* costs $4500 per year, which includes the microcomputer, built-in CD-ROM player, monitor, keyboard, printer (all locked in a security case), software, 12 monthly updates, maintenance, and support service.

End-User Response

Because *Search Helper* was available for five years, several studies of its usefulness were reported in the library literature. At California State University, Long Beach, the service was installed in September 1982. Reference librarians (not end users) received the necessary training. Some attractive advantages included the ease of quickly creating current bibliographies (ideal for undergraduate term papers), and the system's usefulness to librarians seeking quick and current information on library and information science topics (via the *Magazine Index*), for updating information in IAC's microfilm indexes, for providing access to the *Legal Resource Index,* and for retrieving information that is difficult to obtain manually for ready reference. Disadvantages noted were that *Search Helper* could only "AND" terms, that search strategies could not be saved and executed in other databases, and the menu-driven interface was boring for librarians.

Search Helper also was acquired by the Central Reference Department at Louisiana State University at Baton Rouge in 1983. Because IAC's instructions for the novice user were thought to be inadequate, a brochure was developed that briefly described the service and the contents of the databases, and that provided searching tips and an outline of search procedures. All reference staff attended a one-hour workshop to gain familiarity with the service and competency in providing end-user assistance. Although their first experiences were disappointing, mainly due to connection problems, staff decided to give the product another chance so that adequate data could be gathered for a more thorough evaluation. During a subsequent free trial period, use of the service increased substantially, and staff took a closer look at its potential as a reference tool. The new finding was that *Search Helper* was a good end-user public access tool because it was simple to use, and the revised version of the software seemed to have eliminated the connection problems.

At the Queens Borough Public Library in New York, the cost of on-line searching via the major online services restricted access to a few trained librarian-searchers. *Search Helper* was acquired in November 1982 because its low cost and simplicity of use made it possible for all the librarians on the central library staff to conduct online searches. A number of training sessions were given to instruct staff in the use of the microcomputer and *Search Helper*. Since IAC does not fill the need for quick reference aids, brief guides to search strategy and available search modifiers were developed. The system was and is still viewed as an economical and efficient reference tool that complemented the printed indexes. It was heavily used to answer ready reference queries, as a starting point for more in-depth research, and for the creation of quick and current bibliographies of up to 40 citations. *Search Helper* was also used to answer telephone requests for citations of particular articles or facts in the news, and it was sometimes used to control the cost of searching the major vendor services by verifying information about a subject before entering any of the other database services, thus reducing online costs.

Carnegie-Mellon University tested *Search Helper* from April 1984 to January 1985 in order to examine untrained patron reaction to end-user searching. Generally, the results of the survey were favorable and revealed that all the participants like the system, even though two-thirds of the respondents indicated that most or none of the citations obtained seemed to be relevant. Additionally, most expressed a willingness to pay a nominal fee for a search, and most preferred online assistance over printed or staff help. More detailed analysis on the use of *Search Helper* was needed in order to more accurately predict which factors influenced the acceptance of the system, online assistance, help preferences, and acceptance of charges for use.

Studies of *InfoTrac* have been made by the University of California at San Diego, California State University at Chico, and Indiana University. The University of California at San Diego's test of *InfoTrac* revealed that the system was liked by all users—students, researchers, and business people—because of its ease of use and faster retrieval compared with microform or print indexes. *InfoTrac* was in almost constant use during the five months of the test period. Although most users were satisfied with the citations retrieved, the library staff had some concern over relevance and over the possible misconceptions users might have about the comprehensiveness of the database.

California State University at Chico purchased *InfoTrac* in August 1985 after a successful two-month trial period. The students liked the system because of its ease of use and its ability to quickly search a large database and to print citations. Again, the limitations of the database caused some concern, since the librarians believed that users might think coverage is comprehensive and the use of other sources unnecessary. The ability to locate an *InfoTrac* reference in the periodical cited was found to be a significant problem. IAC determined that this was due to page or content differences in regional editions of certain publications. Because of *InfoTrac*'s heavy use, it became necessary to add certain high-demand periodicals to the library's collection. The hardware proved to be quite durable, but a software security problem became evident when the program diskette was replaced by a personal floppy disc. User aids were developed by the university to save staff time. These materials included multiple copies of a list of indexed periodicals; signs indicating that the system indexes selected newspapers, magazines, and journals; simple five-step guides to searching; and signs requesting users to limit search time to ten minutes.

After twelve months of use, a second look at *InfoTrac* at Indiana University found the product to be reliable and that improvements and additions, such as the onscreen list of publications indexed and full text of the *Wall Street Journal* (at an extra cost), had enhanced its usefulness. User reaction at Indiana University has remained high although this study reports that the use of LC subject headings instead of natural language remains a disadvantage. Also, the users (contrary to IAC's pitch) need assistance to understand the system and its limitations. The study concluded, however, that *InfoTrac* is a fine product for the undergraduate library, since this location is where the greatest potential use lies; *InfoTrac* is popular, not scholarly.

Summary

Search Helper, developed when microcomputers were new and exciting, was a fine reference tool that was economical, simple to run, and facilitated downloading of current information from the IAC databases. For a variety of reasons, not all libraries allowed public access due to security problems, cost, patrons' inability to do effective searches, staff time required for assistance, and the need for some training in the use of the equipment, as well as on the use of *Search Helper*. Program limitations, i.e., the system's inability to do more than "AND" terms, save searches, identify problems on screen, etc., led to questions about the real effectiveness of the product. Certainly, the addition of the "OR" operator and a search modifier screen for limiting by date, article type, etc., would have greatly improved *Search Helper*'s utility and increased its use within library end-user programs.

InfoTrac has some attractive advantages for end users in libraries. It allows for quick online searching without the training needed to access remote databases from major vendors; it provides unlimited access to databases without the high cost of searching remote databases; the cost of the system is fixed; and videodiscs and CD-ROM have large storage capacity and durability. *InfoTrac II* was designed to satisfy a particular need for current data from widely used popular sources, particularly for small and medium libraries with limited budgets. Whether this product is as successful as IAC believes it will be remains to be seen. *InfoTrac II* is the first stand-alone CD-ROM product in a planned collection that promises to grow as needs are identified.

IAC values the information, criticisms, comments, and suggestions of users (gathered by brief questionnaires) and of librarians. *InfoTrac* was developed and enhanced by much on-site testing. As the technology advances, IAC is expected to increase *InfoTrac*'s capabilities. Certainly, using the user to develop a product is a most effective marketing strategy.

NOTES

1. Ray Foster, "Wilsearch," in Danuta A. Nitecki, "Databases," *RQ* 25 (Spring 1986): 382–84.

BIBLIOGRAPHY

Bettran, Ann B. "InfoTrac at Indiana University: A Second Look." *Database* 10 (Feb. 1987): 48–50.

Carney, Richard. "Information Access Company's InfoTrac." *Information Technology and Libraries* 4 (June 1985): 149–53.

_____. "InfoTrac: An In-House Computer Access System." *Library Hi Tech* 3 (1985): 91–94.

Ensor, Pat, and Richard A. Curtis. "Search Helper: Low Cost Searching in an Academic Library." *RQ* 23 (Spring 1984): 327–31.

Evans, Nancy, and Henry Pisciotta. "Search Helper: Testing Acceptance of a Gateway Software System." In *National Online Meeting Proceedings—1985*, comp. by Martha E. Williams and Thomas H. Hogan, 131–36. Medford, N.J.: Learned Information, 1985.

Foster, Ray. "Wilsearch: For the Patron, the Age of the One Buck Online Search May Be Here." *American Libraries* 16 (Dec. 1985): 810.

Hall, Cynthia, Harriet Talan, and Barbara Pease. "InfoTrac in Academic Libraries: What's Missing in the New Technology?" *Database* 10 (Feb. 1987): 52–56.

"IAC Introduces CD-ROM Version of Magazine Index." *Information Today* 3 (Dec. 1986): 22.

"IAC Enters Laser Race." *Information Today* 2 (Jan. 1985): 1+.

Kleiner, Jane P. "User Searching: A Public Access Approach to Search Helper." *RQ* 24 (Summer 1985): 442–51.

Miller, Tim. "IAC Workstation Mates Videodisc with CD-ROM." *Information Today* 4 (June 1987): 1+.

Niemeier, Kathy. "Search Helper: IAC's Online Searching Aid." *Library High Tech Special Studies: no. 1.* Ann Arbor, Mich.: Pierian, 1985.

Nitecki, Danuta A. "Wilsonline: A Look at H. W. Wilson's Offerings for Online Access to Its Indexes a Year after Wilsonline's Debut." *American Libraries* 16 (Dec. 1985): 804+.

O'Leary, Mick. "Wilsearch: A New Departure for an Old Institution." *Online* 10 (Mar. 1986): 102–7.

Payne, Greg. "Wilsonline—Worth the Wait." *Information Today* 2 (Feb. 1985): 13+.

Queens Borough Public Library Staff. "Search Helper: The Queens Borough Experience." *Online* 9 (Nov. 1985): 53–56.

Regazzi, John J. "The H. W. Wilson Information System." *Library High Tech* 3 (1985): 29–34.

_____. "Wilsonline: An Introduction." *Library High Tech* 3 (1985): 61–68.

_____. "The Silver Disk-Wilsondisc: Wilsonline on CDROM." *Database* 9 (Oct. 1986): 73–74.

Smith, Bev. "H. W. Wilson Company: Booked for High Tech Advances." *Information Today* 3 (May 1986): 28–30.

Stephens, Kent. "Laserdisc Technology Enters Mainstream." *American Libraries* 17 (Apr. 1986): 252.

Tenopir, Carol. "H. W. Wilson: Online at Last." *Library Journal* 109 (Sept. 1, 1984): 1616–17.

"Wilson Sets Target Date for CD-ROM." *Information Today* 3 (Sept. 1986): 8.

Chapter 7

End-User Services in Business and Related Fields

Steven Smith

INTRODUCTION

This chapter compares online database services available to end users in business and related fields, and addresses the question of how academic, public, and school libraries can serve library patrons who are interested in using them. Services with the greatest utility for end users are discussed first and include *Dow Jones News/Retrieval, DIALOG Business Connection, NewsNet, DataTimes, VU/TEXT, Info Globe Personal Search,* and Mead Data Central's *Lexis/Nexis.* Two specialized services— *WESTLAW* and the *Human Resource Information Network*—are briefly described in a separate section.

Information utilities for business end users fall into three general categories: full-text services, consumer-based information utilities, and financial and statistical databases. The full-text services, such as *Lexis, NewsNet, VU/TEXT, DataTimes,* and *Info Globe,* provide access to the contents of business, trade, and current events publications. These files serve corporate researchers, analysts, managers, and journalists. The information provided in these databases has applications for research on companies, industry trends, competitor intelligence, consumer trends, new products, technological developments, and personal biographical information about executives, directors, and other key business personnel. Consumer-based information utilities (e.g., *CompuServe, Delphi, The Source*), discussed in Chapter 9 offer some business- and investment-related information for personal computer users.

Financial and statistical databases such as *Dow Jones News/Retrieval* serve brokers, bankers, accountants, and insurance people with numeric and statistical data, and economic forecasting information for use in the day-to-day operations of stock, bond, and commodity markets. Vendors such as Data Resources International (DRI), Chase Econometrics, I.P. Sharp, FINET, INSIGHT, and NITE-LINE, which are beyond the scope of this chapter, are important sources of statistical information for in-house use at banks and other financial institutions. Some of these files package information for their clients from Dow Jones, Standard & Poor, and other vendors. (Additional information is available to investors with personal computers through vendors such as Warner Computer Systems, Charles Schwab and Co., and *Huttonline,* marketed to E. F. Hutton clients.) Other utilities, notably *Lexis* and *WESTLAW,* specifically serve the legal community with the full text of laws, regulations, and court decisions.

None of these databases are pure types. Most have succeeded initially by building a steady clientele within a primary occupational group, and have subsequently added services and search features that appeal to the broader corporate and professional markets. The result has been considerable overlapping of database services among these utilities. As these services grow, new ones are introduced to tap additional segments of the overall market. The *Human Resource Information Network* (covering personnel and labor relations) and *DIALOG Business Connection* (covering marketing, sales, and competitor intelligence) are recent examples. Steve Arnold's paper, presented at the National Online Meeting in 1986, identified public relations, strategic planning, marketing, data processing, and personnel and corporate departments as areas where acceptance of end-user searching has lagged in the past.[1] Mick O'Leary's two-part overview of business-information sources for end users, published in chart form, offers a good comparative inventory of many sources discussed in this chapter, as well as others that can only be mentioned here.[2]

Corporate and special libraries maintain access to end-user databases and sometimes have become involved in training executives to use them as part of their information management function. As end-user searching has become more prevalent in the workplace, educators in business schools have seen the importance of training future practitioners in on-line computer literacy. Some online vendors have responded by making their systems available in academic libraries or in classrooms at reduced rates. (This training pattern is already an established part of the curriculum at most law schools.)

Librarians who are aware of the capabilities of these systems have provided access to them in secondary school media centers with some success under some sort of rate structure. Although cost recovery and administration of charges are greater barriers to end-user searching in public libraries, at least one public library is providing access to *Huttonline* for its patrons in Southfield, Michigan, through a grant from E. F. Hutton.[3]

DOW JONES NEWS/RETRIEVAL

Dow Jones News/Retrieval (DJN/R), initiated in the 1970s as an online ticker-tape service, has become an information utility providing easy access to financial and current events information through a menu-driven format. The core of the system is the Dow Jones News Service; a strong selling point of DJN/R is access to Dow Jones financial coverage almost as soon as it hits the wire.

Business and financial databases include:

Dow Jones News. 90-day coverage of information from the *Wall Street Journal, Barron's,* and the Dow Jones News Service.

Dow Jones Quotes. Price quotations on a 15-minute delay for NYSE, ASE, and OTC stocks; for bonds, mutual funds, U.S. Treasury issues, and options; futures quotations for 80 commodities from North American Exchanges; historical quotations by stock, including quarterly (to 1978) and monthly (to 1979) summaries; and historical Dow Jones Averages.

Business and Finance Report. Menu-driven headline search provides digested coverage (two or three screens) of important news events affecting business, and composite market reports that are updated every half hour. News items are added continuously from 6 a.m. to midnight by the Dow Jones News Service.

Dow Jones Text-Search Services. Full text of the *Wall Street Journal* (WSJ), from January 1984 to the current day's publication, available at 6 a.m.; the *Washington Post* in full text, from January 1984, on 48-hour delay; the Dow Jones News Service broadtape, with selected articles from WSJ and *Barron's,* available 36 hours after publication and dating to June 1979; and The Business Library, which contains contents of *American Banker, Financial World, Forbes,* and PR Newswire from January 1985, searchable by Boolean logic through modified BRS protocols as four separate files.

Disclosure 10-K extracts, company profiles, and other SEC findings.

Media General Financial Services. Financial information on the revenues, earnings, dividends, volume, ratios, shareholdings, and price changes of 4,300 companies and 180 industrial groups; option to display a combination of two company or industry choices in adjacent columns for easy comparison of statistics.

Standard and Poor's Online. 4,600 companies, with profiles and statistics on earnings, dividends, and stock statistics for a four-year period.

Investext. Access to Investext reports on major company and industry outlooks by national and regional brokerage firms.

Corporate Earnings Estimator. Earnings forecasts for more than 3,000 companies, provided by Zacks Investment Research's survey of 60 top brokerage firms.

Economic and Foreign Exchange Survey. Weekly survey of U.S. money market and foreign exchange trends; forecasts of monetary and economic indicators from Money Market Services, Inc.

Japan Economic Daily. Same-day coverage of major business, financial, and political news from Kyodo News International, Inc.

Wall Street Week Online. Transcripts of the four most recent PBS television broadcasts of Louis Rukeyser's popular investment program.

Words of Wall Street. An online dictionary of more than 2,000 technical investment terms.

In mid-1985, DJN/R added *TRACK,* a service that permits the user to create and store up to five profiles of twenty-five companies each, and to automatically track the current stock quotations and latest news releases for each company. A new QUICKSEARCH feature provides a composite package of information from DJN/R on a specific company in report format for $39 per report, simply by the user's entering the stock symbol for the company desired.

Consumer-oriented databases, such as *Peterson's College Selection Service, Cineman* movie reviews, *Academic American Encyclopedia,* and a *Medical and Drug Reference* service, have been added. Additionally, the *Official Airline Guide, Compu-u-store Online* home shopping service, *American Express Advance* travel and shopping service, and *MCI Main* have been added for the personal convenience of DJN/R users. In this way, DJN/R has converged with the broader consumer utilities such as *CompuServe, Delphi,* and *The Source.*

Dow Jones News/Retrieval is available through most personal computer-modem combinations and time-sharing terminals. A communications package called *Straight Talk* is available at computer stores and at bookstores to simplify the logon procedures. User aids for DJN/R include a printed manual, a monthly magazine called *DOWLINE,* and a customer hotline available from 8 a.m. to midnight, Monday through Friday, and from 9 a.m. to 6 p.m. on Saturdays.

The DJN/R search is, overall, very easy to use. User prompts are frequent and enlightening, and the user is referred to the "/Help" file for the database on use at the slightest sign of difficulty. "Help" screens are thorough and explicit enough to be self-sufficient without the manual. Once the user gets a feeling for the screen paging commands (e.g., "menu" or "/menu" for a prior menu, "T" or "/T" for a top menu, and

"R" for a previous screen), it is very easy to get around in a file or to go to another file and get more information on an organization or topic.

Using a company stock symbol, one can acquire an enormous amount of information in a relatively short time, especially when compared with the tedious process of handcopying or photocopying investment data and news from printed sources. The "//BUSINESS" service and the Dow Jones News files are cross-indexed to provide codes or file suggestions for additional information on current topics.

Dow Jones has developed an array of software packages that automatically download *News/Retrieval* data for investment analysis functions. Packages include *Home Budget* (financial planning and tax preparation), *Investment Evaluator* (portfolio management), *Investors' Workshop* (portfolio management and charting), *Market Analyzer* (technical analysis of current and historical market quotations), *Market Manager Plus* (portfolio management with audit trail capabilities), *Market Microscope* (fundamental market analysis of companies and groups), *Prospect Organizer* (a sales prospect database- management package), *Spreadsheet Link* (designed specifically to work with Lotus 1-2-3, Multiplan, and VisiCalc data analysis templates custom-designed by the user), and a data communications and management package for the Macintosh called Straight Talk. Additional programs are available from independent software companies that make use of *Dow Jones News/Retrieval* data.

Navigating among the databases after signon is easily accomplished from a reference card that summarizes the database codes. Databases are called up by typing two slashes and the database code. "//INTRO" (for the introductory menu) provides a free overview of the services available on *News/Retrieval,* as well as an online newsletter. Additional general "help" screens are "//MENU," for a master menu of database services, with one-letter choices leading to each; and "//SYMBOL," for a directory of symbols and codes used on DJN/R to obtain information on individual companies, stocks, mutual funds, industry groups, and government agencies.

"Help" screens are available for each database and can be easily obtained by typing the code of the database in question, a space, and then the word "HELP." For example, "//TEXT HELP" will provide assistance on the operation of the full-text service.

The master menu includes pathways to (a) company/industry data and news, (b) quotes and market averages, (c) world news, sports, and weather, (d) shopping, travel, and mail, or (e) education and entertainment. Additional menus guide the user to the information contained in all the databases on DJN/R except the "//TEXT" search. In many files, all company information can be gained by using a ticker symbol. Other general codes are used for broader information categories, such as ".FORGN" for foreign news, ".AFRIC" for news about African countries, ".GOVMT" for general governmental news, and ".LABOR" for labor-related stories. The most complex search protocols on the system are used on "//TEXT," the full-text service. This file was once available on BRS, and still runs with modified BRS commands. Available search protocols for devising strategies include standard Boolean operators and proximity searching with both adjacency (denoting order) and near (where terms can be in either order) commands. Truncation of search terms is accomplished with a dollar sign ($). BRS-based print commands permit the searcher to specify the individual fields of a document for printing and to choose specific document numbers from a retrieved set. The rates for *Dow Jones News/Retrieval* in the 48 contiguous states of the U.S., as of May 1986, are stratified to reflect prime-time vs. off-hour usage, and 300-baud vs. 1200- or 2400-baud access. Basic service to 300-baud subscribers costs $.90 per minute during prime time, and $.20 per minute during off hours. (Prime time is defined as the period between 6 a.m. Eastern Standard Time and 6 p.m. local time.) These rates are multiplied by 2.2 for 1200- and 2400-baud users. Additional charges are made for certain databases, such as the *Official Airline Guide, DISCLOSURE,* and *Media General,* and for access to real-time stock quotes, and for string searches on the *Tracking Service* ($5.00 per month).

Start-up fees and an annual service fee are also assessed, but there are separate plans for the high-volume user. The standard start-up fee is $29.95 for individuals, and $49.95 for corporate locations, plus an annual service fee of $1200, which is waived for the first year. Dow Jones has made arrangements with some educational institutions to provide the service to location for a flat monthly fee—currently $300 per month for three separate passwords. This rate is offered for instructional use on *Dow Jones News/Retrieval.* (Interested libraries should contact Dow Jones representatives for details.)

Studies on the use of DJN/R at the graduate level in business schools have been made because of the increased availability provided by the special academic rate. In a Dow Jones pilot project at Indiana University, for example, the Graduate School of Business, in conjunction with the Bloomington Academic Computer Center, has developed a computer program that permits MBA students and faculty members to book and directly use half-hour blocks of time on DJN/R through the university's VAX computer without a search intermediary. The software permits data to be downloaded and oversees security for the system. (The software also is available to other institutions from the university.) Technical aspects of the local software link and of DJN/R searching are taught in seminars or in class sessions. Since the program begin in 1984, use of the system has increased to the point where three additional telephone lines have been added.[4]

At the Wharton School of the University of Pennsylvania, entering business students receive an orientation to the service at the beginning of the term and can run searches by themselves at library terminals. DJN/R is also included in the finance curriculum there.[5] A successful use of *Dow Jones News/Retrieval* at Purdue University in a pilot project for graduate students in the Krannert School of Management was also sponsored and administered through the library, using programmed instruction and written exercises to prepare students for online searching.[6]

The educational rate for this service is also being used to expose students in elementary and secondary schools to online searching. *Dow Jones News/Retrieval* is being used in the South Brunswick, West Windsor-Plainsboro, New Brunswick, and Princeton public school systems in New Jersey as a general educational tool for secondary students—who use the encyclopedia and weather information as aids to study in geography, find new economic uses of chemical elements as part of their chemistry assignments, locate biographical data on living people, and otherwise learn the capacity of the computer to obtain current information from the larger world outside the classroom.[7] The Center for Learning Technology of BOCES III in New York established a new 40-location program for Long Island schoolchildren in the fall of 1986, using the academic rate structure. In both of the above cases, pilot programs were run with considerable success. Dow Jones has published lesson plans for use of the service in a curriculum guide titled *Educator's Guide to Dow Jones News/Retrieval.*[8]

At both college and secondary school levels, participants felt that exposure to the system was of significant value to students in helping them comprehend what the computer can provide them personally in regard to information, whether they become proficient searchers or not. At the college level, the philosophy seems to be that executives will be able to direct their research better if they have a general knowledge of end-user searching.

DIALOG BUSINESS CONNECTION

DIALOG Business Connection is a menu-driven gateway to the information contained on several DIALOG marketing and statistical databases, particularly for end users in the areas of marketing, sales, finance, and competitor intelligence. Such use represents an interesting reversal to the general pattern of diversification described above. DIALOG, perceiving an end-user market opportunity in a previously untapped area of the total business market, has provided users direct access to its databases to perform simple tasks in a new format. Its success could pave the way for similar interfaces tailored to other end-user-specific business or industry functions.

DIALOG Business Connection eliminates the need for database selection; information from DIALOG databases is supplied to the user through a series of subject-specific menu selections.

Data on corporations and industries is supplied from Business Research Corporation's *Investext,* the *DISCLOSURE* collection of the Securities and Exchange Commission's (SEC) filing abstracts, Dun & Bradstreet *Market Identifiers, Electronic Yellow Pages,* and corporate profiles (including its extensive histories of private companies), the Media General databank, Moody's *Investors Service,* and Standard & Poor's *Corporate Descriptions. CDA Spectrum* provides institutional and individual ownership information for public companies. National Register's *Directory of Corporate Affiliations* covers parent/subsidiary relationships. The *Thomas Register Online* offers manufacturer lists, and the *Trinet Establishment Database* and *PTS Prompt* provide share-of-market reports. *Prompt* and *Investext* also provide analysis and statistics on products, industries, and markets. The *PTS New Product Announcements* are available in full text. Reuters news releases have also been added.

Once connected to the system, the user encounters a main menu with a choice of five search functions: (1) Corporate Intelligence, (2) Financial Screening, (3) Products and Markets, (4) Sales Prospecting, and (5) Travel Planning (the *Official Airline Guide* module). Any of these selections will lead to a set of submenus that provide choices to the user in formulating a well-designed search for the function chosen.

The "Corporate Intelligence" module has a "Corporate Description and Location" menu that permits the user to search for names and addresses of companies, names and addresses of corporate headquarters; corporate family hierarchy; corporate background; company profile; list of company products; and a list of key executives, officers, and directors. By entering a stock symbol or company name, one can obtain the above items or move on to an additional menu that provides access to additional corporate descriptions, financial reports and analyses, reports on publicly traded companies, or a choice for "all available information." A standard report can be selected for a specific company by entering that company's name or ticker symbol.

"Financial Screening" permits analysis of balance sheets, income statements, financial ratios, stock prices, stock volume, and industry comparisons as primary options, using data on publicly traded companies. A choice of any of these options will yield a second menu of specific variables (e.g., price-earnings ratio, beta, etc.), and a choice of the specific option will lead the user to a third menu, which presents a choice from a range of numerical variables, or modify existing variables, by going through the menus again until a multi-variable search is suitably defined.

"Products and Markets" has initial choices of lists of manufacturers for a particular product, market-share data, market information, product design and processes, facilities and resources, unit costs and prices, and analysts' reports on specific industries. Products can be selected by verbal description or by SIC code. Directory information, investment reports, and summaries of articles from the *Predicasts* databases on specific products are available.

"Sales Prospecting" can be performed by geographic location, type of industry by SIC code, size of company, and company status (branch or non-branch). This module leads the searcher through a set of menus that select each criterion, with considerable flexibility, in order to compile a list of sales prospects. Geographical variables, for example, can be at the national, regional, state, county, telephone area code, or zip code level. SIC codes can be 2-, 3-, or 4-digit codes.

"Travel Planning" is the standard *Official Airline Guide* subsystem, and is available on other systems.

Dial-up access to *Business Connection* is available through Tymnet, Telenet, Dialnet, and WATS. Registered users can obtain access to *Business Connection* from *DIALOG* by a "BEGIN DBC" command. The *DIALOGlink* communications package is furnished with *DIALOG Business Connection*.

"Help" screens are available at any point in the search, to explain what is being done and to outline further options or search qualifications to the user, by typing "/H." A few staple commands permit navigation among the various menus: "/menu" to return to current menu, "/M-" to return to previous menu, "/MA" to return to the first applications menu, and "/MM" to return to the main menu. These commands are easy to remember and are also displayed with "Help" functions. "/L" will log the user off the system. "/COST" displays the price of a search, and "/M DIALOG" will return the user to regular DIALOG.

The user can view a list of databases from which information will be derived, along with the price of the information per item, before output is produced from a search. Different formats can be chosen. Output citation charges are the same as they would be from a given vendor in a regular *DIALOG* search. Material can be displayed or printed directly, or downloaded through *DIALOGlink* for reformatting. The output processes are also menu driven.

DIALOG Business Connection is very easy to learn and provides good direction for searching the marketing, financial, and directory databases on *DIALOG* effectively without the user's needing any knowledge of intermediary search commands. The process of moving back through menus to reformulate or modify search strategies might become cumbersome to the frequent searcher, so *DIALOG* has provided a command-stacking function for entire searches.

DIALOG marketing representatives indicate that a pilot program is being conducted with *Business Connection,* to introduce the package to MBA candidates at some U.S. business schools. DIALOG has developed a classroom instruction program for business schools that includes written curriculum materials. The program is supported by the regular DIALOG classroom rate, a flat $15 per hour, including telecommunication charges. Some public libraries have signed up for the service, but it is unclear whether these institutions are using the program as an in-house training and reference tool, or whether library patrons are allowed to use the system. A thorough introduction to the system in *Online* makes several useful points about the possible applications of *DIALOG Business Connection* (e.g., for company research on private companies, industry activities, manufacturing, and market trends). *Business Connection* is similar in function to the *Easynet* gateway service; but as part of the *DIALOG* mainframe, its response time is much better. The significance of *Business Connection* as a product may be that it points up a trend away from disc-based front-end software packages and toward "host-based interfaces."[9]

For the librarian, *Business Connection* is an important new tool for performing certain types of programmatic searches, and any client of a business library (including librarians themselves who do not search often) will want to know its capabilities. *Business Connection* will be an important system for academic libraries in business schools that seek to expose students to the potential payoffs of end-user searching.

Connect charges for *Business Connection* are $1.45 per minute, plus the royalty charges for search results provided. This rate applies to all searches and to some displayed information as well. Additional database charges can be displayed after an individual search is completed.

A $145 sign-up fee is required to obtain access to *DIALOG Business Connection.* As part of its initial sign-up fee, DIALOG is offering $100 in free online time for use within 30 days of registration, a *User's Guide* (priced separately at $50), and the *DIALOGlink* communications software as part of the introductory package. A quick-reference card is also provided. Customer service is available 24 hours per day for *Business Connection.* A CD-ROM version of this database would be very interesting for libraries, especially for public libraries, if the pricing of the system were favorable to heavy use at a fixed price.

NEWSNET

NewsNet provides access to the full text of business newsletters in electronic form, often before they are available in print. The *NewsNet* service has been tailored to the needs of end users since its inception in 1982, offering simple protocols and requiring little recourse to documentation. Enhanced Boolean search capabilities were added to the system during the summer of 1986, but the system can still be used for quick reading without using the advanced search facilities.

More than 300 business periodicals are available through *NewsNet*. Many of these publications are newsletters covering current developments in specific industries: advertising, aerospace, automotive, building and construction, chemical, electronics, energy, farming, health insurance, medicine, metals and mining, public relations, real estate, retailing, telecommunications, tobacco, transport and shipping, and tourism. Coverage is provided of management topics, investing, U.S. regional marketing opportunities, personal recreation and travel, general news, and the political and regulatory environment of business. Several newsletters specialize in coverage of the international business climate in Europe, Africa, the Middle East, or Asia. Coverage of Japan includes the *Jiji Press Ticker* service, *Japan Weekly Monitor,* and several publications reviewing Japanese developments in the technology, computer, aviation, and semiconductor industries.

In addition to newsletters, *NewsNet* offers access to general news services: sixteen subfiles of Gannet News Media Services' *USA Today Update,* including "hotlines" for news, business and finance, weather, and sports; and daily news digests called "Decisionlines" on special subjects, such as technology, law, insurance, real estate, telecommunications, and insurance. Limited access to two weeks of coverage of selected stories from five UPI newswires and from PR Newswire are also provided.

Other special services include access to stock quotes on a 20-minute delay through *VU/TEXT's VU/QUOTE* service, access to the *Official Airline Guide Electronic Edition,* and access to *TRW Business Profile* reports on various companies nationwide. A service called *B.R.A.I.N.,* an electronic referral service to consultants or to databases with expertise on specified research topics is also available. A *Computer Multiple Listing* service provides direction for *NewsNet* clients interested in buying and selling used computer and office equipment.

NewsNet promotional material indicates that subscriptions to all of the printed information available on *NewsNet* would cost $50,000. Some of the sources on *NewsNet* are full-text files that also are accessible on *Lexis* (e.g., *American Banker* and *Commerce Clearing House Tax Day*). Many more of the *NewsNet* sources are unavailable on other online systems.

NewsNet, with its new search capabilities, is advertising its service as being a complement to other services, such as *Lexis, Dow Jones,* and *DIALOG,* for information professionals. *NewsNet* deserves consideration as part of the business curriculum at the college level, as an example of a specialized source of trade information; faculty members might also be interested in the contents of *NewsNet*.

NewsNet has introduced an *Academic Instruction Program,* as of October 1987, which provides special access to educational institutions offering formal, supervised instruction. Most of these institutions are business schools or academic libraries, but one secondary school library is experimenting with *NewsNet*. The instruction package includes documentation, on-site training, and access to the system at $15 per hour, including telecommunications charges.

Most microcomputer and terminal hardware configurations are supported by the *NewsNet* host computer. Users can access the system through Telenet, Tymnet, or a direct line to *NewsNet* at 300-, 1200-, or 2400-baud.

When the user signs on and enters his or her password, the system provides the user with the option of an immediate search or a menu of important commands. The menu choices include options to "Read" full text, "Scan" headlines, "Search" for key words, "Flash" (update the SDI file), go directly to one of the special services (*VU/QUOTE,* OAG, TRW, CMLS, the *Sports Network, B.R.A.I.N.*), or move in the menu structure by entering "Back" (go back to previous prompt), "Quit" (return to main prompt), or "Off" (signoff).

The three basic operations on *NewsNet* are "Read," "Scan," and "Search." Specific journals are coded by a subject group and an individual number. The user can enter "Read" and a newsletter code to retrieve the contents of that newsletter. Without further ado, the system will give the user a choice of seeing the latest issue or of specifying the date of an older item. The full text of the article is then displayed.

Entering the word "Scan" provides the user with a series of headlines; one may select stories to read from these numbered headlines. The word "More" can be used to pull up more headlines to scan. Specific journals are coded by their subject group and an individual number. One can specify up to three title or group codes at a time. When these codes are retrieved, the searcher specifies "Latest," "Earliest," or "All" items retrieved—for Scanning purposes—or gives the system a date (e.g., 01/ 15/85), after which headlines are displayed.

For the convenience of the searcher, the publications on *NewsNet* are grouped into subject categories. Each subject area is assigned a two-letter search code. For example, Electronics and Computers [EC], Finance and Accounting [FI], Government and Regulatory [GT], Investment [IV], Publishing and Broadcasting [PB], and Telecommunications [TE] (all areas of particularly strong coverage) each can be searched as a group. Newsletters from one category can be cross-indexed to appear in another category as well.

NewsNet files can be searched using Boolean logic ("AND," "OR,"

"BUT NOT"). The user enters the "Search" command, combined with two or three specific newsletter or search codes. The system prompts the searcher to enter a range of dates to be searched. An "Enter Key Word(s)" prompt appears, and key words can be entered (e.g., "shuttle" and "challenger"). Key words can be nested within parentheses. String searching of phrases entered within quotation marks (e.g., "prime rate"), and word proximity searching (e.g., Vancouver within/2 fair) are supported. Truncation is performed with an asterisk (*). Queries of up to 76 characters in length may be entered.

If a search produces a large number of hits, the searcher can enter the "Analyze" command. In response, *NewsNet* provides an item-by-item list of newsletters and the number of items retrieved from each by the current search strategy. The searcher can narrow the range of retrieval by using specific newsletter codes, or reformulate the query. Searches of the entire *NewsNet* file can be performed, but they are not recommended. The AP and UPI wires are not searchable by Boolean logic.

A separate SDI service, *NewsFlash,* can notify a client instantly if a newsletter appears with references to a set of pre-established key words. An interest profile of ten key words is established within the limits of the "Search" system and is used to automatically flag new articles for the user. The user periodically signs onto the system, receives a *NewsFlash* message, scans the headlines for the articles, and either stores them for future viewing, reads them immediately, or purges them from the "Flash" profile.

How difficult is the *NewsNet* system to search? In its elementary document-delivery mode, it is as easy to learn and operate as *Dow Jones.* The Boolean logic mode on *NewsNet* is also easy to operate. The system has abundant "Help" screens; the user needs only to type "Help" at any point in the search to obtain information on what to do next.

Any additional instruction on *NewsNet* that might be helpful to the end user concerns the consequences of the system's limitations, inherent in its simplicity. The drawbacks to free-text searching on *NewsNet* include the lack of available paragraph qualifications for searching, and the fact that there is no way to screen documents to determine an article's emphasis based on the frequence with which key words occur, either by ranking or by key word in context. In a length document such as *BNA Daily Tax Report,* for example, a simple Boolean statement without carefully constructed word-proximity indicators is likely to result in false drops buried deep within the text. These are not terrible flaws in a system that is designed primarily for the rapid dissemination of current information, often on industry topics where precise technical jargon and the subject-content of the document being searched will pinpoint the information being sought. These drawbacks are, rather, factors in the use of

NewsNet that an intermediary can pass along to an end user in preparing that person to use the *NewsNet* service.

The basic *NewsNet* connect charge is $60 per hour, at 300- or 1200-baud. There is no discount for use during off-peak hours. A monthly subscription fee of $15 is also levied; subscribers may pay $75 per six-month period, or $120 per year.

The "Read" function invokes a royalty structure, which varies from newsletter to newsletter. This royalty is called a read-rate. Some services bill at a flat rate equal to that charged for the regular database function; other publishers add a 100 percent to 300 percent premium to the cost of reading their publications. In many, but by no means all, cases a subscriber to a printed journal included on the system can qualify for the lowest rate by being "validated" for that journal on the system. Basic per-hour read rates may also vary from database to database on the system. Finally, a charge of $.50 per hit is assessed on the *NewsFlash* search.

User aids include a guide to *NewsNet* searching; a brochure with descriptions of each newsletter and subject grouping, spelling out the cross-referencing procedures for the system; and a monthly newsletter that describes new databases and system capabilities and offers search examples. An overview of the operations of each file on *NewsNet* is available in an 81-page booklet entitled *Guide to News on NewsNet*. This guide also lists all the publications that are available or forthcoming on the service, and breaks them down into categories. An entirely new manual, covering search procedures and database contents for *NewsNet*, will be available in 1988.

DATATIMES

DataTimes is a relatively new regional news service, featuring the full text of the *Arkansas Gazette; San Francisco Chronicle; Chicago Sun-Times; Baton Rouge State Times* and *Morning Advocate; Daily Oklahoman* and *Oklahoma City Times,* an Oklahoma-based business and legal publication; the *Journal Record;* the *Dallas Morning News, Houston Chronicle, Daily Texan* (University of Texas–Austin), *Minneapolis Star* and *Tribune, Seattle Times, Washington Post, Harrisburg* (Pa.) *Patriot,* and *Evening News, Orange County* (Calif.) *Register, St. Petersburg* (Fla.) *Times, San Diego Union* and *Tribune,* and the *Bergen* (N.J.) *Record.* A gateway is available to *Dow Jones News/Retrieval* through *DataTimes,* which allows subscribers to formulate text searches using *DataTimes* protocols. (The Standard & Poor's portion of *DJN/R* is exempt from this agreement.) Another gateway is available to the Canadian *Infomart* service, featuring the full text of eight major Canadian dailies. *USA Today* is available through a cooperative arrangement with Gannett, and addition of at least five more newspaper files from the Gannett group is planned.

Also currently available is the *Austrialian Newspaper Network,* featuring newspapers from Brisbane. Most of the backfiles on *DataTimes* are more recent that 1984, but the Oklahoma City papers date back to 1981, and a *Chicago Sun-Times, Tribune,* and *DataTimes* to January 1976. *AP Newswire, Southwest Newswire,* and the *Legis Trak* system for monitoring activities in state legislatures are also provided, along with *Congressional Quarterly* and the *Bennett News Service.*

The principal clients of *DataTimes* are journalists, companies engaged in business and finance, and educational institutions. The company also has a number of accounts with college and university libraries. Public libraries in the cities where *DataTimes* has newspapers online tend to use the service as a reference tool.

The system is available for searching 24 hours a day, although individual files are not available during daily updates, which are performed between 12 midnight and 6 a.m., one file at a time. User support is available through a toll-free line from 7:00 a.m. to 7:00 p.m., Central Standard Time. The system is supported by Battelle *BASIS* software, and searching is conducted by using *BASIS* protocols.

Once the user is connected with the system, the "Find" and "Display" commands are used to provide most of the search results. Database selection is menu driven at the point at which the user logs onto the system, and searches are conducted in individual newspaper files, one at a time. A "Command" mode is available to bypass menu selection when the user is choosing or changing newspaper or wire files, and to log out of the system. Truncation is accomplished with an asterisk (*).

The "Find" command is basic to all searching on *DataTimes*. Boolean logic ("AND," "OR," "AND NOT") is supported. The "Display" command is used to control output, in conjunction with set numbers of searches and specified portions of articles. A "No Scroll" command can be used with "Display" to format output for viewing screens, including displays of sentences with hits. The "Scan" command allows the searcher to narrow search results after a find, within a specified number of words or adjacent terms.

Word proximity is specified in three ways. Quotation marks (e.g., "abuse* child") specify word proximity but not word order (the terms "abused child" and "child abuse" would both be retrieved in this instance). The ADJ connector requires that the terms be in the order specified. The "Within" command can be used to find terms that occur within a specified number of sentences.

Other important commands include "Look," which provides a dictionary of index terms with a given stem; "List," to display previous searches; "Clock," to display elapsed search-session time; and "Help," for online assistance. "Help" screens for *DataTimes* are extensive and well developed. The user can select online documentation from a menu of explanatory screens, or enter the "Help" command along with the name of a search feature to obtain an explanation of that particular function (e.g., "Help List" for information on the "List" command).

DataTimes is more difficult to use than the menu-driven systems, but it is less complicated than many of the expert ones. Most commands are easily learned and are available on the ready-reference chart. A novice searcher would need to learn Boolean logic and the pitfalls of full-text searching, especially the potential for false coordinations within long news articles; but a novice with some grasp of searching can use the system with a minimum of trial and error.

In January 1988, *DataTimes* is planning to announce a global searching capability, which will allow searchers to apply search statements to more than one database at a time on the *DataTimes* system. This feature may include optional file groupings for different regions of the United States. Also planned is a search option that will allow simple, menu-driven searching of the *DataTimes* network for novice users. This option will be part of the *DataTimes* service, rather than a separate software package or alternate gateway.

Connect charges for the service are either $1.25 per minute with a $75 monthly minimum, or $1.75 per minute with a $12 per month service charge. *DataTimes* representatives say that if planned FCC revisions of telecommunications charges are implemented, *DataTimes* telecommunications charges may be broken out of the overall connect charge, and rates may be revised.

DataTimes does offer an educational rate to colleges and schools, but not public libraries. The cost is $40 per hour, with a one-hour monthly minimum, and it applies to all basic *DataTimes* services but not to gateways maintained cooperatively with separate database vendors.

VU/TEXT

VU/TEXT is an online retrieval service owned and operated by Knight-Ridder Newspapers, Inc., offering access to the full text of newspapers. Originally an automated clippings file for the staff of the *Philadelphia Inquirer,* the database has grown to include many other publications.

Newspapers represented on *VU/TEXT* include the *Akron Beacon Journal; Albany Times-Union; Allentown Morning Call; Anchorage News;* and *Annapolis Capital; Arizona Republic; Arizona Business Ga-*

zette; Boston Globe; Charlotte Observer; Chicago Tribune; Columbia (S. C.) *State,* and *Record; Columbus Dispatch; Detroit Free Press; Fort Lauderdale News* and *Sun-Sentinel; Fresno Bee; Gilroy* (Canada) *Dispatch; Houston Post; Knickerbocker News; Lexington* (Ky.) *Herald-Leader; Daily News of Los Angeles; Los Angeles Times; Miami Herald* (English and Spanish editions); *Orlando Sentinel; Philadelphia Daily News; Philadelphia Inquirer; Phoenix Gazette; Richmond News Leader; Richmond Times-Dispatch; Sacramento Bee; San Jose Mercury-News; Seattle Post-Intelligencer; Washington Post;* and *Wichita Eagle-Beacon.* As these newspaper files grow, they are divided into separate files of one to two years each for easier searching. Time depth varies for each file, depending on when the newspapers were added to *VU/TEXT.*

The Associated Press, Mediawire, PR Newswire, KNT Newswire, Knight-Ridder Financial News, and Business Wire services are available through *VU/TEXT,* along with *VU/QUOTE,* a stock and commodity quotation service. The *Wall Street Transcript* service provides verbatim transcripts of round table discussions among corporate officers and industry analysts, as well as brokerage reports. The *Academic American Encyclopedia* has also been added. *VU/TEXT* is adding *Business DateLine,* with a full text of articles from 100 regional publications in the United States and Canada, as well as the magazines *Discover, Fortune, Life, People, Money, Sports Illustrated,* and *Time.*

VU/TEXT has condensed versions of the *ABI/Inform* and *PTS Prompt* databases available as separate files. Descriptor and product-code fields are attenuated on *VU/TEXT,* in contrast to the versions available through other major bibliographic utilities. The DISCLOSURE databases are now also available on *VU/TEXT.* An agreement with Datasolve, Ltd., provides access to such international journals *The Financial Times of London, The Guardian, The Economist,* Asahi News service, BBC External Service News, BBC Summary of World Broadcasts, and TASS. Canada's QL service is available through a reciprocal agreement to users who obtain separate passwords from *VU/TEXT. VU/TEXT* is also accessible from *WESTLAW.*

VU/TEXT has documented some of the uses that its corporate clients have devised for the system in a newsletter. Law firms use the system to collect background information on clients, judges, or companies, and to track recent developments in law, legislation, regulation, or taxation in different parts of the country. Banks use the databases to collect credit information on small local companies, to assemble background information on clientele, and to track innovative banking practices in various markets. Corporate libraries use *VU/TEXT* for competitor intelligence, client information, and to track local industry and consumer trends.

When logging onto *VU/TEXT,* the user will see a signon message that includes an option for listing the *VU/TEXT* files simply by entering a carriage return. At this point, the searcher enters a three- or four-letter code to select a specific database to search.

Since October 1987, Global Group codes have been made available for multifile searching. These include a code (NEWS) for a complete search of 32 newspapers and six wire services from 1983 to the present. Other codes permit exclusive searches of the wire services, the magazine databases, a cluster of business databases, training databases, or the full contents of each newspaper (as opposed to two-year segments of each paper). (The Miami and Detroit papers, *VU/QUOTE, DISCLOSURE, Wall Street Transcript,* and *ECS Marine* databases cannot be searched with global commands.)

A session global command (SSNGBL) can be used to create a combination of up to 128 fields for searching during a specific session. Up to eight customized combinations of multiple files can be used per session, but these global groupings cannot be saved for use in subsequent search sessions without being re-entered. Once a file on global grouping has been selected, the system prompts the user to enter a search query.

The search software for *VU/TEXT* is *QL Search.* Searches on *VU/TEXT* are performed by using simple key word combinations involving word proximity indicators, as well as Boolean logic ("AND," "OR," "NOT"). Up to 63 terms can be used in a strategy. The system defaults to "OR" logic if a string of words is entered with no logical operators between them. Automatic searching of plurals ending in "-s" is performed by default on *VU/TEXT*, unless an "Option Plurals Off" command is issued. (Suppression of pluralization of a single word within a search statement is accomplished by placing a space symbol in front of the word, e.g., #aid.)

Searches can be performed on the full text of the articles or on selected segments of text. Articles are segmented into numbered fields; the fields may vary from one file to another, but typically they will be coded as follows: (1) Date, Page, Section and Edition, (2) Type of Illustration (3) Source, (4) Memo, (5) Headline, (6) Lead Paragraphs, (7) Rest of Text, and (8) Key Words. To restrict a search to particular fields, the searcher enters an "@" sign, followed by the field number and the terms to be searched. Data searching and date ranging are accomplished with a special code for that purpose.

Word adjacency is indicated with a slash, and word proximity is specified by placing a number next to the slash (e.g., "new /3 product"). Additional proximity indicators are available on some of the newspaper files ("/p" can be used to specify the occurrence of two words in the same paragraph, for example). Phrases can be highlighted in quotes (e.g., "prior restraint").

VU/TEXT permits entry of only one search query at a time. The order of processing for Boolean connectors in a query is "OR," then

"AND," then "NOT." Once a statement has been entered, the system automatically processes it and displays the results. One-line search statements can be executed in more than one newspaper file without being re-keyed. Using the "Save" command, the user can store a one-line search statement for further modification or future use during a session.

Descriptors are intended to enrich the retrieval capacity of the electronic record, rather than to stand alone as controlled vocabulary for exclusive searching, although they can be searched effectively by themselves in some special cases. Descriptors are assigned to each article from thesauri of terms that vary from newspaper to newspaper.

Flexible truncation features are provided to assist the searcher in coping with the variations of word forms that are inherent in full-text searching. Open-ended truncation is performed with an exclamation point (!), e.g., "indust!" An asterisk (*) is employed for internal truncation to represent a universal character, e.g., "wom*n." By placing specific suffixes within parentheses after a search term, the user can retrieve compound variations of a word, along with its root, e.g., "predict(ing, ed, ion)." Retrieval of the root word can be suppressed entirely by including the word "noroot" with the suffixes, e.g., "project(ing,ed,ion,noroot)." (This statement would retrieve the terms "projecting," "projected," and "projection," but not the word "project.")

If the searcher wishes to view all of the terms that have been generated through truncation, an optional command "Option Termlist On," enables *VU/TEXT* to display them. A menu then prompts the user to either search all the terms, to enter item numbers for terms to be included or excluded from the final search, or to modify the search entirely. The "Option Termlist" feature allows the searcher to detect unforeseen twists in truncation, and displays any examples of "dirty data" that have escaped the proofreaders in the editorial process. The "Dict" command permits the user to view all of the terms with a given root-word spelling, without entering a formal search command.

Items can be displayed in full text or in partial formats, including simple titles. Full-text displays include highlighting or the occurrences of search terms, either by inverse characters or asterisks, at the user's discretion. Specific fields can be chosen for display before a search is run, or a general command can be issued to display a full bibliographic citation. Citations and full text can be typed directly—without additional charges— or printed offline. Specific pages within a document can be chosen, as well as specific documents within a set, or documents can be printed in part or in full by accession number from a citation. Multifile search results are listed in tabular form, and can be displayed or printed by individual file name, or the number of documents in the document set for that file.

The system will rank (sort) retrieved items in one of three ways: in chronological order, in reverse chronological order, or in order by the most frequent occurrence of search terms in the document. The command to invoke this last feature is "Rank Method A," which is entered before the search query. This last feature allows the user to display articles in which the emphasis on the chosen terms is the greatest—a useful tool in a full-text file, where relevancy of retrieval is a special challenge.

How easy is *VU/TEXT* to search? The command structure is more difficult to use than a simple menu-driven format, and more complex than *NewsNet* or *DataTimes*. Basic searching on *VU/TEXT* is probably easier than on some of the larger bibliographical utilities, but to use the system effectively, the searcher needs to be familiar with its more powerful search and display features, which involves some training and practice. As in the case of *DataTimes,* the complexities and pitfalls of extended full-text searching need to be mastered. The *VU/TEXT in Education* program described below is the company's approach to the training of future end users in an academic setting.

Rates for the system are two tiered and vary from one database to another. For a $10-per-month maintenance fee, users can access the system with no monthly minimum service charge. The newspapers in the system cost $105 per hour in this mode. For subscribers who guarantee $90 per month in usage, the same files are available at $90 per hour on the average. A 50 percent surcharge is added for 2400-baud access. Offline prints costs $.55 per page. Each page contains two screens of information.

A sign-up fee of $50 covers the cost of the password and the *VU/TEXT User's Manual,* updated blue sheets giving information on the content of each file, and a semimonthly newsletter. *VU/TEXT* customer service staff will train new subscribers. Search assistance is available through a toll-free line, from 8 a.m. to 10 p.m. Eastern Standard Time weekdays. "Help" screens are currently available to explain commands and procedures online.

VU/TEXT offers a special educational rate package, geared to academic institutions at the graduate or undergraduate level. The *VU/TEXT in Education* (VIE) rate is a flat fee of $15 per hour, including telecommunications costs and instructional aids developed by *VU/TEXT* especially for the classroom. The database must be used only for classroom instruction for this rate to apply; students may not use it for outside research. Schools of journalism and business are currently taking advantage of these special rates for classroom instruction.

INFO GLOBE

Info Globe is the online service for the full text of Canada's *Globe and Mail,* which has been greatly augmented by the addition of other business services. The *Globe and Mail* online has been available for searching since 1978. The full text of the newspaper is online at 6:00 a.m. each day of publication.

Other services include the *Canadian Financial* database, providing the full text of auditing reports for large publicly held Canadian corporations and crown corporations competing in the private sector; and *MARKETSCAN*'s stock market quotations from the Toronto, Montreal, Vancouver, Alberta, New York, and American Stock Exchanges. The *INSIGHT* databases, provided by Canada Systems Group, provide separate information files on Canadian businesses: (1) Corporate Names, (2) Bankruptcies (corporate and personal), (3) Inter-Corp Ownership (holdings in Canadian concerns), (4) Trademarks (including 200,000 registered and pending Canadian trademarks), (5) Canadian Federal Corporations and Directors (covering ownership, revenues and assets, and identities of corporate directors), and (6) the *Canadian Trade Index,* an industrial directory of Canadian firms. In addition, the *Report on Business* corporate database offers detailed financial data covering a ten-year period for 1,500 can companies, and quarterly reports for 350 major Canadian corporations. *Info Globe* also is the Canadian marketing entity for *Dow Jones News/Retrieval, Finsbury Textline,* and the *DataSolve* world reporter.

The *Info Globe* utility serves journalists, as well as business managers, accountants, lawyers, sales people, and researchers. Record formats are similar to those on *VU/TEXT,* but the specific command language differs from that of *QL Search;* and general search capabilities vary between the two systems in some details. For example, natural language (rather than field codes as employed by *VU/TEXT*) can be employed to invoke *Globe and Mail* online paragraph searching, e.g., "drought in head, lead" for the term "drought" in headlines and introductory paragraphs of an article. Considerable flexibility in truncation is provided by a feature that permits the searcher to specify multiple word-endings for a word stem between brackets (e.g., "product⟨s⟩" will exclude any other suffixes to the search term "product"). Limited command stacking is possible by entering the steps for a search with a colon (:) between them. Output is controlled from a menu after a search is run, and the user may select from the standard short formats, KWIC (Key Words in Context), a display of fields chosen by the searcher, or the full-document display. Sophisticated print command-strings can be used to introduce considerable flexibility into the displaying of documents.

Info Globe and *VU/TEXT* offer similar degrees of difficulty for the prospective end user, despite the variations in procedures; to gain complete mastery of each system's possibilities, the user needs considerable training. *Info Globe* includes extensive online "help" screens, which describe almost every aspect of searching or displaying documents on the system, grouped by function.

To accommodate its expanding base of end users, however, *Info Globe* has developed new products that provide end users with easier access routes to the basic information provided by the *Globe and Mail* online portion of the *Info Globe* search. *Info Globe Personal Search* is easy to learn, making it suitable for classroom use at the elementary or secondary school level, much as *Dow Jones News/Retrieval* has been adapted to schools.

After signing on to *Personal Search,* the user can select any one of thirteen files from an introductory menu simply by selecting the number of the file. Files cover current events and continuing issues, current events and hot topics, world politics, Canadian national news, news from the provinces, foreign countries, personal investment information, science, sports, entertainment, the environment, and health, and there is a special file on happenings in Toronto. The choice of any file leads to additional selections from numbered menus. Continuing issues, for example, include acid rain, abortion, education, terrorism, disarmament, free trade, atomic accidents, strikes, capital punishment, drug abuse, and sexual discrimination and harrassment.

Investment information in the file includes articles on specific Canadian companies and general information on personal finance, mutual funds, bonds, options and futures markets, pensions, registered retirement savings plans, gold prices, insider trading, corporate reports, dividends, interest rates, income taxes, and general investment news, all searchable as separate topics.

The choice of topic leads to a list of fifteen headlines. Choosing the number of a headline causes the article to be displayed immediately in full text. The user can bypass the first set of headlines in order to obtain a further list of headlines on the same topic. Articles are arranged in reverse order of publication, with the most current listed first. Some articles are brief news releases, one screen in length; others may include four or five screens of text.

Aside from choosing numbered selections, the user needs to use only one of the six single-letter commands to navigate among the screens: "F" to page down, "Utility" to page up, "T" to obtain the top menu of a particular file, "P" to obtain the previous menu, "X" for main menu, or "?" for the "help" screens. The only situations that depart from the menu-driven format are searches for investment articles on companies—which require the entry of stock symbols—and the movie- and theater-review module—which requires the user to enter the name of the production in order to obtain a list of reviews.

Rates for the regular *Info Globe* search are billed in Canadian dollars: $2.82 per minute and $.30 per article displayed online, or $.01 per line printed offline, as of June 1987. Telecom Canada telecommunications charges are an additional $.18 per minute. Charges for the other databases on the system vary considerably; details are available from *Info Globe*'s customer service office. Volume discounts are available with an initial commitment. Public libraries and schools are eligible for an automatic discount for the *Globe and Mail* and the *Canadian Financial Database*.

Initiation fees vary according to the database or combination of databases chosen. Training is available at workshops offered in major Canadian and U.S. cities, for $150 per person, and includes practice time on the system. Customer assistance is available for searchers from 9:00 a.m. to 5:00 p.m., Monday through Friday.

Rates for *Info Globe Personal Search* are $1 per minute during prime hours (8 a.m. to 8 p.m. Toronto time), and $.50 per minute during off-hours. The initiation fee for personal search is $49.95, which includes 60 minutes of free time on the system.

MEAD DATA CENTRAL

The Mead Data Central (MDC) databases consists of a vast collection of full-text information on law, current events, and medicine. The principal MDC databases are *Lexis* (the legal module), *Nexis* (the current events module), and *Medis* (a medical file discussed in Chapter 8).

Lexis libraries include the United States, United Kingdom, French, Australian, and New Zealand libraries. The U.S. library alone contains separate files on admiralty law; banking; bankruptcy law; Delaware corporate law; federal laws, regulations, and decisions pertaining to energy, the environment, communications, securities, and taxes; international trade; labor; military justice; federal patent, trademark, and copyright laws and regulations; public contracts; and trade regulations. Also included are law reviews from six prestigious university law reviews, ABA ethics opinions and bylaws, Commerce Clearing House federal and state tax reports, and the complete docket of the Baldwain United bankruptcy litigation. *Lexis* also includes a complete set of state laws files for the United States, which typically include state supreme court, appeals court, and tax court opinions, and opinions of the state attorney general. *Lexis* is the oldest and most financially successful of Mead's data libraries, having as its principal competitor the *WESTLAW* system. *Lexis*, along with *WESTLAW*, has been the model for the incorporation of end-user training for professional practitioners into both the workplace and the academic curriculum.

NAARS, the *National Automated Accounting Research System,* is provided through *Lexis* by the American Institute of Certified Public Accountants, and includes New York and American Stock Exchange and some over-the-counter annual reports, and selected information from proxy statements and proceedings of the Securities and Exchange Commission (SEC) and of various accounting standards boards and committees. *LEXPAT,* a library of the *Nexis* search, includes the full text of utility patents from January 1975 to the present, plant and design patents from 1976 to the present, and listings of every patent ever issued, categorized by class and subclass. The *Manual of Classification* and the *Index to U.S. Classification* are also available online.

The *Nexis* libraries include separate files for newspapers, magazines, newswires, and newsletters, which can be searched separately as document types. In excess of 250 publications are represented. In addition, the publications in *Nexis* can be searched in libraries organized by subject groupings: business, finance, government, news, and trade and technology. Daily newspapers such as the *New York Times, Washington Post,* and *Christian Science Monitor;* magazine articles from general interest journals such as *Newsweek, Editorial Research Reports, Facts On File, U.S. News and World Report;* and many trade and technology newsletters are included in this encyclopedic library. Recent additions to the basic *Nexis* file include the full contents of the magazine *ASAP* and *Trade and Industry ASAP* files from Information Access Company as part of the general magazine file. These files include such magazines as *Time, People, Business Week,* and other Time publications. Two general interest files on *Nexis* are *TODAY,* a file of concise summaries of same-day news from the *New York Times* (daily summary, business day, and 1:30 p.m. updates, or a combination of these), and *APOLIT,* an election search from the AP wire from biographies of candidates and summaries of campaign and election items.

EXCHANGE is a full-text economic library consisting of ECONO, with proceedings of research from ABECOR (a committee of ten banks from eight European countries) and information from the Evans Economics electronic news service; VIEWPT, a massive collection of company research reports from 23 leading brokerage firms; plus the DISCLOSURE SEC filing and a separate file of SEC 10-K, 10-Q, and Update reports. Some of the firms included are Merrill Lynch; Argus Research Corp.; Paine Webber; the Pershing Division of Donaldson, Lufkin, and Jenrette; Drexel Burnham and Lambert; J. C. Bradford; Yamaichi Research; and Zacks Investment Research. Firms are chosen to provide strong regional coverage as well as national focus.

MDC databases are accessible through special terminals available from Mead or through certain MS-DOS-compatible computer terminals with special software assistance. Users with CROSTALK XVI, Version 3.6, may now access MDC using IBM, AT&T, Columbia, Compaq, Corona, Data General, Eagle, Hewlett Packard, Sperry, TeleVideo, Texas Instruments, Victor, Wang, and Zenith machines, and additional machines are being added.

Documentation for the MDC databases includes the *Reference Manual* for searching; a "Quick Reference" brochure outlining commands, and record segments, and giving examples of appropriate command statements; a two-volume *Lexis Libraries Guide;* and a thick one-volume *Guide to Nexis and Related Services.* The last two publications list every file in the entire database, show their contents, and indicate what segments are searchable on each file. A 35-page *Learning Lexis* handbook provides a detailed description of the system, a series of case-study examples in law to illustrate different types of search strategies, and additional tips for searches-by-situation in chart form.

Abundant assistance is available to the user through Mead. "Help" screens are available at most points in the search—to provide a basic description of a problem—and some screens lead to additional "Help" screens, providing a more detailed treatment of a given system function. Customer service for *Lexis/Nexis* users is available through a toll-free line, 24 hours a day, seven days a week.

Additional help is available to assist users in learning to formulate database searches. Three tutorial databases are available online to the user, free of charge (except for telecommunicatons charges). The *CAI* (Computer-Assisted Instruction) database provides the user with basic interactive instruction in "AND," "OR," and word-proximity operations; gives examples of problems for the user to work out; and provides correct answers. *Tutor,* an advanced tutorial database, runs the user through instructional modules that review advanced aspects of searching *Lexis/Nexis* (e.g., segment searches, search modification, and command stacking). *Tutor* can be used as an education program for the MDC searcher with established basic skills, or for a review of functions that a searcher has not encountered in a while. Finally, *Debut* provides an overview of the contents of new databases on the system with a few screens of information.

Each Mead Data Central database is divided into "libraries," or subject groupings. The libraries are composed of "files," corresponding to the contents of a specific publication on *Nexis*, or a specific class of court documents or findings on *Lexis* (e.g., Supreme Court decisions, or Opinions of the Attorney General of the United States). Files are composed of "documents," such as court cases, sections of a statute, annual reports, specific patents, or individual news stories. Documents, in turn, are divided into "segments," i.e., data fields that can be searched or displayed independently. Headlines of news stories, author names, and legal case citations are examples of segments. Searches on MDC databases may be run at any level of specificity within individual libraries.

After logon, a Mead Data Central search usually involves selecting a library from a menu list, selecting a file from a "help" menu for that library, entering the search request, and pressing the "Transmit" key. (The special service charges are incurred at this point in each search.) After viewing the initial search results in a display format, the searcher proceeds to modify the search (narrowing or qualifying it), and displays or prints the results before logging off the system.

On the Mead Data terminals, most of the above operations are accomplished through the use of special function keys. For example, there is a "change libraries" key, a "change files" key, a "modify search" key, a "print" key, etc. For users of the IBM-PC and some other hardware, the access software provided by Mead enables searchers to use the function keys on their machines to emulate the dedicated terminal functions. A terminal overlay is provided, showing what each function key will do. On all non-Mead terminals, the functions can be executed using a three-letter code, typed on a standard ASCII keyboard: e.g., ".CF" for "change files," ".CL" for "change libraries," ".TR" for "transmit," etc. These three-character commands can also be "stacked" to create shorthand messages to circumvent the use of function keys—even on the MDC hardware—in the interests of saving time.

Searchable segments (fields) on *Lexis* are: case name, docket number, court, case citation from published source, date of decision, source of appeal (lower court), judge hearing appeal, counsel, opinion by (last name of judge writing the legal opinion), text of opinion, concur by (last name of the judge writing the concurring opinion), text of the dissent, and a separate field allowing the searcher to locate on the system all the opinions written by a particular judge.

Searchable segments on *Nexis* include byline, dateline, headline, and date of publication, as well as the full text of the article. Output on *Nexis* can be sorted by date and length of articles for printing. Searching is performed through the use of words (up to twenty characters) and "connectors," specifying word proximity or Boolean relationships among search terms. Proximity operators include "W" (for "within"), where words can appear in either order and be within a specified number of words of each other, and "PRE" (for "preceding"), which denotes word order.

The above expressions of word proximity can be used along with standard Boolean operators ("OR," "AND," "AND NOT"), or the Boolean operators can be used independently. To request that a search be conducted in a specific segment of the document, the user specifies the segment at the beginning of the search statement, and the search strategy is simply entered in parentheses. Parentheses can also be used to express priorities within a search statement.

Truncation of individual words is indicated through the use of an exclamation point (!), and an individual "wild card" character for one letter can be indicated through the use of the asterisk(*) (e.g., "WOM*N" for "WOMAN" or "WOMEN").

Search results from Mead Data Central databases can be displayed or printed in KWIC format, showing the 15 or 30 words to either side of the search term's occurrence (on *Nexis*), or the 25 or 50 words to either side of the search term (on *Lexis*). Other options include full display of the document, display of the basic bibliographic reference or legal case citation, or a list of parts into which the retrieved documents may be displayed. This latter "Segmts" (segments) option presents users with a menu from which they may choose specific segments of retrieved documents to be displayed or cited.

Mead Data Central is considering rate revisions for January 1988 that may affect both its costs and its rate structure. Current rates as of December 1987 include a subscription charge ($50 per month for *Nexis,* $125 for *Lexis*), a $20 per hour connect—charge (with Telenet or Meadnet access costing an additional $12 per hour), and a variable charge for each initial search of the system. The charge per search ranges from $7 to $30, depending on the size of the file that is selected. Printing costs $.02 per line, offline or online, but there is no additional charge for printing a single screen. Volume discounts of up to 34 percent are available to frequent searchers.

Many professional searchers have found costs to be difficult to contain on Mead databases, because each new search statement that is transmitted to a *Nexis* or *Lexis* file in prime time results in at least a $7 charge. Modifications of a search (narrowing or qualifying the strategy) result in an additional $3 charge during prime time. An additional variable that tends to inflate costs is the assessment of additional charges if a group of databases is chosen.

Strategies for cost containment suggested by J. Paul Lomio in his 1985 article "The High Cost of Nexis and What a Searcher Can Do about It" include careful planning of searches offline, scrupulous proofreading of each search statement before pressing the "Transmit" key, selection of as small a file as possible, use of broad initial strategies that can be modified rather than re-entered, and use of MDC's customer services.[10]

The cost-containment problem is more challenging on *Nexis* than on *Lexis,* because *Nexis* searching tends to involve free-text strategies rather than legal shorthand, and free-text searching is more likely to require search modification. The *Lexis* module lends itself to precise searching because of the nature of its subject matter. Much legal research is by nature citation searching, cross-referencing of cases, or pinpointing of precise phrases specific to the field of law. One of the *Lexis* system's greatest benefits, as compared with old-fashioned manual searching, is its automated tabular cross-referencing of legal citations (AUTO-CITE), and its online access to *Shepard's Citations,* which traces the history of legal decisions.

Nexis, with its rich and massive resources, good scanning, and print capabilities compatible with its full-text retrieval capacity, still presents all the perils and pitfalls of a straight full-text system without key words. Learning to use *Nexis* involves a carefully designed sequence of programmed instruction tailored to the future specialized information needs of the student, and similar in character to the occupational instruction that is offered on the *Lexis* files.

Aware of the complexities of its system, and wanting to maintain a maximum level of quality in the training of its users, Mead Data Central has in the past made it a policy to train its clients and to discourage distribution of its databases by intermediaries not supported or trained by Mead. Also aware of the fact that attorneys in small private practices might want to use *Lexis* without maintaining a terminal in their offices, Mead has set up a Membership Group Program, which permits local law libraries and bar associations to act as billing agents for a group of *Lexis* users, who can be trained locally or by Mead at their own option. The University of North Carolina at Chapel Hill runs a library service program for North Carolina attorneys, which includes reference assistance, photocopying and interlibrary loan service, a message board, consultations on setting up and maintaining law libraries, and walkup access to *WESTLAW* terminals (from 2:30 p.m. to 5:30 p.m.) for a flat fee. Part of the service includes access to *Lexis* through the Mead Data Central program. Attorneys can use personal computers in their own offices or homes to gain access to *Lexis* and its allied services, with the library providing the billing.[11]

Law schools have been entrusted with training new attorneys through a contract that provides *Lexis* to law schools at a flat fee.[12] As another example, the University of North Carolina-Chapel Hill law school requires all first-year students to attend two-week training sessions on *Lexis* during the fall semester and on *WESTLAW* during the spring. Training includes hour-and-a-half online sessions, with two students per terminal.[13] Law firms have come to expect such training of students; it has become a professional standard. Such training arrangements are not limited to law schools, however. For example, at Bentley College in Waltham, Massachusetts, a four-year private college that specializes in business administration, students of business law and paralegal students receive one-on-one tutorials on the use of *Lexis,* which is offered for use in the library at the educational rate.[14]

Mead is currently conducting pilot programs in business schools at major universities, involving the possible use of *NAARS, EXCHANGE,* and the *Lexis Tax Library* by graduate business students through a law school contract. Auditing sections of accounting schools experiment with *NAARS,* for example, to obtain statistics and information on business events for use in annual reports. Also on the horizon, Mead has announced that it is testing CD-ROM technology in order to evaluate its use in law practices.

In regard to *Nexis,* no wholesale pricing arrangement is currently available. Mead educational representatives have stressed the difficulty that is involved in providing *Nexis* at a discount to any client; such an arrangement would involve renegotiation of all of the company's royalty contracts with every database producer that supplies a component of *Nexis.* (*Lexis* is produced by Mead Data and can be easily discounted at will for use by educational institutions.) As long as this policy holds, searching of *Nexis* by end users at academic libraries will probably not be practical from a budgetary standpoint. Nonetheless, *Nexis* remains an extremely important research tool for obtaining background information and information on current events pertaining to business, and for use by journalists and other researchers.

OTHER SERVICES

WESTLAW, marketed by West Publishing Company of St. Paul, Minnesota, is a comprehensive legal research service of comparable scope to *Lexis. WESTLAW* is widely used in law offices by attorneys and other legal researchers, through a variety of hardware. The key word and key number system that has made West's legal publications famous is incorporated into the online system. For current events research, gateways to *VU/TEXT* and *DJN/R* are provided. Rates for *WESTLAW* as of October 1986 include a $125-per-month flat-rate subscription fee and a simple $100-to-$150-per-month service fee, with discounts available for educational institutions.

The *Human Resource Information Network* (HRIN) is a new full-text information retrieval network dedicated to serving the personnel and human resource professional. The system is designed to be searched by end users, and includes timely news, database research material, and regulatory information pertinent to all aspects of personnel administration and human resource management, including affirmative action, employment and recruiting, training and staff development, safety and health, and labor and employee relations. HRIN also offers electronic communications services, interactive software, and online services for seminar registrations and airline reservations. It has recently added *PAYLINE*, an online national salary survey with continuous updates for human resources professionals and attorneys. Also planned for 1988 is a college recruiting database with electronic resumés for university students in the personnel and human resources professions, which may later include working professionals as well.

The system is available to corporations by annual subscription. An average installation costs around $2,700 per location, plus hourly access fees and print charges. A subset, *Human Resource Library Network,* is available to libraries for a $125 annual subscription, plus connect charges of about $36 to $91 per hour, and additional citation charges.

SUMMARY

Online databases for end users provide essential information for business personnel for performing their everyday job functions. Most of this information is in finished form, rather than in bibliographic form. Full texts of information relating to investments, the activities of clients and competitors, technical advancements within specified industries, directories of potential sales contacts, and numerical data on real and projected industrial performances are available.

The national and regional newspaper data files contain valuable company information on earnings trends; interviews with officers and executives; information about key personnel changes and biographical information on key persons; information on contract awards, plan expansions, relocations and closings, new products and ventures, stock splits and dividends, mergers and acquisitions; plus industry information on local property values and real estate trends, technological and research breakthroughs, credit and mortgage conditions; background information on government regulations, investigations, and court proceedings or lawsuits; and foreign dispatches on multinational operations.

Marydee Ojala, in her article "End-User Searching and Its Implications for Librarians," provides some examples of what activities a special librarian might expect practiced end users to be able to perform in a corporate setting. Searches for routine stock quotes or stories from *DJN/R,* frequently repeated searches for updated information on a topic, searches for daily news reports, more complex searches restricted to one database on one system, highly specialized searches requiring specialized knowledge on the part of the user about particular services, or "quick-and-dirty" searches for a few articles to brainstorm a new topic are all examples of appropriate end-user searching in the day-to-day operations of a company, in her view, and librarians should expect more people to be interested in these activities in the future, due in part to an increase in the marketing of and classroom exposure to end-user systems.[15]

Despite the potential benefits of this wealth of online information, the use of business information services by corporate end users lags behind technological innovation, according to Steve Arnold of Data Courier, Inc., who has monitored the training of corporate end users for several years. Factors cited by Arnold as contributing to resistance in the adoption of online tools by corporate end users are lack of standardization in search protocols; failure of online database producers to upgrade the quality and consistency of and support services for online products to benefit end users as opposed to libraries; lack of standardization of PC hardware within corporate data processing departments; a lag in training behind hardware capabilities; and a basic human tendency among some potential end users not to take it upon themselves to learn how to use personal computers on their own. A possible consequence of this resistance among corporate end users might be the centralization of the information function in corporate data processing departments, rather than the diversification and "democratization" of online research that has been foreseen by the visionaries of the online industry.[16]

Aside from the problems of standardization of data within computer networks at the company level, and within the industry as a whole, the problems described in Arnold's paper are basic computer literacy problems that libraries can help address. In view of the gap between technological invention and end-user comprehension in the area of database searching, there is a definite need for the training of professionals in the characteristics and use of these systems. This activity can be performed at any of three levels of commitment: (1) providing a computer port in the library for classroom programs, (2) offering bibliographic instruction in the structure and function of business databases, their rates and search procedures, and their similarities and differences, and (3) providing actual instruction and experience for the end user in the basic mechanics of searching.

Throughout this chapter, we have seen that some database producers have been responding to the problem of training end users by attempting to reach future practitioners while they are being educated in order to impress upon them the value of online systems. In law, we have seen that the ability to perform online legal research has become practically a prerequisite for employment in many large law firms. Business schools have been exposing students to some of the financially based online systems. Some journalism schools are integrating online newspaper services into the curriculum. Finally, secondary schools are beginning to perceive that, for the majority of their students, the teaching of computer literacy may have more to do with using computers to gain access to information than with learning mathematics-based programming skills.

The role of public libraries in this development is less obvious than that of academic and school libraries, but it is no less rich in possibilities. Public librarians might use some existing cases of successful computer literacy instruction to devise programs that will expose adults to the potential of databases in business. Real problems exist with structured training and with accountability for costs for the implementation of timesharing services in public library settings. Large vendors might be amenable to providing subsidized time for demonstrations of their systems; however, they cannot be expected to provide regular public access to their systems at a wholesale rate, thereby undermining their own potential markets for clients. Public libraries will especially want to closely monitor the development of CD-ROM products that simulate these online products. The economics of CD-ROM closely approximates the sort of rate concept that public libraries can use most effectively: fixed charges for a product with a very high usage among a large group of users.

One promising innovation that may alleviate the practical problems of logistics, particularly for public libraries, is the *Answer Machine,* a product being beta-tested in late 1987 by Telebase Systems at the Bryn Mawr (Pa.) Public Library. *Answer Machine* is designed to provide access by debit card to the *Easynet* gateway system at a flat rate. *NewsNet, VU/ TEXT, Datatimes,* and *Dow Jones News/Retrieval* are among the databases available to *Easynet* searchers. A number of rate structures are being contemplated for library installations of the *Answer Machine.*[17]

The point to be made is that, as technology makes access to databases easier for more and more users, the individual librarian's knowledge of the contents and functions of the actual databases becomes more important in attaining the informational objectives of the prospective database searcher, in any and all library settings.

Well-informed librarians at all levels of the continuing education process have a responsibility to educate information users, who may have high expectations about what information ought to exist on computers, about the limitations of existing computerized information sources and the complexities of using them. The area of online end-user databases represents a promising one for the application of this sort of expertise.

NOTES

1. Steve Arnold, "End Users: Old Myths and New Realities," in *National Online Meeting Proceedings—1986*, comp. by Martha Williams and Thomas H. Hogan, 5–10 (Medford, N.J.: Learned Information, 1986).

2. Mick O'Leary, "Business Information in the End User Databanks—Part 1," *Online* 10 (May 1986): 108–111.

3. "E. F. Hutton: Huttonline," *Library Hi Tech News* 27 (May 1986): 2.

4. Joseph Pica, personal communication.

5. Michael Halperin, personal communication. Students' responses to the end-user

searching program at the Lippincott Library of the Wharton School are discussed in: Alice C. Littlejohn, "End-User Searching in an Academic Library—The Students' Views," *RQ* 26 (Summer 1987): 460–66.

6. Nancy Garman and Judith Pask, "End-User Searching in Business and Management," in *National Online Meeting Proceedings—1985*, comp. by Martha Williams and Thomas H. Hogan, 161–66 (Medford, N.J.: Learned Information, 1985).

7. Joseph F. Sullivan, *New York Times,* March 16, 1986, Section 1, p. 52.

8. Alan H. Walker, Coordinator of Instructional Services, Center for Learning Technology, 3rd Supervisory District of Suffolk County, personal communication.

9. Mick O'Leary, "DIALOG Business Connection: DIALOG for the End User," *Online* 10 (Sept. 1986): 15–24.

10. J. Paul Lomio, "The High Cost of Nexis and What a Searcher Can Do about It," *Online* 9 (Sept. 1985): 54–56.

11. Timothy L. Coggins, Associate Librarian, Law Library, University of North Carolina, Chapel Hill, personal communication.

12. J. Edwards, "Lexis and WESTLAW Instruction in the Law School: University of Oklahoma," *Law Library Journal* 76 (Summer 1983): 605–31.

13. Michael Campbell, *Computerized Legal Research. Final Report.* ERIC ED 242 872

14. Tjaldo Belastock, Associate Library Director, Bentley College, personal communication.

15. Marydee Ojala, "End User Searching and Its Implications for Librarians," *Special Libraries* 76 (Spring 1985): 93–99.

16. Arnold, 1986.

17. Nancy Herther, "The 'Answer Machine'—Online's Answer to CDROM?" *Database* 10 (Dec. 1987): 114–15.

BIBLIOGRAPHY

Arnold, Steve. "End Users: Old Myths and New Realities." In *National Online Meeting Proceedings—1986,* comp. by Martha E. Williams and Thomas H. Hogan, 5–10. Medford, N.J.: Learned Information, 1986.

Bamford, James. "The Electronic Edge." *Forbes* 135 (May 6, 1985): 102–9.

Breslow, Jordan. "Lawyers on Line." *PC World* 3 (Oct. 1985): 216–23.

Campbell, Michael. *Computerized Legal Research. Final Report.* ERIC ED 242 872

"E. F. Hutton: Huttonline." *Library Hi Tech News* 27 (May 1986): 2.

Edwards, J. "Lexis and WESTLAW Instruction in the Law School: University of Oklahoma." *Law Library Journal* 76 (Summer 1983): 605–31.

Franklin, Carl. "Searching Lexis and WESTLAW—Part I." *Database* 9 (Feb. 1986): 13–20.

Fried, Michael. "NewsNet: An Offering of Current and Specialized Information." *Online* 9 (July 1985): 99–105.

Garman, Nancy, and Judith Pask. "End-User Searching in Business and Management." In *National Online Meeting Proceedings—1985,* comp. by Martha E. Williams and Thomas H. Hogan, 161–66. Medford, N.J.: Learned Information, 1985.

Herther, Nancy. "The 'Answer Machine'—Online's Answer to CDROM?" *Database* 10 (Dec. 1987): 114–15.

Littlejohn, Alice C. "End-User Searching in an Academic Library—The Students' Views." *RQ* 26 (Summer 1987): 460–66.

Lomio, J. "The High Cost of Nexis and What a Searcher Can Do about It." *Online* 9 (Sept. 1985): 54–56.

McCleary, Hunter. "VU/TEXT: Full-Text Daily Newspaper Information...and More." *Online* 9 (July 1985): 87–95.

Melville, Karen. "Info Globe Databases." *Online* 10 (July 1986): 124–28.

Ojala, Marydee. "End User Searching and Its Implications for Librarians." *Special Libraries* 76 (Spring 1985): 93–99.

O'Leary, Mick. "Business Information in the End User Databanks—Part 1." *Online* 10 (May 1986): 108–11.

_____. "Business Information in the End User Databanks—Part 2." *Online* 10 (July 1986): 119–20.

_____. "DIALOG Business Connection: DIALOG for the End User." *Online* 10 (Sept. 1986): 15–24.

Pelto, Michael A. "Human Resource Information Network." *Database* 9 (Aug. 1986): 114–20.

Willman, Donna. "First Look: VU/TEXT Databases." *Online* 9 (Mar. 1985): 61–68.

Chapter 8

End-User Searching in Science, Technology, and Health

Debra Ketchell and Susanne J. Redalje

INTRODUCTION

End-user searching in the science, technology, and health fields is not a new phenomenon. Librarians began advising and training scientists and health professionals to conduct their own online searches long before the advent of "user-friendly" systems in 1982. Early in the history of on-line searching, search system developers and many librarians felt that end users would be the primary searchers.[1] Sewell reported on a program that began training pathologists and pharmacists in 1974 to search the *Medline* and *Toxline* databases using the National Library of Medicine's command-driven *MEDLARS* system.[2] Haines reported on teaching chemists to search DIALOG databases at the Kodak Research Laboratories.[3] However, until 1982, librarians and other information specialists performed the majority of online searching.

The appearance of end-user search systems marketed to health, science, and technology professionals related not only to the increasing availability of electronic information sources, but also to the need for current information, the widespread use of microcomputers, and the availability of other services, such as electronic mail, online continuing education programs, and electronic bulletin boards. Two different models of end-user searching have been developed. In the library-based model, the end user searches on a terminal in the library, on a system chosen by the library, and is trained and assisted by the library staff, and in some cases even subsidized by the library. In the consultant mode, the equipment and search system is located in the end user's office, and the librarian acts as a consultant and trainer. Some libraries offer both models. This chapter covers both those systems best suited for the library-based model and those systems best suited for the individual end user.

End users cannot be placed in a single category, nor can they be assumed to have the same abilities and needs. For users who have only an intermittent need or who do not want to devote much time to searching, menu-driven or simplified systems, such as BRS's *After Dark, BRS Colleague,* DIALOG's *Knowledge Index,* or *PaperChase,* are appropriate. For users who want more powerful capabilities or access to different databases, command-driven systems, such as *CAS ONLINE, DIALOG,* and *MEDLARS,* are a better match. Users who need to use the command-driven systems but who do not feel comfortable doing so may opt to use front-end software programs that provide special assistance, such as *SciMate, Grateful Med, Med-Base,* or *ProSearch.* Thus, any system can be considered an end-user system. This chapter covers all systems of potential value to end users regardless of format. It is divided into two sections, covering: (1) systems in the science and technology fields, and (2) systems specifically designed for the health sciences.

GENERAL SCIENCE SERVICES

CAS ONLINE

CAS ONLINE is produced by the Chemical Abstracts Service (CAS). It is a fully capable, command-driven system. *CAS ONLINE* is divided into three major databases: *CA,* the primary bibliographic database covering the chemically related literature from 1967 (the abstracts are available and searchable, a feature unique to this system); *CAOLD,* a unique retrospective file covering the literature dating back to 1966; and the *Registry* file, which may be used as a chemical dictionary or searched by substructure.

CAS ONLINE is now part of an international network called the Scientific and Technical Network (STN). Begun in 1983, STN is the result of a cooperative agreement between Fachinformationszentrum Energie, Physik Mathematik GmbH (FIZ Karlsruhe), and the Chemical Abstracts Service. Additional support came from the Japan Association for International Chemical Information. A new full-service center soon will be established in Tokyo at the Japan Information Center of Science and Technology. Besides *CAS ONLINE,* the STN network provides access to a variety of databases in the sciences and technology, including *Compendex* and *BIOSIS.* Several of the databases are unique files, including

DIPPR, produced by the American Institute of Chemical Engineers, a non-bibliographic database describing the physical properties of more than 1000 commercially important compounds.

CAS ONLINE offers a variety of training programs, including one designed for chemist end users—*CA FILE. CAS ONLINE* is designed for end users who are new to online searching, stresses the use of the bibliographic file, and includes hands-on time. The fee for a full-day session is $150 ($75 academic); half-day session costs $100 ($50 academic). In addition to workshops, *CAS ONLINE* holds users' meetings in conjunction with major national meetings, such as the American Chemical Society meetings. The company is beginning to hold regional users' meetings as well. These meetings are intended to help the user keep up to date with new capabilities and enhancements to the system, and to allow time for questions and recommendations.

To supplement training, *CAS ONLINE/STN* has begun developing a series of tutorial diskettes called *STN MENTOR,* which run on IBM microcomputers. The first two to be developed are *STN Overview* and *Introduction to CAS ONLINE.* These tutorials are simple to use and give an excellent overview of the system. The *Introduction to CAS ONLINE* is sufficient for many beginners to learn to perform basic searches. The diskettes include excellent sample searches, coverage of Boolean logic, and information about choosing subject terms. A parallel tutorial has been developed by the American Chemical Society for its full-text database—*Chemical Journals Online.* This database is unique to STN and is the first of a group of full-text journal databases to be added to the system.

There are a variety of additional search aids that are helpful to the user. The system manuals are designed for self-instruction, providing many examples, along with sample questions and answers. *Chemical Abstracts* uses controlled subject headings that are listed in the printed *Index Guide,* along with helpful cross-references. The *Index Guide* is also useful for locating registry numbers and chemical names. Since 1985, *Chemical Abstracts* has published an additional subject heading list in two parts covering (1) general subjects, and (2) plants and animals. Other helpful aids include *Qualified Substances in the CA File* and *Name Segments in the Registry File.* A complete list of user aids may be obtained by calling the CAS toll-free customer service number. In addition, there is an excellent online help structure. At anytime during the search, a "?" or the command "Help" will produce a list of appropriate options, an explanation of commands, or a more in-depth explanation of an error response.

The command system for *CAS ONLINE* is called "Messenger" and functions essentially as an invisible gateway allowing access to databases on the host computers. The command system is simple to use and comprises two levels: the novice mode and the expert mode. The novice mode functions almost as if the system were menu driven, prompting the user for the needed information. For example, if the user enters the command "Display" with a carriage return, the user is asked first for the statement number to be displayed, then for the desired format in which the citations are to be printed, and then for the number of citations to be printed. The expert mode allows these steps to be completed in one step simply by stacking the commands. Either abbreviations or full commands may be used. There is no need to "Enter" a particular mode. A user may be familiar with the commands but forget all the elements needed in the "Display" command above. In this case, the novice mode can be entered simply by typing the full command and pressing the carriage return. Once the display of citations is completed, the user can return to the expert mode by using either the full or abbreviated command and all the information needed in one step.

The basic pricing structure for *CAS ONLINE* is competitive with the other systems. The *Chemical Abstracts* database costs $106 per hour on *CAS ONLINE,* and $94 for subscribers of the printed *Chemical Abstracts. File 399, Chemical Abstracts'* equivalent to *DIALOG,* costs $105.

For academic institutions, the Chemical Abstracts Service subsidizes 90 percent of search costs. This subsidy means that a search costs $9.40 per hour, and bibliographic citations online cost $.03 each, $.06 each if abstracts are included. Telelcommunications charges are additional. The full-text *ACS Journals* database is offered at a 50 percent discount. Other STN databases are not covered by the academic plan. The academic plan pricing structure makes the *Chemical Abstracts* database extremely attractive for academic users. A $50 sign-up fee to STN is required to establish an academic account. Payment may be made from a deposit account or by monthly billing. With each account come five "logonids" (passwords) that allow access to the system for five searchers at one time. The passwords are a convenient feature for libraries that must charge back costs to patrons. When entering a database, the user can also enter a "Cost" center by using an eight-character alphanumeric code. The charges for each search then will appear on the invoice according to the code that was entered. Academic searchers can use the system at reduced rates during the following non-prime time hours: Sunday through Thursday, from 5 p.m. to 8 a.m.; Friday from 5 p.m. to 8 p.m.; and Saturday from 8 a.m. to 1 p.m. EST. The computer is down on the first Saturday of the month. Customer service is available from 8 a.m. to 6 p.m. EST via a toll-free number. Using the "Send" command, the search can send messages to the *CAS ONLINE* staff—a nice feature, especially if an immediate answer is not needed or it is after hours.

The literature includes several studies using *CAS ONLINE* or other systems with chemical files. Most of these studies have been done in industry.[4] One example of an end-user program study in academe is taking place at the University of Arizona. Because of the persistence of one member of the chemistry faculty, in 1984, a program was begun that now involves more than 21 academic departments and two libraries. Users include undergraduates through faculty in almost all areas of science, including pharmacy and pharmaceutics, planetary sciences, and, of course, chemistry. The program is both an in-house program and an advisory program, allowing patrons to use *CAS ONLINE* from their office or from a terminal made available in the Science and Engineering Library. The program uses the academic plan offered by the Chemical Abstracts Service.

From the beginning, it was felt that the system should be available to all users at no charge, and the system was to be an integral part of the reference search offered by the Science and Engineering Library. First a trial period of three months was established, paid for by the chemistry and biochemistry departments. After the trial period was over, the library was able to obtain a $10,000 grant from the Office of the Vice-President for Research, which carried the program for more than a year. Money for the program now comes out of the library's budget, with search costs averaging $1,000 per month.[5]

The chemistry and biochemistry departments were given a logonid for their faculty and staff. The other three logonids were retained by the library. To sign up to use the system, the user calls or stops by the reference desk and is assigned a time and a logonid.

Training for use of the system is offered by the Science and Engineering Library staff for those who want it. These sessions run for two hours and cover the basics of searching the bibliographic files, along with a little coverage of the *Registry* file as a dictionary. Manuals are available for those who prefer to learn on their own. A newsletter was established to provide a stable form of communication as the program grew. The newsletter provides hints and help in developing search strategies, and it announces change in the program and new features on the system.

No formal evaluation of the results of end-user searches was made. However, a survey was sent out to evaluate the success of the program, and the results were positive. The original goals of the program were to provide easy access to online searching at a low cost. The Science and Engineering Library staff feel that the program has successfully met these goals, and, judging from informal comments, they also feel that most users have been successful and satisfied with the results of their searches.[6]

DIALOG and BRS

DIALOG and *BRS* are the major online systems used by professionals today. Between them, these two systems have many unique and valuable databases. Sophisticated end users and end users who may have little other choice because the databases they need are available on no other system may wish to choose the regular online services of *BRS* and *DIA-LOG*. These systems are fully command driven, although *BRS* does offer an option to use menus on its main system. *DIALOG* contains more than 200 databases, most of them in the sciences. For users interested in the geosciences, fisheries, oceanography, and many other specialized areas, *DIALOG*'s main system should be considered. *BRS* contains more than 100 databases, many of them in the sciences and technology.

At an American Chemistry Society meeting, DIALOG representatives pointed out that in the previous 5-year period, those attending DIALOG seminars have changed from being almost entirely information professionals (e.g., librarians) to being 90 to 95 percent end users from every discipline. For end users who choose to use the main *DIALOG* system, the company has developed two specialized workshops—one for chemists, and one for health professionals. The sessions are basically the same as DIALOG's regular beginning workshops, but they take the specialized needs and subject interests of health and science users into consideration. Requestees are screened before individuals are placed into one of these sessions, and intermediaries are not encouraged to attend.

Knowledge Index, BRS After Dark, BRS Colleague

Both DIALOG and BRS felt there was a market for easy-to-use, relatively inexpensive systems geared primarily to end users. To fill this need, DIALOG's *Knowledge Index* and BRS's *After Dark* systems were developed. Both are after-hours systems, which is one reason why the costs are much lower than for the main systems. Details concerning these systems can be found in other chapters.

As of August 1987, 15 of *Knowledge Index*'s 65 databases covered the science, technology, and health-related fields (see Table 1). Agriculture is nicely covered with *Agricola, CAB Abstracts,* and *Agribusiness USA*. Technology and computer science are also well covered with *Compendex, INSPEC, NTIS, Microcomputer Index,* and the *Computer Database*.

Unfortunately, there is a very large gap in the coverage of the basic sciences due to the lack of *Chemical Abstracts* and *BIOSIS Previews*. The agricultural files support some areas of the life sciences, including botany, forestry, and animal science. However, this coverage is not sufficient to overcome the lack of *BIOSIS*.

The only chemistry-related databases are *Heilbron* and *Merck,* both excellent full-text databases that provide information on chemical compounds. As is the case in the life sciences, there are some related files for those interested in the agricultural applications of chemistry, such as the *Engineering Index* and *NTIS*. However, there is no substitute for the gap created by the lack of *CA Search*.

TABLE 1:   Selected List of Science and Technology Databases

Databases	Knowledge Index	BRS After Dark	BRS Colleague
Agricola	X	X	X
BIOSIS		X	X
CA SEARCH		X	X
CAB Abstracts	X	X	X
Compendex	X		X
INSPEC	X	X	X
MATH SCI	X	X	X
Medline	X	X	X
Merck Index			X
NTIS	X	X	X
Pollution Abstracts			X
SPORT	X	X	X
Superindex			X

BRS has developed several systems dedicated to use by end users. Both *BRS After Dark* and *Colleague* have many databases that are of interest to those in the sciences and technology. *BRS Colleague* offers the full complement of BRS databases, including such varied files as the *Drug Information Full-Text* (DIFT) and *Robotics* (RBOT). For those who need to deal with standards and specifications, several databases produced by Information Handling are offered, including *Industry and International Standards* and *IHS Vendor Information Database*. The *Colleague* search system originally had been marketed primarily to health and biomedical professionals and will be discussed in more detail along with other health services later in this chapter.

BRS After Dark includes fewer databases than *Colleague*. As of August 1987, there were more than 20 databases of scientific and technical interest (see Table 1). The basic sciences are covered well on *After Dark,* including both *Chemical Abstracts* and *BIOSIS*. One unfortunate gap is the lack of *Compendex* (containing the *Engineering Index*), the most comprehensive of the engineering databases. Some areas of engineering are still well covered through *NTIS* and *INSPEC.*

Each of the systems included in this section has much to offer, but choosing a system could be difficult. One way to choose is by examining the subject areas covered by the system. For chemical engineers, the choice is not difficult. For many areas of chemical engineering, both *Chemical Abstracts* and *Compendex* are needed, and *Colleague* is the only system that offers both. Cost, though, may become a factor, as *Colleague* is the most expensive of these systems. There is also the choice to be made between the menu-driven systems of *BRS* and the simplified command-driven system of *Knowledge Index.*

OTHER SCI-TECH PRODUCTS AND SYSTEMS

Not all vendors have developed specialized end-user systems such as *After Dark* and *Knowledge Index*. This lack of availability, however, does not mean that these systems are inappropriate for end users. End users must make the same choices that librarians and other information specialists make when choosing a system. Each system has databases that overlap, but each also has unique databases that may be of value to the end user. Other databases have unique search features that might make the time invested by the end user to learn a full system worthwhile.

Telesystemes Questel

Telesystemes Questel is a French-based vendor that is particularly strong in chemistry. This manufacturer's search system, called *Darc*, provides chemical structure and substructure search capability. A new feature called *Darc In-House* allows the creation of personal files describing chemical structures and reactions.

Pergamon Orbit InfoLine

Pergamon Orbit InfoLine, a British-based system, is at present undergoing many changes, having recently purchased the *Orbit* search system from SDC. The business databases will continue to use the *InfoLine* software. This software is particularly strong in the area of patents. For end users who might already be familiar with another search system such as *DIALOG, InfoLine*'s command system should prove easy to use. The system allows the use of synonyms of commands, for example, "Expand" or "Neighbor" may be used to examine alphabetically similar terms from the online index. All non-business databases will migrate to the *Orbit* software during 1987. Among their newer databases that might be of interest to end users is *CHEMQUEST. CHEMQUEST* consists of the catalogs of major chemical producers and is searchable by a variety of access points, including structure and substructure. *Pergamon Orbit InfoLine* is currently providing free training for *InfoLine* users on the *Orbit* software.

CIS

Chemical Information Systems offers unique databases in the areas of environment and chemistry. Formerly a government-owned system, *CIS* is now privately owned by Fein-Marquart. In addition to unique files, the company has developed a new training method that might be useful for end users with specialized needs. Training, however, is expensive and time consuming, one of the drawbacks for many end users (and online professionals as well!). CIS also has developed a training program that takes advantage of remote searching capability. The needs of the participants are determined beforehand, and a tailor-made session is designed. The instructor at CIS and the participant at his or her home terminal then signson at a prearranged time, and the lesson proceeds on an interactive basis.

BIOSIS Bits

The *BIOSIS Information Transfer System* (BITS) is a selective information dissemination service available from Biosciences Information. What makes this service different from the average SDI is that instead of monthly updates arriving on paper, *BITS* updates are distributed in machine-readable formats. Most formats for diskettes and magnetic tape are supported, as are most operating systems.

Citations received from *BITS* are easily searched using any database management software, such as the *Sci-Mate Manager*. *BioSuperfile* is a software package that was developed for *BIOSIS* to use *BITS*. *BioSuperfile II*, an updated version, allows for even more sophisticated searching.

Several distribution options are available to *BITS* subscribers. *MICRO/BITS* is for use on the microcomputers and is limited to a single-user site. *MACRO/BITS* is designed to be used with a minicomputer or mainframe, and comes on magnetic tape. Multiple users and user sites are allowed. A third option is *INTER/BITS*, which allows for multiple users with a single-subject profile.

Users can set up their profile as if it were to be searched online. *BIOSIS* has developed a "Profile Development Form" to assist users with the process, and for difficult searches, *BIOSIS* offers a profile search. For $250, the *BIOSIS* staff will develop and test an appropriate strategy. Once a profile has been turned in, the staff will estimate the annual size of the retrieval. Strategies can be extensively changed only once a year. During a subscription year, strategies can be moderately changed as long as retrieval does not vary more than 10 percent from the original estimation. *BIOSIS* also has developed a list of twenty pre-profile searches, including such topics as plant breeding, human ecology, and bioengineering.

Charges for a *BITS* search vary depending on the format of the citations (i.e., with or without abstracts), the number of citations expected per year, and the distribution format chosen. There is a required minimum of 500 citations per year, and costs range from $110 for 500 citations without abstracts to over $3000 for 10,000 citations with abstracts.

BIOSIS Connection

BIOSIS is developing an end-user system for the life sciences. The system has two levels of access: a basic (menu-driven) mode, and an expert (command-driven) mode. The system does not include the *BIOSIS* database, but it does provide a current awareness file that includes citations before they are abstracted, indexed, and placed in *BIOSIS*. Additionally, the system includes databases of conference proceedings, forthcoming meetings, new books in the life sciences, and employment opportunities, as well as electronic mail capabilities.

Sci-Mate

The *Sci-Mate* software system, produced by the Institute for Scientific Information (ISI), is an integrated front-end package designed for end users with microcomputers. It consists of three parts: *The Searcher* (for assistance with online commands), *The Manager* (a database management package), and *The Editor* (for reformatting bibliographic citations). For more information on *Sci-Mate,* refer to Chapter 10.

TEX

The American Mathematical Society offers a group of software products based on the program *TEX*. These programs allow the user to convert *TEX*-encoded records from the *MATHSCI* database into correct mathematical formulas. Without this conversion, users of the *MATHSCI* database often find the search results incomprehensible.

CD-ROM Services

There are many new compact disc and other new microcomputer-based technologies that will prove useful for the end user. Several versions of *Medline* (see below) have been out for some time now. DIALOG and SilverPlatter have announced that they will be providing *NTIS* on CD-ROM. In addition to CD-ROM versions of bibliographic databases, publishers are producing many non-bibliographic databases. For example, Wiley now offers the *Kirk-Othmer Encyclopedia of Chemical Technology* and the *Encyclopedia of Polymer Science and Engineering* on CD-ROM, the *McGraw-Hill Encyclopedia of Science and Technology* also is available on CD-ROM, and Sadtler has many of its chemical spectra collections available in digital format. For more information on CD-ROM, see Chapter 11.

MEDICAL SEARCH SYSTEMS

Health sciences libraries began providing "self-service" searching to their clientele before the advent of "user-friendly" systems and have become active proponents of both library-based and office-based searching. Sewell reported on a program that began training pathologists and pharmacists in 1974 to search the *Medline* and *Toxline* databases using the

National Library of Medicine's command-driven *MEDLARS* system.[7] *PaperChase,* a user-friendly version of the *Medline* database, was developed in 1979 at Beth Israel Hospital in Boston for hospital staff to run their own online searches without training.[8] The *MiniMedline System,* an in-house, user friendly subset of *Medline,* became available to faculty, students, and staff at Georgetown University Medical Center in 1981.[9] Other health sciences libraries began offering end-user search services that employ general systems, such as *BRS After Dark,*[10] or systems aimed specifically at health care professionals, such as *Colleague,* as soon as they came on the market.

Most health sciences libraries offer consultative and training services for end users.[11] Articles and publications on how to choose a search system, what equipment is required, and how to search specific databases and systems have been written by health professionals and health sciences librarians, and articles on the development of consultative services are commonplace in the current literature.[12] Print, video, and computer-based training aids for end users have been developed by both search system vendors and librarians.

The primary search services marketed to health sciences librarians for end-user services or to health professionals directly for bibliographic searching are: *BRS Colleague, DIALOG Medical Connection,* the National Library of Medicine's *MEDLARS,* and Beth Israel Hospital's *PaperChase.* Each of these systems offers *Medline,* the primary bibliographic database for biomedical literature in the United States. These four systems will be described below in detail and compared. A description of other medical information services—*AMA/NET, Medis,* minicomputer-based *Medline,* and *Medline* on CD-ROM—will conclude this section.

MAJOR MEDICAL SERVICES

Colleague carries the broadest range of bibliographic and full-text databases (see Table 2). Unique sources for the medical field include the *AIDS Library* and *Journal Watch,* offering summaries by physicians of key clinical articles from 20 journals and health-related news headlines. *DMC* (DIALOG Medical Connection) offers the *Occupational Safety and Health* database, nine general interest databases, and five sci-tech databases. *MEDLARS* offers only health-related databases, with unique coverage in cancer and toxicology. *PaperChase* is a database system offering access to *Medline.*

Colleague's full-text journals include such titles as the *Annals of Internal Medicine, British Medical Journal, Harvard Medical School Health Letter, Lancet, Nature, New England Journal of Medicine,* and *Science.*

TABLE 2:   Database Availability, December 1987

Databases	Colleague	DMC	MEDLARS	PaperChase
AIDS Library	X			
BIOETHICS			X	
BIOSIS	X	X		
CAB	X	X		
CANCERLIT	X	X	X	
CINAHL (nursing)	X	X		
Drug Information Full Text	X	X		
EMBASE	X	X		
HEALTH	X	X	X	
Intl Pharm Abstracts	X	X		
Medline	X	X	X	X
Med/Psyc Previews	X			
PDQ	X		X	
Psycinfo	X	X		
SPORT	X			
Toxline, Toxnet			X	
Total Databases	140	28	20	1
Full-Text Journals	69	0	0	0
Full-Text Books	24	0	0	0
Online Reprint Ordering	yes	yes	no	yes
SDI Service	yes	yes	yes	no
Electronic Mail	yes	yes	no	no

Most of its full-text are core textbooks that are readily available in their printed format. Full-text databases contain text only—no tables, graphs, or images are included. This may decrease their value for some health professionals and researchers. An experiment conducted by the author of this article found that it took five minutes to "download" six text pages from *Lancet* on *Colleague,* using a 1200-baud modem in non-prime time. The "downloaded" article cost approximately $3 during prime time and $2 during non-prime time. While the process was inexpensive, a look at the original article revealed that two of its six pages were tables, and thus were not included in the full-text print, in this case a significant loss. On the other hand, the article was identified and printed in less than ten minutes. For a physician in his or her office or on the hospital floor, the full-text journal turnaround time could certainly outweigh any missing data.

All four systems can be searched almost 24 hours a day, seven days per week. *Colleague* and *MEDLARS* offer reduced rates during evenings and on weekends. All of these systems except *PaperChase* are accessed through Telenet or Tymnet; *PaperChase* is accessed through Compu-Serve. *DMC* is also accessible through Dialnet, and *MEDLARS* can be accessed via a toll-free number for users without a Telenet or Tymnet number. *Paperchase* requires VT52/100 terminal emulation and offers a free communications software program, or the system will step through a customization process online for popular communications programs. *DMC* is designed to work with *DIALOGlink, MEDLARS* offers a search aid program called *Grateful Med,* and *Colleague* offers a free telecommunications software program called *Colleague Express.*

Multiple-user accounting is available only on *Colleague* through its group account with individual passwords. *DMC* is not designed for multiple-user accounting. The *Med-Base* software program provides up to 50 local passwords and accounting for the *MEDLARS* system. The program also allows a library to enter a core journal list for marking printouts with local holdings information. *PaperChase* is designed as a multi-user system and allows the library or institution to set up local individual accounts. A user can also establish an account with the library and have all costs billed to his or her credit card. The University of Washington Health Sciences Library and Information Services offers faculty, staff, and students an account option and charges $50 a year to maintain the direct billing account.[13] The University of Nebraska Medical Center Library offers the same search to its clientele; however, rather than assessing an account fee, the library charges the user $3 more per connect hour.[14] *PaperChase* also allows the local institution to add its own core journal collection as a limiter for searching.

Each service offers options for training and support. *Colleague* offers an online instructional database and a video tutorial is available. *Colleague* supplies a manual, a reference card and a monthly newsletter. Customer service is available from 8 a.m. to 1 a.m. Monday through Friday, from 8 a.m. to 5 p.m. Saturday, and from 8 a.m. to 2 p.m. Sunday EST via a toll-free number. *DMC* supplies a manual and customer service is available 24 hours a day.

MEDLARS offers an instructional database and supplies a reference card and monthly newsletter. Initial and advanced one-week training classes are offered regularly throughout the United States at no charge. These sessions have been modularized to allow attendance for training on a single database. User services is available from 8 a.m. to 5 p.m. Monday through Friday EST via a toll-free number.

PaperChase offers no training. The system was designed for users with no prior instruction. Customer service is available from 8 a.m. to 6 p.m. Monday through Friday EST via a toll-free number. The University of Nebraska Medical Center Library has developed a short instructional guide called *PaperChase: An Introductory Manual,* which is available for purchase at $5.

The pricing structures are quite different for each of these systems. Volume discounts are available for *Colleague, DMC,* and *PaperChase.*

Special student packages are available for *Colleague* and *PaperChase*. There is a $95 sign-up fee for *DMC* which includes a $100 usage credit. *DMC* database usage rates are the same as the full *DIALOG* system. For *Colleague,* there is an initial sign-up fee of $95 plus a minimum monthly charge of $15. A new user receives two hours of free time on the *Instructional Service* practice databases. Group accounts are $150 and $50, respectively. Database usage rates are usually less for *BRS Search* and all databases are discounted depending on the database used ($32 for *Medline*), plus a charge for each record after 6 p.m. local time and weekends.

MEDLARS has a complex pricing algorithm composed of connect hour, time of day, search statement, online citation, interaction, computer resources disc access, and online characters charges. Some of the toxicological databases are priced higher due to royalty charges from outside commercial producers. There is no sign-up or minimum monthly charge, and new users receive two hours of free time.

PaperChase has no sign-up or minimum monthly charge. The database usage rate includes a connect hour, search set and display fees. *Paperchase* offers a free trial-period. For an average *Medline* search (12 connect minutes and display of 30 records, 15 with abstracts), rates run from low to high as follows: *MEDLARS, Colleague, PaperChase, DMC.* Specifics on the use of each of these services are noted below:

Colleague

Colleague is a menu-driven system providing the user with menus for choosing databases and prompts for performing commands. Online help is available in a descending-level menu, and covers all commands in detail. The system allows an experienced user to "stack" commands and answers to system prompts in order to speed the search process. Four display formats are available: title only, short, medium, and long. The short format displays a citation; the medium format displays a citation with the descriptors, or in full text, a citation and the relevant paragraphs where the search terms appeared; and the long format displays the complete record, including abstract, or in full text, the entire text of the article or chapter. There are five special display features: continuous output, rather than screen by screen; expand from short to medium format, or from medium to long format, when displaying screen by screen; "zoom," which jumps to the references cited in the full text and then resumes display; key word, which displays on those paragraphs of a full-text document where the requested search terms appear; and a sort command to display the retrieval material in alphabetical order by author, document title, or journal or book title.

Connectors to link search terms are the usual "AND," "OR," and

"NOT." In addition, "SAME" finds terms in the same field, and "WITH" finds terms in the same sentence. In *Colleague,* unlike the full-service *BRS Search,* adjacency of terms is assumed when no other connector is present. The system retrieves search terms in all record files unless limited by a qualifier(s). *Colleague* allows both left- and right-hand truncation by a designated number of ending characters. Authors, journal titles, subject headings, and other fields must be typed in a particular format. There is no subject heading, language, year, or age menu. British spelling and plural forms are automatically added on medical databases.

DIALOG Medical Connection

DMC is a menu-driven system with a simplified command option similar to *Knowledge Index.* Both options offer help on demand. The menus, prompts, and "help" screens step the user through choosing a database, connecting search sets, and limiting a search. The main menu provides the user with the options of choosing the *Medical Reference Library,* the *Bioscience Reference Library,* the *General Reference Library,* or *Science Technology Reference Library,* help in formulating a search, and *Dialmail.* Further menus allow the user to choose a specific database, to select a menu-driven or command mode, and to enter search terms.

For refining a search, the user can choose from menu options that include narrowing the search with an additional concept, or processing the search. A wild card character or truncation is also available. No selection assistance is provided for medical subject headings (MESH), although the system will notify the user when a MESH term match is made. A quick overview of search strategy formulation is available from the main menu. Three display options are available: short (titles only), medium (citations), and long (citations plus abstracts). Menus also step the user through offline printing (either via U.S. mail or *Dialmail*) and through online reprint ordering.

MEDLARS, Grateful Med, and Med-Base

MEDLARS is a completely command-driven system. There is an "Explain" command that identifies the available commands and how to use them, and there is a "Help" command that provides basic assistance on how to proceed. The user may display a single or several fields or choose from three standard formats. The connectors are limited to "AND," "OR," and "AND NOT," although the "String Search" command will allow proximity searching in a two-step process. Only right-hand truncation is possible without "string searching."

MEDLARS is a product of the mainframe search software of the seventies, with modification-made to upgrade it to the eighties. Despite the apparent complexity of the system, many health care professionals choose the system because of its low cost and the wide availability of support from health sciences librarians.

In response to demands from health professionals, NLM offers a front-end software program called *Grateful Med,* which serves as a communications and menu-driven interface to the *Medline* and most other *MEDLARS* databases. Hardware requirements for *Grateful Med* are an IBM-PC or IBM-compatible system, and a 100 percent Hayes-compatible modem. *Grateful Med* costs $29.95 plus $3 for shipping and handling. Updated versions are available free to registered users. *Grateful Med* requires a communications port, a monochrome or color monitor, a telephone number for Telenet or Tymnet, and a user code or password. In use, *Grateful Med* first asks whether the user wants to search *Medline* or *Catline,* or whether the expert searcher mode is desired. Choosing a database causes the main or input menu to appear. The input menu is a work form on which the user fills in names and terms next to appropriate fields, which are listed along the left side of the screen. In addition, a user may browse or select Medical Subject Headings and cross-references by pressing a key on the "subject words" line.

"Help" screens explaining how to enter terms on each line are available by pressing the "Home" key. After completing the input screen, the user is asked, "Do you want to retrieve abstracts (y/n)?," and then "OK to go on to search (y/n)?" At this point, the user sits back, and waits until the search has been completed. *Grateful Med* automatically connects to *MEDLARS,* runs the search, downloads the retrieved references (downloaded records automatically include record number, author, title, source, subject headings, language, and abstracts, if requested), disconnects from *MEDLARS* and from the telecommunications network, and beeps when the search results are ready for the user to review. The user is prompted to send the set of references to a printer or to display the references one at a time while choosing which to save and print. Once the current *Medline* retrieval has been reviewed or printed, *Grateful Med* asks if the user would like to run the same search on earlier years, and if so, going how many years back. Following this step is the only way to go back beyond the current *Medline* file of three years.

Grateful Med automatically puts author names in the proper format, truncates all subject words, and selects Medical Subject Headings if a direct or near alphabetic match is made. An experienced searcher can also use the program as a straight telecommunications program for direct access to the full *MEDLARS* system in command-driven mode. *Grateful Med* is a good program for introducing end users to *MEDLARS*. Most users will spend less time then usual online, because the program runs the search. The *Grateful Med* program provides a different approach to novice users of the *Medline* database.

Med-Base is a sophisticated PC-based software interface program for *Medline, CANCERLIT,* and *Health* databases. An "expert mode" is available to bypass "help" and menu screens.

Med-Base includes two floppy disks and an on-disk manual which may be printed. The program, marketed by Online Research Systems, costs $399. Quantity discounts and a $10 demonstration program good for four weeks of searching are available. Hardware requirements are an IBM-PC or IBM-compatible with at least 256K RAM, DOS 2.0 or later version and a 100 percent Hayes compatible modem. The program can be set up for 1200 or 2400 baud for a local Telenet or Tymnet number. It does not support the NLM toll-free WATS sign-on, and it runs most effectively on a hard disk system.

Med-Base automatically signs on to the NLM computer when the "Search for Information" is selected from the main menu. Although the program masks its interaction with *MEDLARS,* the user is directly connected to the NLM computer during the entire search process. The user is then prompted to enter a subject. *Med-Base* then attempts to map it to a *MeSH* term. It also prompts the user with broader and narrower *MeSH* terms, to see related terms, or to explode a term. After retrieving the results for a term, the program lists the number of articles for the term and the number with the term as a focus of the article, and then lists the results for each subheading. The user chooses from these refinements and a search set is established. "Help" screens or menus pop up on demand to combine sets; limit sets by language, age, or publication year; search by author name, journal name, registry number, free text terms, or unique identifier. The browse function allows the user to scan titles or other fields of a search set. While browsing or by using an autosearch option, the user can ask *Med-Base* to retrieve any similar references to chosen titles.

Display options are menu-style and the user may pick any combination of fields. References may be sorted by author, name of journal, or date of publication. The user may also add a library's journal codes to the program disc. When displaying, *Med-Base* will then note if a reference is available in the library. A record editor to review or edit search results while offline and a cost log to track time, date duration, and cost of the preceding 200 searches are also included.

PaperChase

PaperChase is a completely menu-driven system that allows an end user to search *Medline* with little or no instruction. The entire *Medline* database from 1966 to the present is searchable as a single database, which makes searching a bit slower. All assistance is provided online. If at any time the menu prompts are not understood, typing a question mark (?) will supply specific help. Brief instructions for system use are also available online. A document request service allows the user to order a photocopy of a journal article while online by pressing a key when the record is displayed.

PaperChase takes the user through the search process step by step, supplying an automatic default for the most commonly used option on each menu. It translates natural language input into an appropriate format. The user need not be concerned about singular or plural word forms, British spellings, or the format for author names or journal title abbreviations. Each term is entered separately at a "Look For" prompt, and the system responds with a list of related Medical Subject Headings and title words. Search sets can then be combined using the connectors "AND" and "OR." Retrieval may be limited to a customized subset of journals, such as the library's holdings, or to the *Abridged Index Medicus* subset. The system makes it difficult to retain title words and will not search for terms in abstracts, preferring instead to emphasize the use of Medical Subject Headings (abstracts, however, can be displayed). This feature creates a potential problem when the user is searching for less common topics.

PaperChase's usefulness as a medical end-user program has been demonstrated at the University of Washington Health Sciences Library and Information Center (UWHSLIC) in Seattle, co-sponsor of a curriculum-based end-user service.[15] In the spring of 1985, the UWHSLIC began offering online search experience, using *PaperChase*, to medical students as part of the "Introduction to Clinical Medicine-2" (ICM-2) course. This course is built on a team approach—the microcomputer system is on loan from the course coordinator, *PaperChase* costs are billed to a general non-library fund, and the library contributes space, supplies, and user assistance. The ICM-2 course requires each student to run a search on a patient care problem. Students first attend an hour hands-on instructional lecture that is presented by a reference librarian to the entire class of 180 second-year medical students early in the academic year. Students then complete the search assignment at their discretion. Although *PaperChase* is self-instructional, reference librarians spend a significant amount of time assisting users with equipment and logon problems, because many of the students are not familiar with microcomputers. In addition, the usual learning curve for using the system does not occur with more than 200 first-time users running a single search. To save time, reference librarians encourage medical students to work in groups, with a knowledgeable student coaching first-time users—satisfying the needs both of students and librarians. The continuing success of the program and the demand for access to *PaperChase* by other students, staff, and faculty have led to the establishment of an expanded end-user search service for all library clientele. The library charges an annual administrative fee to cover handling costs for each user. Usage costs are billed by the library if charged to a university budget, or billed directly by *PaperChase* to a user's credit card if a budget number is not used.

OTHER MEDICAL SYSTEMS

AMA/NET

AMA/NET is a service of American Medical Computing, a wholly owned subsidiary of the American Medical Association, and Softsearch, Inc. The system offers several categories of online services designed for physicians: information bases, public information services, electronic mail, and interactive applications. Information databases include *Paper-Chase*; *MEDLARS*, via *Grateful Med; Empires*, (a subset of the *Exerpta Medica* database covering more than 300 English-language journals published since 1984), and searchable by topic, author, title, source, and AMA specialty; the *Associated Press Medical News Service*, with news of medical interest; *Disease Information*, with descriptions of more than 3500 diseases, disorders, and conditions (based on the AMA's *Current Medical Information Technology*); *Medical Procedure Coding and Nomenclature*, adapted from the AMA's *Current Medical Information Terminology;* and *Medical Socio/Economic Bibliographic Information*, which includes selected references on health care delivery and economic issues in medicine drawn from more than 700 journals, newspapers, books, and other publications. Public information services include the Center for Disease Control, Food and Drug Administration, and Surgeon General's information services, and the AMA's news and library services. Interactive applications include *DXplain*, a diagnostic decision-support system based on the associated signs and symptoms of 2000 diseases, and covering 470 medical terms and more than 65,000 disease-term relationships; and Massachusetts General Hospital's *Continuing Medical Education Programs*, which include interactive courses ranging from free-form simulated patient encounters to structured self-paced tutorials.

Medis

Medis, a service of Mead Data Central, was reconfigured in May 1987 to meet the needs of business, media, and legal professionals in locating information on health care subjects. This service was previously marketed solely to health care facilities. A subscription to *Medis* is available only through *Nexis* or *Lexis* subscriptions. In its new configuration, *Medis* has archived several medical journals. The system offers 40 full-text journals and two books, *Drug Information Full Text, Medline*, and *PDQ*. *Medis* is primarily a full-text system consisting of five libraries: *GENMED* (general medicine), *PHARM* (drug information), *ADMIN* (administration), and *Medline*. Within each library, journals, books, and bibliographic databases are further divided into clinical specialties, such as cardiology, dermatology, and family medicine. *Medis* requires special dedicated Mead Data terminals or software.

Minicomputer *Medline* Systems

The Georgetown University Medical Center Library developed the *MiniMedline* system, a user-friendly subset of the *Medline* database, in 1982 to meet the in-house educational and clinical searching needs of students, residents, and faculty. *MiniMedline* is supplied on magnetic tape and runs on a minicomputer. More than thirteen health sciences libraries have installed the system for in-house use in their own institutions. Because records are downloaded from *MEDLARS,* an institution may select a larger or smaller subset of journals and retrospective coverage. Abstracts are not included. Most libraries offer a dial-up capability, as well as in-library search terminals. The system is menu driven and accepts natural language queries.

CL-Medline by CLSI is a turnkey system using a DEC VAX II minicomputer and high-capacity optical disc drives. Configurations can be designed to serve six or more users. The *CL-Medline* database includes all English-language journals published in the last four years, with abstracts and local journal holdings information. The rest of *Medline* is available through dial-up access to *BRS Search*. Updates are produced monthly or quarterly on optical disc, with a cumulative revision each year. The system is menu or command driven and has full search capabilities. A library can set its own information displays and the amount of use allowed to each searcher.

CD-ROM *Medline*

Another local option for end-user searching is compact-disc read-only memory (CD-ROM). Many academic health sciences and hospital libraries offer *Medline* on CD-ROM for users. Several vendors offer *Medline* on CD-ROM. These products all require a fully configured IBM with a hard disc drive to run effectively, and use standard CD-ROM players such as Hitachi, Sony, and Philips. Most vendors offer a lease or purchase option for the equipment and free trial-periods.

Compact Cambridge/Medline by Cambridge Scientific Abstracts offers one complete year of *Medline* per disc dating back to 1982. The current year's disc is updated quarterly. The search software either contains pop-up menus or is command driven. Subscribers to *Cambridge* journals receive special discounts.

Medline on CD-ROM by SilverPlatter Information offers a five-year set (one year per disc) of the complete *Medline* database. The current year's disc is updated quarterly. The set is remastered each year to reflect changes in medical subject headings. The search software is command driven. Other health-related SilverPlatter products are *PsycLit* (psychology), *CA-CD* (oncology), *OSH-ROM* (occupational safety and health), and *CHEM-BANK* (toxic substances).

Colleague onDisc by BRS offers an English-language subset of *Medline* (one year per disc) dating back to 1985. The current year's disc is updated three times a year. The search software is the same as for the menu-driven online *Colleague* search system. A tutorial is included with the software.

Ebsco offers two CD-ROM options: *Comprehensive Medline* and *Core Medline*. *Comprehensive Medline* offers a three-year English-language subset of *Medline* on two discs. Two CD-ROM players are required. *Core Medline* offers a three-year subset of the *Abridged Index Medicus* titles and all nursing and dental records on one disc. Both options are updated quarterly. The search software is command driven with Lotus-style selection bars. A menu option will be added in the near future. A library can load its own journal titles for limiting or marking retrieval. A statistical package is also included to monitor use.

Medline onDisc by DIALOG offers one complete year of *Medline* per disc back to 1981. The current year is updated quarterly. The search software is menu-driven.

Compact Med-Base by Online Research Systems divides the entire *Medline* database from 1966 to the present into four segments. The search software is an enhanced version of the *Med-Base* program.

CONCLUSION

This chapter has illustrated the wide variety of options available for end users in the health, science, and technology fields regardless of whether the searching is done in their offices or within the library. Five major considerations for choosing a system—subject coverage; access; cost; search interface and features; and training and support—have been discussed. The ranking of the considerations, however, will vary from user to user and perhaps from search to search.

DIALOG has identified three categories of scientific end users: (1) those who are aware that computer-searching services are available from a qualified technical information specialist; (2) those who are aware of information retrieval but who feel that there is something available beyond what their non-technical librarian is providing; and (3) those coming from organizations that lack a library or information department.[16]

For whatever reason, health, science, and technology professionals are becoming online searchers, and it is evident that their numbers will increase. Librarians will continue to play an important role in online search services, whether it be as a searcher, as a consultant, as an instructor, or as an administrator of an in-house system.

NOTES

1. Sylvia Faibisoff and Jitka Hurych, "Is There a Future for the End User in Online Bibliographic Searching?" *Special Libraries* 72 (Oct. 1981): 347–55; Charles Meadows, "Online Searching and Computer Programming: Some Behavioral Similarities...," *Online* 3 (Jan. 1979): 49–52.

2. Winifred Sewell and Alice Vevan, "Non-Mediated Use of Medline and Toxline by Pathologists and Pharmacists," *Bulletin of the Medical Library Association* 64 (Oct. 1976): 382–91.

3. Judith Haines, "Experiences in Training End User Searchers," *Online* 6 (Nov. 1982): 14–23.

4. Robert Buntrock and Aldora Valicenti, "End User Searching: The Amoco Experience," *Journal of Chemical Information and Computer Science* 25 (1985): 422–25; Cheryl Kirk, "End User Training at the Amoco Research Center," *Special Libraries* 77 (Winter 1986): 20–27; Martha Reiter, "Can You Teach Me to Do My Own Searching...," *Journal of Chemical Information and Computer Science* 25 (1985): 419–22.

5. A budget cut has forced some reduction in the program. Remote searching is now limited to those using the chemistry and biochemistry department loginids. These departments have also been limited in the amount of searching the library will cover each month. If they go over that amount, the departments pick up the cost. For more details on this program, contact: Kathy Whitley, Science–Engineering Library, University of Arizona, Tucson, AZ 85721.

6. Susanne Redalje, "Proposal for Funding of CAS ONLINE" (Univ. of Arizona, 1984) and "CAS ONLINE User Survey" (Univ. of Arizona, 1984).

7. Sewell, 382–91.

8. Gary Horowitz and Howard Bleich, "PaperChase: A Computer Program to Search the Medical Literature," *New England Journal of Medicine* 305 (Oct. 15, 1981): 924–30; Gary Horowitz, Jerome Jackson, and Howard Bleich, "PaperChase: Self-Service Bibliographic Retrieval," *Journal of the American Medical Association* 250 (Nov. 11, 1983): 2494–99.

9. Naomi Broering, "The MiniMedline System: A Library-Based End User Search System," *Bulletin of the Medical Library Association* 73 (Apr. 1985): 138–45.

10. Deborah Slingluff, Yvonne Lev, and Andrew Eisan, "An End User Search Service in an Academic Health Sciences Library," *Medical Reference Services Quarterly* 4 (Spring 1985): 11–21.

11. Rex G. Bickers, "Online Medical Information Systems," *Primary Care* 12 (Sept. 1985): 459–82. Jayne M. Crofts, "Reaching the End User: The Education and Training Program at the William H. Welch Medical Library," *Medical Reference Services Quarterly* 4 (Winter 1985/1986): 77–82; J. Homan, "End User Information Utilities in the Health Sciences," *Bulletin of the Medical Library Association* 74 (Jan. 1986): 31–35; R. Haynes,

"Computer Searching of the Medical Literature: An Evaluation of Medline Searching Systems," *Annals of Internal Medicine* 1-3 (Nov. 1985): 812-16; Peg Hewitt and Thomas Chalmder, "Using Medline to Peruse the Literature," *Controlled Clinical Trials* 6 (Mar. 1985): 75-83; Debra Ketchell, *Online Searching by Health Professionals*, 6th ed. (Seattle: Washington Health Information Network, 1987); Joanne Marshall, "How to Choose the Online Medical Database That's Right for You," *Canadian Medical Association Journal* 134 (Mar. 15, 1986): 634-40; Claudia Perry, "Online Information Retrieval in Pharmacy and Related Fields," *American Journal of Hospital Pharmacy* 43 (June 1986): 1509-24; Lawrence S. Rivkin, "Using Database," *Computers in Veterinary Practice* 16 (July 1986): 647-68; Robert Rutledge, "Physician Use of Online Databases," *Urologic Clinics of North America* 13 (Feb. 1986): 65-89.

12. Sandra M. Wood, Ellen Brassil Horak, and Bonnie Snow, eds., "End User Searching in the Health Sciences," *Medical Reference Services Quarterly* 5 (Summer 1986). Special issue.

13. *PaperChase* fee schedule (University of Washington Health Sciences Library and Information Center, 1987).

14. Marie Reidelback, *PaperChase: An Introductory Manual* (Omaha: McGooghan Library of Medicine, 1986).

15. Kay Denfeld, personal communication, 1986.

16. MaryAnn S. Palma and Charles Sutherland, "Meeting the Needs of the End User," *Journal of Chemical Information and Computer Sciences* 25 (1985): 423.

BIBLIOGRAPHY

Bickers, Rex G. "Online Medical Information Systems." *Primary Care* 12 (Sept. 1985): 459-82.

Broering, Naomi. "The MiniMedline System: A Library-Based End User Search System." *Bulletin of the Medical Library Association* 73 (Apr. 1985): 138-45.

Buntrock, Robert, and Aldona Valicenti. "End User Searching: The Amoco Experience." *Journal of Chemical Information and Computer Science* 25 (1985): 422-25.

Crofts, Jayne M. "Reaching the End User: The Education and Training Program at the William H. Welch Medical Library." *Medical Reference Services Quarterly* 4 (Winter 1985/1986): 77-82.

Faibisoff, Sylvia, and Jitka Hurych. "Is There a Future for the End User in Online Bibliographic Searching?" *Special Libraries* 72 (Oct. 1981): 347-55.

Feinglos, Susan. *Medline: A Basic Guide to Searching*. Chicago: Medical Library Assn., 1985.

Haines, Judith. "Experiences in Training End User Searchers." *Online* 6 (Nov. 1982): 14-23.

Haynes, R., et al. "Computer Searching of the Medical Literature: An Evaluation of Medline Searching Systems." *Annals of Internal Medicine* 1-3 (Nov. 1985): 812-16.

Henderson, B. "Computers and Medicine: The Physician Online." *Canadian Medical Association Journal* 131 (Nov. 15, 1984): 1286-92.

Hewitt, Peg, and Thomas Chalmers. "Using Medline to Peruse the Literature." *Controlled Clinical Trials* 6 (Mar. 1985): 75-83.

Homan, J. Michael. "End User Information Utilities in the Health Sciences." *Bulletin of the Medical Library Association* 74 (Jan. 1986): 31-35.

Horowitz, Gary, and Howard Bleich. "PaperChase: A Computer Program to Search the Medical Literature." *New England Journal of Medicine* 305 (Oct. 15, 1981): 924–30.

Horowitz, Gary, Jerome Jackson, and Howard Bleich. "PaperChase: Self-Service Bibliographic Retrieval." *Journal of the American Medical Association* 250 (Nov. 11, 1983): 2494–99.

Ketchell, Debra. *Online Searching by Health Professionals.* 6th ed. Seattle: Washington Health Information Network, 1987.

Kirk, Cheryl. "End User Training at the Amoco Research Center." *Special Libraries* 77 (Winter 1986): 20–27.

Leipzig, Nancy, Marlene Kozak, and Ronald Schwartz. "Experiences with End User Searching in a Pharmaceutical Company." In *National Online Meeting Proceedings—1983,* comp. by Martha E. Williams and Thomas H. Hogan, 325–32. Medford, N.J.: Learned Information, 1983.

Marshall, Joanne. "How to Choose the Online Medical Database That's Right for You." *Canadian Medical Association Journal* 134 (Mar. 15, 1986): 634–40.

_____. "The Physician in the Information Age: Interim Results of the CMS INet Trial." *Canadian Medical Association Journal* 133 (Nov. 15, 1985): 1045–48.

Meadows, Charles. "Online Searching and Computer Programming: Some Behavioral Similarities (or . . . Why End Users Will Eventually Take Over the Terminal)." *Online* 3 (Jan. 1979): 49–52.

Medical Library Association. *Confluence: Source of New Energy. Abstracts.* 87th Annual Meeting, Portland, Oregon, May 15–21, 1987. Chicago: MLA, 1987.

National Library of Medicine. *The Basics of Searching Medline: A Guide for the Health Professional.* Bethesda, Md.: NLM, 1985.

Ostrum, G., Diane Yoder, and Kenneth Yoder. "Chemists as End User Searchers—Training and Follow-up." In *International Online Information Meeting, 9th,* 313–40. Oxford: Learned Information, 1985.

_____. "Training in CAS Online for End Users." In *National Online Meeting Proceedings—1985,* comp. by Martha E. Williams and Thomas H. Hogan, 344. Medford, N.J.: Learned Information, 1985.

Palma, Mary Ann S., and Charles Sutherland. "Meeting the Needs of the End User." *Journal of Chemical Information and Computer Sciences* 25 (1985): 422–25.

Perry, Claudia. "Online Information Retrieval in Pharmacy and Related Fields." *American Journal of Hospital Pharmacy* 43 (June 1986): 1509–24.

Reidelbach, Marie. *PaperChase: An Introductory Manual.* Omaha: McGooghan Library of Medicine, Univ. of Nebraska Medical Center, 1986.

Reiter, Martha. "Can You Teach Me to Do My Own Searching? or Tailoring Online Training to the Needs of the End User." *Journal of Chemical Information and Computer Science* 25 (1985): 419–22.

Rich, Carol. "Searching STN International." *Database* 9 (Oct. 1986): 116–20.

Rivkin, Lawrence S. "Using Database." *Computers in Veterinary Practice* 16 (July 1986): 647–68.

Rutledge, Robert. "Physician Use of On-line Databases." *Urologic Clinics of North America* 13 (Feb. 1986): 65–89.

Scheidt, Stephen S., Helene Goldstein, and Linda S. Blackburn. "Application of the Office or Home Computer to Searching the Medical Literature." *Journal of the American College of Cardiology* 8 (Nov. 1986): 1211–17.

Sewell, Winifred, and Alice Vevan. "Non-Mediated Use of Medline and Toxline by Pathologists and Pharmacists." *Bulletin of the Medical Library Association* 64 (Oct. 1976): 382–91.

Slingluff, Deborah, Yvonne Lev, and Andrew Eisan. "An End User Search Service in an Academic Health Sciences Library." *Medical Reference Services Quarterly* 4 (Spring 1985): 11–21.

Chapter 9

Consumer End-User Services

Sarah B. Watstein

INTRODUCTION

Emerging...innovative...successful...responsive...trailblazers... these are the words that appear in the literature on consumer information online systems. Systems that promise to be the "most powerful resource any personal computer can have"[1] deserve our attention. The following chapter might best be labeled "Miscellanea," for its focus is on general-purpose consumer information online systems currently available on a public or semi-public basis. Such systems differ from research information systems in their emphasis, market, less sophisticated search software, and variety of services and information offered.

Consumer information online systems range in emphasis from providing "personal information for the at-home user"[2] to providing information that addresses "professional and business needs."[3] Such systems have been developed for the home computer market; their potential value, place in, and adaptability to academic or research libraries thus are debatable. Research information systems, such as *BRS* and *DIALOG,* are distinguished by their "encyclopedic" nature. Such systems generally are complex information or bibliographic retrieval systems. Offering large, research-oriented databases, these systems lend themselves to serious but often occasional users who have specific research or information needs. Research systems tend to be more single-focused than their general-purpose counterparts, providing thorough coverage of limited areas or specified disciplines, rather than providing "a smorgasbord of many services."[4] Consumer information systems are attempting to reach a mass market, specifically "well-educated and affluent micro/personal computer users."[5] Services are directed to users in their business, professional, organizational, and consumer roles. In this way, users' professional and personal or individual needs are met. In contrast, research information systems take the requirements of academic or scholarly use more seriously.

Access to research information systems has tended to be more complicated than access to consumer information online systems. One reason for this trend is that the former have traditionally not been menu driven. Control and navigation are often not accomplished without recourse to printed manuals or lengthy documentation. In contrast, consumer information systems are designed to be quick and easy to use, with simple-to-follow instructions both online and in print documentation. Menu selection is the primary means of accessing the various features offered by consumer information online systems. The main menu usually comes up automatically when the end user logs on. Menus can be used to: (1) present options in the system, such as categories of service or lists of actual services themselves; (2) organize the sections of particular services; or (3) list the information retrieved. By traveling the menu route, the end user arrives at a specific service, feature, or option. Most consumer information online systems also offer end users the option of bypassing menus via direct commands or other shortcuts, which differ from system to system. Suppressing the menus at each of various levels saves time.

Consumer information online systems also differ from research information systems in the quantity and variety of services and information they offer. Informational, transactional, and communications are three basic types of online service offered by these systems. Communications services are prominent features of consumer information online systems. Electronic mail, bulletin boards, chatting online, voluntary online directories, message services, member publishing, CB radio simulators, and computer conferencing are examples of some communications services currently on the market. Two equally prominent features of consumer information online systems are new services, and business and financial services. The former may include the hour's top news stories; stories from United Press International or the Associated Press; or daily coverage of news and features as reported in diverse national or local news media. The latter may include time-sensitive data obtained from up-to-the-minute coverage of commodities, money market funds, stocks and bonds, and investments, and demographics relevant to organizations that wish to relocate, establish locations for new businesses, or add new facilities in new areas. Besides offering communications, general news, and business and financial services, consumer information online systems also offer education-related services and transactional services such as travel, shopping, banking, and brokerage. Online quizzes, encyclopedias, college planning information, and computer-based tutorials constitute but a few of the education-related services on the market. Airline schedules and bookings, and restaurant and lodgings' guides constitute standard travel services on the market. Extensive shopping services that facilitate shopping from the home or office, bartering, and job-searching services are examples of some of the personal services on the market. Remote consumer information thus can easily be provided to the online community. The systems discussed here in depth include, in alphabetical order, *CompuServe, Delphi,* and *The Source.* A newer service called *GEnie* and the general use of electronic bulletin boards are also briefly discussed. Because of their many similarities, comparing or contrasting the systems discussed is neither an obvious nor an easy task. Careful reading of the systems' documentation is the key to choosing the right utility. Before reading the remainder of this chapter, it is wise to keep in mind the fact that any discussion of system features and services can very rapidly become outdated. Continual expansion and modification of services is characteristic of each system discussed. Falk's concluding sentence to his article comparing *The Source* and *CompuServe* is worth repeating here: "for information utilities, as well as for all other aspects of computer-based services, rapid change and development seem to be the continuing rule."[6]

COMPUSERVE

The first consumer information online system to be considered is *CompuServe*. With corporate headquarters in Columbus, Ohio, *CompuServe* is an H & R Block Company. *CompuServe* remains the largest and most diverse of the systems. Its variety of services and innovative operating features are aimed at a broad consumer base, including entrepreneurs, investors, business people, professionals, and others with personal needs. It is obvious that *CompuServe* has expanded, since it has been the "premier supplier of business information and communication services for Fortune 500 companies since 1969."[7] In 1984, Brian J. Murphy noted that *CompuServe* "covers a lot of territory,"[8] and this is still true. Because of its scope and diversity, *CompuServe*'s market and appeal are virtually limitless.

The following sections are currently available from *CompuServe:* Home Services, Business and Financial Services, Personal Computing Services, Services for Professionals, and User Information Services. The Home Services area is "focused on the information that will enhance your home life, bring you enjoyment, and maybe save you a few of your hard-earned dollars."[9] Selections include News, Weather, and Sports;

Reference Library; Communications; Home Shopping and Banking; Discussion Forums; Games; Education; Home Management; Travel; and Entertainment. The Business and Financial Services area provides information and services to streamline users' retrieval of stock market data, company reports, and more, including the following categories: News and Financial Analysis, Investments and Quotations, Career Planning, Brokerage and Banking, Reference Library, Discussion Forums, Travel Services, and Personal Finance. Personal Computing Services put subscribers in touch with others who have the same equipment or programming challenges. As of this writing, such services include: News, Reference, Communications, Shopping, and Group and Club Membership. The Services for Professionals category is geared toward specific professions, but it may also be useful to others interested in learning more about these professions. Currently offered are services for specialists in Aviation, Communications and Data Processing, Engineering and Technology, Environment, Law, Medicine, and Jewelry. The User Information menu provides users with a number of selections from which they can obtain information, ask questions, order *CompuServe* products, and so on. The User Information menu at this writing includes: What's New; Command Summary and Usage Tips; Feedback to *CompuServe*; Order Products, Guides, etc.; Change Terminal Settings; Change Your Password; Billing; Logon Instructions and Numbers; and Electronic Bounce Back.

Additional services include Forums, CB Simulator, and National Bulletin Board. Forums allow subscribers to discuss and exchange information on specific subjects of common interest. This service generally provides management bulletins, message posting and retrieval, conferencing, member interest files, and a data library. Forum membership usually is provided on request at no additional charge. Forums can be found under each of the main menu selections (discussed above as services). A *Forum User's Guide* provides more detailed information on Forums than does the *User's Guide*. Additional forums are announced weekly online in What's New. The CB Simulator is a public communications service that can be used like a CB radio, but without the radio. This service allows subscribers to talk to other subscribers "live" through their terminals. The National Bulletin Board provides a national audience for general notice, items for sale, and items and services wanted.

A telephone; a computer, terminal, or communicating word processor; and a modem are the three elements needed to connect with the *CompuServe Information Service*. This equipment is provided by the customer. A variety of terminals and personal computers can be used to access *CompuServe*. Four terminal types are supported: VIDTEX, Software Compatible, ANSI Compatible (VT100), Teleray 1061, and OTHER (for anything else!). Most communications software packages can emulate one of these standard terminal types. *CompuServe* produces and distributes communications software that offers customers "the best link-up with genuine *CompuServe* communication[s] software.[10] This software, called *VIDTEX Enhanced Terminal Communications Software,* includes "instant" free software updates online, error-free uploading and downloading, high-resolution graphics, automatic logon and menu navigation files, programmable function keys, full printer support (including "print screen"), capture buffer, adjustable communication settings, cursor positioning, and support of Hayes-compatible modems.

To get started, potential subscribers must get a *Starter Kit.* The kit cost is a one-time sign-up charge; there are no subsequent subscription fees. The kit includes the *Information Service User's Guide,* and sign-up ID and password, along with full instructions for completing the subscription while online; five free hours to facilitate getting to know the service; an introductory subscription to *CompuServe's* monthly magazine, *Online Today,* and to *CompuServe's Update* newsletter; a poster-sized "Service Configuration Diagram"; a *Forum and EasyPlex User's Guide;* convenient "Reference Cards" for various areas of the service; and an alphabetized "Quick Reference Word Summary." These kits are sold at many retail computer stores, electronic equipment stores, and mass merchandise stores, and even through the *Sears Catalog.* Subscriptions may be completed during the user's free time or up to 90 days afterward. Once online information is completed, *CompuServe* wil generate and mail a "second" password. Detailed subscription steps can be found in the *User's Guide.*

The *CompuServe Network* can be reached indirectly via Tymnet, Telenet, or DataPac; an additional communications surcharge is incurred when using these networks. The most current list of network numbers is maintained online and is also included in the *User's Guide.* Logging on may also be done directly through the *CompuServe Network;* access made through this network incurs communications surcharges. This network can be reached by a local phone call from most metropolitan areas of the contiguous United Statess. Hours of service availability are either standard time (from 6 p.m. to 5 a.m. local time on weekdays, and all day on weekends and on announced *CompuServe* holidays) or prime time (from 8 a.m. to 6 p.m. local time on weekdays). The time zone is determined by the local time at the point of *CompuServe Network* connection.

The *CompuServe User's Guide* is organized into sections on Subscribing, New User Information, Menus, Services, and Command Summaries. A *User's Guide* Index completes the publication. User information is also available on the User Information menu. Through this menu, users can obtain information, ask questions, or order *CompuServe* products. Users may want to find out what's new, obtain summaries of commands or other usage tips, change their terminal settings, change their passwords, verify logon instructions and numbers, or ask about billing.

In addition to referring to the *User's Guide,* reading *CompuServe's Update* newsletter, *"Online Today,"* and the online "What's New" articles, searchers can get assistance online in a variety of ways. At most online prompts, a list of commands, information, and instructions can be obtained by entering the word "Help." Customer Service staff are also available if a question requires attention or research. Such questions can be submitted through the online feedback service; questions that require an answer are responded to via electronic mail from a Customer Service representative within a few days. Problems can also be directed to the Customer Service staff by telephone. Representatives are on duty Monday through Friday from 8 a.m. to midnight, and on weekends from 2 p.m. to midnight (Eastern time). Last, the Forums serve as a way to get assistance, as does the CB Simulator, which provides "live" communications with other subscribers who may be able to help.

Like other consumer information end-user systems, *CompuServe* uses the menu approach to information selection, and display is quite simple. "Most features of this service are available through page-numbered menus."[11] This trail goes from general to more specific topics, called sub-menus. Various commands are available to make service access more direct or to allow users to move around in the menus, get help, display information in a particular format, and logoff. Menu/Navigational commands navigate users through the menus. Control Character commands cause certain actions when the user enters them by pressing the "Control" key while simultaneously pressing a single letter key. Some of the services have unique commands that will work within a particular service. A summary of frequently used service commands is located in the *User's Guide.* Online, a list of commands, is obtained at a menu prompt or within a specific service by entering the word "Help" as a prompt.

Currently, the following selections are on the main menu: Home Services, Business and Financial Services, Personal Computing Services, Services for Professionals, and User Information Services. A flowchart in the back of the *User's Guide* illustrates the menu structure for User Information. The final section of the *Guide,* Command Summaries, contains lists of frequently used commands.

The most current consumer information service rates can be found online under the User Information menu selection "Billing: Your Charges, Rates, Options, and Making Changes." Billing options include the Charge Card Option and the CHECKFREE Option. Several reports are available that facilitate reviewing charges; Week-by-Week Summary, Usage Analysis by Week, Transaction/Session Analysis, Current Week's Information, and Hardcopy Listing by Week. Billing details are kept online for up to eight weeks to encourage users to try to answer their own billing inquiries via feedback, or via a letter or phone call to the Customer Service department. Connect time, purchases, supplementary communications charges, and premium program charges are totalled and billed once a month. A Business Account is available to businesses and other organizations with credit. This account provides a single monthly invoice, listing the total charges for each separate User ID Number.

DELPHI

"Delphi is innovative, providing a quality product to its customers, and is striving to be a leader in the Videotex industry."[12] *Delphi,* the full-service communications and information network, is operated by General Videotex Corporation (GVC) of Cambridge, Massachusetts. Characterizing itself as a "young, aggressive telecommunications company providing state-of-the-art online utility service to businesses, associations, and consumers,"[13] GVC was founded in 1980. Its purposes are: (1) to provide cost-effective online utility services of the highest quality, (2) to promote the concept of online services to individuals and organizations, and (3) to continue to expand penetration of the fast-growing market for online services and wide-area networks. *Delphi* came online in 1983, a few years after *CompuServe* and *The Source.* This service is designed for use by the whole family and the entire office. In his review of *Delphi,* Andy Eddy notes that "this is a service that isn't focused on one group,"[14] and that "subscribers can find a service to satisfy almost any taste."[15] While it might be said that the network has a definite slant to some of its offerings to attract specific markets, such as the business user or the home subscriber, in general, businesses, consumers, and associations are equally treated.

Delphi resembles *CompuServe* and *The Source* closely, and offers a range of services to satisfy almost any taste. "Bulletin Boards" allows members to post and read notices regarding just about anything: meetings, opinions on social issues, record swaps, etc. "Conference" connects users with other members for simultaneous conversations. *"Delphi* Mail," an electronic mail service that is compatible with virtually any terminal or personal computer, lets users send electronic messages to other members. "MAILTHRU" enables *"Delphi* Mail" users to send electronic messages to users of *The Source* or *CompuServe* electronic mail systems. In "Entertainment," users can play games, participate in a collaborative novel, read an online comedy magazine, or browse the entertainment newswires. "Financial Services" includes information on investments, personal finances, the latest financial news and quotes, and buying and selling securities. "Groups and Clubs" enables groups sharing a common interest to get together. The "Library" is *Delphi*'s main resource center, boasting a complete online encyclopedia, access to Lockheed's *DIALOG* databases, an interactive "Automotive Comparison and Pricing Guide," newsletters, and other databases. "Merchants' Row" consists of shopping services with sophisticated interactive capabilities. "News, Weather, and Sports" offers news and sports from the Associated Press and forecasts from Accu-Weather. Applications and services to help users manage their business activities are available from "Office Manager." "Travel Services" offers complete travel information and reservations capabilities. Two other services include "Using *Delphi*" and "Workspace." "Using *Delphi*" includes settings so that users can change screen settings, their password, prompt, etc., a guided tour, lists of the closest telecommunications phone numbers, and information on the rates and prices of *Delphi* are also included. "Workspace" offers a place to upload, write, edit or otherwise prepare material for sending to others electronically. The *Delphi Handbook* notes that just about any communications software will do for accessing *Delphi*, and advises subscribers to contact their computer dealer for recommendations. "Registering" involves thinking of and registering a *Delphi* name that will identify users to others for electronic mail receipt and conferencing, and that will serve as their account number for customer service and billing. A *"Delphi* Membership Agreement" must also be signed and returned.

A local access phone number, password, and user name (member's name) constitute access information needed to connect to *Delphi*. Dialing up and signing on may be done directly or via subscribers' local Tymnet or DataPac telephone numbers. Appendixes in the *Handbook* provide local numbers for these systems, and the numbers are also listed online using *Delphi*.

An easy-to-use, complete, and factual *Handbook* is the primary system documentation. Notations used in the *Handbook* are explained in the "Getting Started' section of the handbook. This section also discusses signing on, the *"Delphi* Guided Tour," taking control of *Delphi* (i.e., through commands, control characters, prompts), typing ahead, echo, and passwords. The main selection of the handbook, "The *Delphi* Main Menu," cover each of the menu items in detail. Appendixes cover Tymnet and Datapac numbers, as mentioned earlier, and an index completes the *Handbook*.

The "Using Delphi" section of the "Main Menu" gives members access to online information about using *Delphi*, prices and rates, telephone access numbers, answers to commonly asked questions, ordering manuals, and using the various gateway services. This section also describes the means for sending comments, suggestions, and questions to the *Delphi* Product Development Group. An online newsletter informs members about recently implemented *Delphi* features. A "Guided Tour" also provides a review of the fundamentals. *Delphi* Customer Service is available daily via a toll-free number, staffed from 8 a.m. to 1 a.m. Eastern Time. Customers can also access Customer Service of the "*Delphi* Oracle" online.

There are a variety of ways to get assistance online. The information contained in the *Handbook* is available directly from *Delphi*. By using the tutorial section, called the "Guided Tour," subscribers can let the system explain itself. Online information is accessible by using the "Help" command, by picking menu items named "Help," or simply by answering *Delphi*'s questions with a question mark. "Help" information is updated online. Most of the other information is also available online under the "Using Delphi" selection of the "Main Menu." Sending "*Delphi* Mail" to "Service" results in the company's professional customer service staff providing information pertaining to subscribers' needs. Last, *Delphi*'s "Conference" serves as a way to connect subscribers with other members for simultaneous conversations and assistance, when needed. General Videotex Corporation's processing center is located at its Cambridge, Massachusetts facility. The center houses several Digital Equipment superminicomputers. GVC is adding processing power to meet demands.

Connecting to *Delphi* for the first time initiates a tour of the utility for the new *Delphi* user. This online tutorial, compliments of a tour guide named "Max," serves both to help the user become familiar with the needs of the service and to guide the user through various functions. Actual, hands-on practice during the tour shows new users how everything works, how to respond to prompts from *Delphi*, how to use simple commands, and how to get help.

The service presents a menu of commands or database selections. Commands are simple and straightforward, and are of two types—interrupts and responses. Interrupts are relatively few in number and are used when *Delphi* is in the middle of doing something. Responses are given after *Delphi* asks what the user wants; responses usually consist of items on a current menu or a list of choices. The variety of valid responses to *Delphi* prompts is wide and includes commands or information that is specific to the user's situation, rather than items from a list in the system. Once users become familiar with the commands, they can suppress the menus at each command level. The "Main Menu" is the "Table of Contents" for all of *Delphi*. Everything branches out from this point. The "Menu Items," or *Delphi*'s "Main Menu," are described in detail in the *Handbook*.

A one time sign-up fee of $49.95 includes the *Delphi Handbook* and two free hours of evening use. "*Delphi* Starter Kits," which include a command card and two free hours of evening use, available at retail computer dealers, sell for $29.95. Connect time is billed in one-minute increments. Home time and office time have different rates. Home time is from 6 p.m. to 7 a.m. weekdays in subscribers' local time zones in the continental United States, Mexico, and Canada. Office time is from 7 a.m. to 6 p.m. in subscribers' local time zones in the continental United States, Mexico and Canada. There is no surcharge for 1200- or 2400-bps transmission. Basic rate time covers the use of standard *Delphi* services and includes domestic network charges. Charges may be applied to customers' credit cards; direct billing carries a $3.50 service charge per month. Monthly storage and some *Delphi* services carry additional fees.

THE SOURCE

The Source is a servicemark of Source Telecomputing Corporation, a subsidiary of the Reader's Digest Association. *The Source*'s services are offered in participation with Control Data Corporation. *The Source* provides services that are directed to users in their business, professional, and consumer roles. The main orientation of *The Source* is toward personal and individual needs.

Service categories are similar to those of *CompuServe*, but exist on a much smaller scale. Today, News, Business, Communications (Communications Services), SIGS (Special Interest Groups), PC (Personal Computing), Travel, Home (Education, Shopping, and Games), and INFO (Member Information) constitute service categories currently offered. The hour's top news, business updates, sports news and scores, the day's features, and an overview of what's new on *The Source* constitute the Today service. The News service has continuous feeds from the wire services, and offers news, weather, and sports from United Press International, the Associated Press, the *Washington Post,* Scripps-Howard News Service, Accu-Weather, United Media Features, and Financial Market Reports and News. The News service also offers news indexed by subject, and a concise daily news and feature magazine. Business services include Investor Services (Quotes, Portfolio Manager, and Spear Securities trading Online); Business Update (up-to-the-minute business and investment information); Investext (research reports from companies to help users formulate their own personal investment strategies; STOCKVUE (information on the performance of common stocks over periods ranging from one to five weeks); UNISTOX (stock commodity reports from the financial wire of United Press International); Stockcheck (Associated Press price quotes on issues traded on the New York, American, and OTC exchanges); Commodity World News (price information and news on the trading activities of the most active commodities); *Donoghue Moneyletter* (an electronic edition of the *Financial Newsletter* published by the Donoghue Organization); Tax Notes Today (an electronic tax database providing coverage of all federal tax developments); Information on Demand; and Employment Services (an online listing of candidates and jobs available in 40 industry categories). Communications Services includes SourceMail; Bulletin Boards; Chatting Online; Computer Conferencing; a Members' Directory; a Mailgram Messaging Service; and Member Publishing. Sending correspondence in many ways; listing and posting notices; conversing between two members; introducing and learning about members; sending West Union Mailgrams; publishing; and conferencing are some of the communications options these services provide users. Special Interest Groups offers users free text searching; file transfer; software exchange; a members' directory; bulletin boards; newsletters and product or service order forms; and links to other services on *The Source*. Selected Personal Computer Services includes: *Microsearch Buyer's Guide; PC Industry News; PC Member Publishers;* and Special Interest Groups. Selected Travel Services includes the *Official Airline Guide; Mobil Travel Guide; A-Z International Hotel Guide;* and *Accu-Weather.* Together, these services constitute a full complement of travel services for business or pleasure.

Home Services ranges from education (an online encyclopedia) to shopping at home (for brand-name products, books in print, and tapes and records). Members' Bulletin Boards and Publishing Catalogs facilitate shopping between members. Games, movie reviews, and access to information and periodically updated columns complete the Home Services line.

The Source can be reached using any terminal or personal computer equipped with a modem and communications software. The parameters to use when setting up a modem and software to connect to *The Source* are provided in the manual. An access number, host computer system number, I.D. number, and password constitute access information needed to connect to *The Source.* Network selection depends on the subscriber's location and the availability of telecommunications service in his or her area. Network choices are Telenet, Sourcenet, and WATS (which is tollfree but carries an additional charge). Details about signing on through each of these networks are provided in the manual.

The Source offers extensive printed and online documentation. New subscribers receive a lengthy manual that includes chapters on "Getting Started," as well as descriptions of each of *The Source*'s databases, a "Files and Features" chapter, and an index. Included in the manual pockets are a "*Source* Quick Reference Card," an invitation to a "Tutor" tour, a "Command Guide," and a fold-out "Source Menu" (a handy guide to the layout and location of services on *The Source*). *The Source* Customer Support, an 800-number, is available from 8 a.m. to 1 a.m. daily, Eastern Standard Time. Customer Support via SourceMail is also an option.

Online, the most important way to get questions answered is simply by using the command "Help," which displays a menu designed to assist both the new and experienced subscriber. A second way to obtain customer support online is via *The Source*'s free online service. Thirdly, general information about the system is available via "Member Information" (INFO), a free online service. One of the items on this menu is "Tutorial and Introduction," a guided, step-by-step tour. Last, the Special Interest Groups category is a means of getting assistance from system subscribers who share common professional or personal interests.

Getting around *The Source* is done by selecting from listed choices on display menus and using basic navigation commands. Menus are the basic organizational forms used to present options in *The Source*. These options include categories of service and lists of actual services themselves. Menus can also be used to organize the sections of particular services and to list information retrieved. *The Source* menus are the keys to the layout and location of services on *The Source*. A menus "map" enclosed with the manual gives the complete structure. From the Main Menu of services, any service category on *The Source* can be entered by typing the corresponding number and pressing "Return." Once familiar with the layout of the services, the user can access services even quicker via the Command Level. At the Command Level, all that needs to be done is to type in the Command Name for the service desired and to press "Return." Basic commands aid in the routine use of the programs and services. Basic commands include commands to get out of a service, sign off from *The Source*, get the menus of services, and get help. Prompts are the questions, phrases, or command lists that allow users to control the information coming from *The Source*. Responses determine what is displayed next. Prompts are used to move from one section of a service to another, through pages, or down a list of items; to leave one service and go to another; or to get assistance, if needed. Various shortcuts are available to save users time and money. These shortcuts include command stringing (bypassing prompts) and "automated" commands, or abbreviated commands, that activate commands automatically at logon.

Membership is $49.95 and includes a *SourcePak* manual. Users may select one of three desired billing services: credit card billing, automatic checking account payments, or direct billing (for corporate accounts). Aside from the initial registration fee, there are two basic types of charges. Usage charges are those for the time users are connected to *The Source*. All usage charges are computed based on the users' local time at their billing address, and are calculated to the next minute. Hourly charges are broken down by time of day, and by weekday or weekend and holiday rates. The billing periods are prime time (from 7 a.m. to 6 p.m.) and non-prime time (all other hours of the week). Storage charges are based on the number of characters users store on files on computers of *The Source*. Text files, correspondence, and programs can be stored in files on *The Source*. Monthly charges are based on the number of "records" stored in file storage areas, such as users' file directories, Source-Mail directories, Sharefiles areas, or investor services portfolios. Other charges are incurred when additional manuals or software are ordered. Surcharges may be applied to certain types of "value-added" services, such as the *Official Airline Guide,* Investext, and STOCKVUE. WATS access carries a 25 cents-per-minute surcharge.

GEnie

Competing with *CompuServe, Delphi,* and *The Source* is *GEnie*. Begun in October 1985, *GEnie* (General Electronic Network for Information Exchange) is a product of General Electric's Information Services Company. *GEnie*'s target market is the narrow audience of serious personal computer users, as its range of consumer services illustrates.

The emphasis of *GEnie* is on communications, and there are no fancy databases to search as on the other information utilities. Instead, the centers of activity on *GEnie* are called "Round Tables" (special-interest bulletin boards).[16] The Round Tables, a service category that electronically brings together local, regional, or national users with a common interest, are either conducted by private individuals knowledgeable in the subject, or sponsored by microcomputer hardware and software manufacturers. The private individuals operate as independent contractors to *GEnie*. A message area and a software library constitute the two basic sections of each Round Table.

Many of the Round Tables are microcomputer user groups with large libraries of public-domain software that can be downloaded by users. Included are a number of Macintosh computer-specific services— "Macazine" and two Macintosh Round Tables. Other forms of computer communications available on *GEnie* include electronic mail; a CB radio simulator; a conferencing area; games; and electronic "yard sale" section where users can buy, sell, and trade items; and the ISIS (International Syndicated Information Services) electronic newswire. ISIS includes summaries of news stories from several major industry newsletters. *GEnie* has also added several informational databases, most of which are targeted at personal computing. Recently, *GEnie* has added several transactional services, including an airline schedules and reservations service; a service from American Express that provides account inquiry, shopping, and travel services; and a "Quotes" service covering securities.

Getting started is easy, and can be done by calling (800) 638-8369. Miastowski notes, "Set your communications software for half-duplex; have your Visa, Mastercard, or checking account number ready; and once you're connected, enter 'HHH' and press 'Return.' Wait, and at the 'U# = prompt,' enter '5JM11999' and press 'Return' again. *GEnie*'s main menu will appear, allowing you to explore a bit while you decide if you want to sign up. If you want, you can become a subscriber, and a representative will call you back in a day or so with your local access ID number. Choose a password and a mailbox name, and you're ready to go."[17] The manufacturer claims that getting onto *GEnie* requires a local call in 90 percent of the United States; some 450 local access numbers are noted in the United States alone. By bypassing telecommunications networks, *GEnie* has been able to keep its prices low.

Searching techniques are similar to those of other consumer information online systems, although menus don't list all of the features. To select a service option directly and avoid the menus, the user types "M," followed by the service's number. Typing a second number and a comma allows one to choose a specific service option directly. *GEnie* also responds to natural language commands, such as "Read" to read a message transmitted through electronic mail.

GEnie's customer base is pleased with its well-chosen and well-designed services, fast response time, range of features, ease of use, and online help and instruction manuals. A low sign-up fee of $18, a basic rate of $5 per hour for non-prime time access at either 300 or 1200 baud (without a surcharge), and no monthly minimums are other features that are attractive to potential *GEnie* customers.

BULLETIN BOARD SYSTEMS (BBS)

Bulletin boards are, traditionally, boards for posting notices, as at a school. Within the context of consumer information online systems, bulletin board systems (BBS), are, in fact, separate homegrown information services. (BBS are not to be confused, however, with bulletin board services offered by various consumer information systems discussed earlier. *The Source*, for example, provides scores of categories for listing notices in its "Post" bulletin board program. Users can read or scan notices from any of these categories, as well as post notices themselves. Similarly, on *Delphi*'s "Bulletin Boards," users can post or read messages in a variety of categories.) Currently, thousands of bulletin boards on a myriad of subjects exist. These database message systems can be local, regional, or national in scope. They can be general or specialized; feature built-in capabilities such as uploading, downloading, separate files for features, etc.; or focus on professional or business interests or hobbies. The databases can boast of vast storage capacity with dozens of files (with some of the files set up for key word searching), or the databases can consist of passwords. Most database message systems are open all night. Bulletin board systems may be commercial, but they are usually noncommercial ventures. As such, bulletin board systems are under no commitment to continue operation. Users therefore should not depend on any free bulletin board for continuing information.

Pioneered by Ward Christensen and Randy Suess back in 1978, the first electronic bulletin board operated for one month, from January 16, 1978, to February 16, 1978.[18] The first bulletin board system to become commercially available was the Apple Bulletin Board System (ABBS), which is still widely used.

Who's behind these systems? Generally, individual system operators, or SYSOPs (for "system operators"), with lots of enthusiasm, commitment, time, money, and patience are behind bulletin board systems. Putting a public access system on and keeping it running takes time and money. Setting up a bulletin board involves searching hardware and software, deciding what information to put on it and how to organize the information, organizing daily routines, and soliciting volunteer help. BBSs have the advantage of running unattended for several days at a time, depending on the system's storage capacity. Heavy demand at peak times, however, can lead to disc crashes, telephone problems, and storage problems. Patience is required to handle these realities and to cope with vandals attempting to "crack" private bulletin boards. Resistance to crashes and good support are features to look for when selecting a BBS.

Keeping up with bulletin boards and related online systems is possible by reading *PLUMB* and *Bulletin Board Systems,* two newsletters that cover this area. Features in the latter include: an annual survey of bulletin board news; ham radio networks; schools and bulletin board systems; job hunting by computer advice; free software sources; online health and medical boards; tips on how to start and maintain bulletin boards; advice on obtaining technical information; free online farm reports; updates on various microcomputer user-group bulletin boards; and key names, addresses, and telephone numbers. An annual directory, *National Directory of Bulletin Board Systems,* also helps users keep current with the world of bulletin board systems. Lastly Patrick R. Dewey's comprehensive guide to starting and running an electronic bulletin board system, *Essential Guide to Bulletin Board Systems,* offers a complete overview of the bulletin board systems network.

NOTES

1. *1986 Source* (brochure) (McLean, Va.: The Source, 1986).
2. Carol Tenopir, "Library Use of the Source and CompuServe," *Library Journal* 110 (Apr. 15, 1985): 58.
3. Ibid.
4. Avery Jenkins, "Online Databases," *PC Week* 3 (Mar. 11, 1986): 83.
5. Howard Falk, "The Source v. CompuServe," *Online Review* 8 (1984): 214.
6. Falk, 224.
7. *1986 CompuServe* (brochure) (Columbus, Ohio: CompuServe, 1986): 1.
8. Brian J. Murphy, "Telecommunications Talk," *Creative Computing* 10 (Apr. 1984): 196.
9. CompuServe, *Information Service: The First Choice of a Network Nation* (Columbus, Ohio: CompuServe, 1986): 24.
10. CompuServe, *Starter Kit* (Columbus, Ohio: CompuServe, 1984): 3.
11. Compuserve, *Starter Kit,* 2.
12. Letter to Sarah Watstein from General Videotex Corporation, May 1986.
13. General Videotex Corporation, *Company Background* (brochure), undated.
14. Andy Eddy, "Delphi," *Analog Computing* (Dec. 1985): 78.
15. Ibid.
16. G. Barton Latamore, "GEnie: Out of the Bottle," *PC World* 4 (July 1986): 280.
17. Stan Miastowski, "The GEnie in the CRT," *Macworld* 3 (Nov. 1986): 141–42.
18. Patrick R. Dewey, "A Professional Librarian Looks at the Consumer Online Services...," *Online* 7 (Sept. 1983): 40.

BIBLIOGRAPHY

Bulletin Board Systems (formerly *PLUMB*). 8/year. Westport, Conn.: Meckler, 1983– .

CompuServe User's Guide. Columbus, Ohio: CompuServe, 1984.

Delphi Handbook. Cambridge, Mass.: General Videotex, 1985.

Dew, Robert. "Delphi: A Good Value in On Line Services." *Infoworld* 6 (Aug. 13, 1984): 59–61.

Dewey, Patrick. "A Professional Librarian Looks at the Consumer Online Services...The Source, CompuServe, Apple Bulletin Board, et al." *Online* 7 (Sept. 1983): 36–41.

Eddy, Andy. "Delphi." *Analog Computing* (Dec. 1985): 77–78.

Engel, Margaret. "AIDS Sufferers Find Solace in Computer Network." *Washington Post,* D1, D7, col. 3 (Jan. 26, 1986).

Falk, Howard. "The Source v. CompuServe." *Online Review* 8 (1984): 214–24.

Ferrarini, Elizabeth. "Making the Most of Your Online Minutes." *LinkUp* 2 (Mar. 1986).

General Videotex Corporation (GVC) Delphi. Delfan, N.J.: Datapro Research Corp., 1986. Mimeographed

Jenkins, Avery. "On Line Databases." *PC Week* 3 (Mar. 11, 1986): 83–89.

Katzeff, Paul. "Video Magazine Comes to Boston." *Boston Herald* (Jan. 23, 1986).

Kesselman, Martin. "Online Update." *Wilson Library Bulletin* 61 (June 1987): 53–54.

Latamore, G. Barton. "GEnie: Out of the Bottle." *PC World* 4 (July 1986): 280–86.

Lesko, Matthew. "Low Cost On Line Databases." *Byte* 9 (Oct. 1984): 167–74.

Louden, William. "Consumer Databanks: What We've Learned about the End User." In *Online '86 Proceedings,* edited by Jean Paul Emard, 143–48. Westport, Conn.: Meckler, 1986.

Manning, Ric. "Bulletin Boards: Everybody's Online Services." *Online* 8 (Nov. 1984): 8–9.

Miastowski, Stan. "The GEnie in the CRT." *Macworld* 3 (Nov. 1986): 141–42.

Murphy, Brian. "Telecommunications Talk." *Creative Computing* 10 (Apr. 1984): 196–202.

————. "Telecommunications Talk." *Creative Computing* 12 (Feb. 1986): 226–30.

O'Leary, Mick. "CompuServe and The Source: Databanks for the End User." *Database* 8 (June 1985): 100–106.

————. "GEnie and BIX in the Online Vanguard." *Online* 10 (July 1987): 76–78.

Schepp, Brad. "Delphi: The On Line Industry's Oracle." *Datapro Directory of Online Services* 5 (Apr. 1986): 1–2.

The Source Manual 1986/1987. McLean, Va.: Source Telecomputing, 1986.

Tenopir, Carol. "Library Use of The Source and CompuServe." *Library Journal* 110 (Apr. 15, 1985): 58–59.

Chapter 10

Front-End and Gateway Software for End Users

Martin Kesselman

INTRODUCTION

The advent of more powerful computers, such as the microcomputer, has led to the development of software that makes the search process easier and more accessible to an untrained user. These front-end software packages, if selected and used with care, can provide several advantages to online searching. Front-ends are basically interfaces, at the front between the user and the online service. Front-ends can be part of the online service itself, as with *BRS After Dark;* aids to searching on a user's microcomputer, such as *Searchmaster;* or part of an intermediary gateway computer, such as *Easynet*. This chapter will focus both on the features to look for in selecting a microcomputer front-end package that is appropriate for end users, and on the major front-end packages that are currently available and appropriate for library end-user search programs.

Like many communications software packages, front-end software provides features for storing phone numbers and passwords, for automatically logging on, for preparing a search strategy offline and uploading it to the online search service, and for downloading search results to disc. Additional features provided by front-ends include database selection, assistance with setting up a search strategy, and help with saving search strategies and results. A wide range of front-end packages are now available; some are geared for use by end users with no online experience, and others have features that require a knowledge of the online search process. Front-ends can be used to offer short searches on current topics to end users, for training and introducing online searching to new searchers, and by more experienced searchers for searching unfamiliar and little-used systems easily.

Most front-end features are used before the searcher goes online, such as assisting with choosing a suitable database and setting up a search strategy. Ideally, in database selection, front-ends should attempt to narrow down the field of possibilities but leave the final choice up to the user.

As to developing a search strategy, front-ends can be either menu driven or command driven. Menu-driven formats are easier to use and less error prone than command-driven formats, but they are slower and often do not take advantage of a system's full capabilities. With command-driven interfaces, however, the user may need to have more knowledge of Boolean logic, appropriate field tag selection, and what format to use to search (e.g., correctly inputting an author's name). One advantage menus have for end users is that they keep the new user on track, making him or her less likely to ask inappropriate questions.

A very simple menu-driven system is one offered by *Search Helper*. *Search Helper* first asks the user to select the database he or she wishes to search, and then asks whether the user is interested in a person or a subject. The user can then choose additional terms to narrow down the search. For multi-word phrases, the software automatically adds the *DIALOG* "WITH" proximity operator. *Search Helper* keeps the costs of searching low but does so at the expense of not allowing for any online interaction. However, for short reference searches to obtain current information on a topic, *Search Helper* can be an effective search assistant for undergraduates and for end users in public libraries.

The use of a graphic search work form is a more advanced menu-driven interface offered by several front-ends, including *Wilsearch*. On its work form, *Wilsearch* prompts the user to type in terms, authors' names, journal titles, years, and other specifications next to the appropriate field designations. The software then puts each of these terms in the correct format. Additionally, *Wilsearch* ignores apostrophes, articles, and prepositions so that only significant terms are searched. *Wilsearch* also automatically masks the Boolean operator "AND," and it automatically truncates to search for both the singular and plural forms of a word. Terms on each subject line are "AND"ed together. For "OR" logic, the user must begin a subject line with the word "Any." (See Chapter 6 for more information on *Search Helper* and *Wilsearch*.)

When the user is through with his or her search, most front-end packages offer several options for saving search strategies and for downloading search results. Successful search strategies can oftentimes be saved on the package, rather than with the online service, and be reloaded and used at a later date. This feature can provide a significant savings over online

SDIs, because there are no online storage charges, the strategy can be easily updated offline, and the strategy can be run online as frequently or infrequently as desired. *Wilsearch* also provides a feedback function where the user is asked whether or not a citation retrieved is relevant to his or her search. Based on the user's response, the subject headings for relevant citations are displayed for the user to try in order to help increase his or her search precision and recall.

FRONT-END AND GATEWAY PRODUCTS

The choice of an appropriate front-end should be based on the services accessed and the needs of the user. Packages that are devoted to just one online service, such as *Wilsearch,* or to one database, such as *Micro-DISCLOSURE* (for the *DISCLOSURE* database on *DIALOG*), may provide more specialized features than do packages that offer access to many databases and services. For example, *MicroDISCLOSURE* allows one to compute financial ratios and create specialized reports on companies from downloaded records. Most packages include communications capabilities for accessing additional online services. Search assisting functions, however, may be available only for specific services or databases.

Several front-end and gateway services are currently on the market. Some are marketed directly to end users through personal computer and professional journals. The weekly newsletter *Infoworld* and the *Online Chronicle* are good sources for librarians who want to keep up with new products and developments. The selected bibliography at the end of this chapter cites some general articles on front-ends that compare or discuss several services. Reviews of specific packages can be found in various online and library periodicals, such as *Library Software Review, Library Hi-Tech, Online,* and *Online Review.*

Many front-end packages, such as *Wilsearch* and *Search Helper,* are appropriate for library end-user search programs. However, librarians should also be familiar with packages such as *Sci-Mate* and *ProSearch,* which are geared toward personal purchase, in order to advise appropriate end users in their organization. Some of the major front-ends that are appropriate for both novice and experienced end users are discussed alphabetically below, followed by a discussion of the *Easynet* gateway service.

PC Net/Link

PC Net/Link, from Informatics, offers access to twelve different online services, including *BRS, DIALOG, Dow Jones, Lexis* and *Nexis, NewsNet,* NLM, OCLC, Questel, RLIN, SDC, and *WESTLAW.* The strength of *PC Net/Link* lies in its menu-driven database selection process. The user is first offered a choice of 26 primary headings, each of which is further divided into as many as 26 subheadings. A search can include one main heading and up to two subheadings. Descriptions of the resultant databases are displayed, and the user makes a final selection. *PC Net/Link* can easily be customized or updated, because the package includes word processing capabilities. Libraries can add their own database descriptions and index terms. Libraries may also wish to delete descriptions, and notes, or add cost information, depending on local needs.

Although *PC Net/Link* provides a great deal of assistance with database selection, the only help given with searching is a listing of the online system's commands to be searched. Users therefore must have familiarity with the various online services *PC Net/Link* provides access to. Before logon, the system asks if the user wants a summary of the basic commands of the service about to be searched (for example, how to scan or expand a database term; how to truncate a term, or, for the *Medline* database, how to search a tree number). *PC Net/Link* does allow the user to prepare his or her initial search query offline, upload it, and then download search results.

PC Net/Link requires an IBM-PC XT or an IBM-PC with a hard disc drive, 128K Ram, a Hayes Smartmodem or compatible, and the *Genesys Telios* communications software, available from Informatics. The package sells for $400 to $550, depending on available discounts (the greatest discount is provided to library schools and federal libraries).

ProSearch

ProSearch, from Personal Bibliographic Software (PBS), also provides a great deal of assistance with database selection. *ProSearch* was originally developed by the now defunct Menlow Corporation, the same company that developed *DIALOGlink*. *ProSearch* and *DIALOGlink* use exactly the same interface, except that *ProSearch* offers many more features and can be used fully for both *DIALOG* and *BRS*. *ProSearch* provides color graphics and windowing that create the illusion of searching through library catalog cards in selecting *DIALOG* and *BRS* databases to search. The user first chooses from four categories, such as the one for biology and medicine, and then selects from 30 to 40 subject terms within each of these categories. These terms can be either topics, such as electronics, or a document type, such as a dissertation. The user then examines selected database descriptions on the screen and chooses those files of interest to search. For $100 per year, one can receive a subscription to updated database category discs, as well as any new releases of the software.

After selecting a database, users have the option of searching with *ProSearch* in their native command language or through the use of a high-level interface. The high-level interface provides a graphic search work form with columns for set number, key words and phrases, paragraph qualifiers, and number of postings. A very nice feature is that changing an item in an earlier search statement will also change any following statements affected. Searchers can also easily switch between the high-level interface and searching in the online system's native language.

Another method of search assistance is the cross-emulation feature available on *ProSearch*. Several *BRS* commands can be searched using *DIALOG*, and much of *DIALOG* can be searched via *BRS* for those users who are familiar only with one of these services. Some of the commands that can be emulated include adjacency, truncation, print, and expand. Cross-emulation can be used in both the native and high-level interface modes. Because *ProSearch* contains all of *DIALOG*'s "Blue Sheets" and the *BRS* "Aid Pages," the software can provide the searcher with a sample of the proper format to use for an index field at any time. In addition, a status line at the bottom of the screen shows if the searcher is online, if the printer is online, the disc space available, and the percentage of space available in the buffer. A very useful cost-saving feature is that *ProSearch* allows the user to type ahead of the responses received from *BRS* and *DIALOG* while online, and to edit any previous search statements that have not yet been uploaded.

ProSearch offers a great deal of versatility in that it can be used by both novice searchers through the high-level interface and by experienced searchers through the native interface. For search services, *ProSearch* also contains accounting features that enable libraries to track usage by particular clients or searchers, or for billing individual search sessions. Besides *BRS* and *DIALOG*, *ProSearch* contains logon macros for other online services, including *Dow Jones, BRS Colleague, Knowledge Index,* and *CompuServe*. To use these services, the searcher needs only to add their passwords. Other services can also be added by the user, up to a maximum of 20 services.

ProSearch is now being marketed by PBS as part of the *Searcher's Tool Kit*. The other components of the *Tool Kit* include *ProCite,* which is a bibliographic formatter for translating citations into the proper format for various style sheets, and various *Bibliolinks* packages (one for each online service), which translate online records into the *ProCite* package format. These packages allow searchers to eliminate duplicate records, and to sort and create indexes by key word or phrase. Version 1.05 of *ProSearch* is now available and has added the new two-step logon procedure, and copy protection has been dropped. The *ProSearch* package sells for $495, and a trial disc is available for $19.95. Discounts are available to purchasers of other PBS packages. *ProSearch* requires an IBM-PC or IBM-compatible computer, and a Hayes Smartmodem or compatible. A hard disc drive is recommended.

Q Base

Q Base is a new front-end designed to assist novice searchers with *DI-ALOG*. *Q Base* follows a fairly consistent menu structure, and the cursor keys on the IBM keyboard are used to make selections throughout. All *Q Base* features are accessed online, and database selection is made through *DIALOG's Dialindex* database. "Help" screens can be displayed at any time by pressing one of the IBM function keys.

To start the program, one chooses the "search for information" option from *Q Base's* main menu. The user is then logged onto the *Dialindex* database and asked to first choose from more than 80 subject-related database families. After one types in search terms, databases are ranked by *Q Base* as to the number of hits for each of the terms. Afterwards, the user can press one of the function keys to obtain a brief description of any of these databases that are of potential interest.

When inputting a search strategy, users may create up to 50 search sets with *Q Base.* Although *Q Base* assists with *DIALOG* commands, the user must still have some knowledge of Boolean logic to know how to combine sets effectively. The *Q Base* manual, which is online and must be printed in order for the user to obtain a hard copy, covers only the rudiments of searching. *Q Base* searches the Basic Index (usually the title, abstract, and descriptor fields) by default unless the user specifies a particular index field by pressing one of the function keys. A listing of additional index fields that may be searched is displayed by pressing another function key. In typing in a search statement, if a user puts in a phrase, *Q Base* automatically adds the "3N" proximity operator, meaning that each word is within three words of the other in any order. Users have the option of overriding this feature and putting in another proximity operator.

After completing a search, *Q Base* allows records to be printed or browsed. *Q Base* also includes a record editor that allows users to review or edit search results. Results can be viewed one at a time, and unwanted items can easily be deleted before printing. Records from more than one database search can also be merged into one file with *Q Base.*

Two very useful features for library end-user services are *Q Base's* accounting and maintenance features. Through the accounting and maintenance option on the main menu, one can obtain cost reports for one or several search sessions, and one can easily change telephone numbers and passwords. With *Q Base,* a main *DIALOG* password is added by the library, and then up to 50 local passwords can be created to access *Q Base.*

However, maintenance and full accounting features are protected and accessible only through the main password.

Q Base requires an IBM-PC or compatible and a Hayes Smartmodem or compatible, and sells for $249. A demonstration diskette that is good for four weeks of searching is available from Online Research for $10. Online Research also markets *Searchworks,* a front-end for intermediaries, which has several post-processing features, such as indexing and ranking completed searches; and *Med-Base,* a front-end for searching NLM's *Medline* database and assisting with medical subject headings. Online Research maintains a technical support desk that is available from 1 p.m. to 5 p.m.

Sci-Mate

The *Sci-Mate Searcher*, from the Institute of Scientific Information (ISI), provides a common menu-driven interface that offers access to SDC, *DIALOG,* NLM, *BRS,* and Questel. *Sci-Mate* provides assistance with command language, but the user must know the database he or she intends to search and must have some familiarity with database structure. Listings of searchable fields are displayed for ISI's databases, as well as for other selected heavily searched files, such as *ERIC* and *Medline*. With these files, the searcher is assisted automatically in using the correct format for various fields, such as searching by language. After the searcher inputs a term, the menu asks if he or she wishes to end query construction, refine the query with "AND" logic, extend the query with "OR" logic, limit the query with "NOT" logic, or specify proximity to another term. The *Sci-Mate Searcher* also allows searching in each online service's native command mode.

When the user is through with a search, the "Save" strategy command allows him or her to retain the entire search strategy or just the portion that proved most useful. Saved profiles can be edited easily through menus for inserting or deleting lines, reorganizing the sequences, or appending lines to an existing profile.

Post-processing is a key feature of *Sci-Mate* when the *Manager* and *Editor* software packages are purchased as well. With the *Manager,* citations are structured immediately according to templates that the user has the option of redesigning. The user can also add his or her own records, search the records in his or her personal database, and flag particular items, such as those ordered through a document delivery service. With the *Editor,* bibliographic references, including those from an online search, can be reformatted to specific requirements and to the formats of 15 standard style manuals and journals.

Sci-Mate requires 128K RAM, an IBM-PC or compatible with two drives (floppy or hard disc), and any modem. Each component lists for

$399. The three components can be purchased separately, or together as a package. ISI recently instituted a special academic program whereby the company will provide one copy of the *Sci-Mate* package to a library for free. In return, the library agrees to provide some first-level support to the teaching faculty at their institution who purchase any of the packages. Teaching faculty at participating universities also receive a 40 percent discount toward the purchase of any component. ISI has even organized *Sci-Mate* users' groups and publishes a newsletter called *Sci-Mate Matters*.

Searchmaster and *Microsoft Access*

Another approach to developing search strategies is the use of scripts, which is offered by *Searchmaster* and *Microsoft Access*. Writing scripts is in many ways akin to programming, and requires time and skill. On *Searchmaster*, which offers access to *DIALOG*, SDC, *BRS,* and NLM, scripts are written in the command language of the system one intends to search. The librarian can provide instructions and leave blanks in the scripts for the user to fill in. Scripts can also offer branching, with menus of options taking the user to different parts of a script. Scripts can also be developed to meet the needs of some end users, who, as they gain experience with online searching, can bypass much of the assistance provided by the system. Another potential use of scripts is for repetitive searches on a topic such as one required for a class term paper assignment. Smaller scripts can also be linked together into a larger master script, and a search performed online can be saved as a script. To some extent, libraries can also save parts of repeatedly used searches as a "hedge," through a permanent "saved search" on *DIALOG* or *BRS*. Scripts on *Searchmaster* can be interrupted easily at any time when the user chooses to search the database directly. *Searchmaster* also provides a "talk" and "search" mode online. The search mode is menu driven, and the talk mode allows direct searching in the native command language.

Microsoft Access comes with prepared scripts to search, and uses various consumer-oriented online services, such as *CompuServe, Dow Jones,* and *NewsNet*. Simple scripts can easily be written by using the "Learn" command, which actually stores a particular search strategy or logon procedure. More complex scripts can be created with the *Microsoft Access Script* command language, and a script developer's kit is available for use by more serious scriptwriters.

Searchmaster sells for $299 and requires 128K RAM, an IBM-PC or compatible, and a Hayes Smartmodem or compatible. *Microsoft Access* sells for $250 and also requires an IBM-PC or compatible, and a Hayes Smartmodem or compatible. The *Microsoft Access Custom Menu Developer's Kit* sells for $25.

Searchware

Searchware is a front-end that is sold in more than 50 subject modules (e.g., medicine), each offering access to approximately eight to twelve *DIALOG* databases. The package includes a *DIALOG* password, and online charges are paid to *Searchware* rather than to *DIALOG*. The database selection process is performed online. In a preliminary search, *Searchware* searches the topic on *Dialindex* and downloads the postings for each of the files in the module purchased.

Searchware offers three levels of searching. The easiest of these levels uses a simplified menu system. At the simplest search level, *Searchware* provides screens requesting (1) all terms the user wants included in a search (AND" logic), (2) some terms the user wants included in a search ("OR" logic), and (3) terms the user does not want included in a search ("NOT" logic). However, these menus cannot be coordinated together, as might be done through the use of parentheses for nesting when the user is searching *DIALOG* directly. In level two searching, the searcher uses *DIALOG* commands, but the search is entered offline and then uploaded. Level three searching provides direct online access with *DIALOG*. The *Searchware* manual provides some instruction on using basic *DIALOG* commands and includes descriptions of each of the databases in the subset purchased.

Because *Searchware* provides access to only a limited number of *DIALOG* files, it is best suited for personal purchase by end users who need to access only a restricted number of subject-related databases. Unfortunately, *Searchware* does not even provide basic communications functions for accessing *DIALOG* directly or, for that matter, any other online service. *Searchware* requires an IBM-PC with one disc drive and a minimum of 128K. The first *Searchware* disc costs $290. Each additional subject module purchased costs $100.

Easynet

As an alternative to front-end software packages, the *Easynet* gateway service also provides a transparent interface for online searching. The *Easynet* interface is also available as *Infomaster* on Western Union's Easylink electronic mail service, as *IQuest* on *CompuServe,* and as *Alanet Plus* on Alanet. In fact, the *Easynet* gateway, because it is based on a mainframe, can provide a great deal more transparency than do other systems to the casual end user who is not familiar with accessing online information resources. *Easynet* is accessed through a toll-free number with any microcomputer or terminal.

Easynet first provides subject category menus for users to choose from, first asking the user to select either a subject, person, place, organization, or "Help," until his or her choice is narrowed to a particular database. After the user inputs a single search line, *Easynet* selects a vendor and database, performs the search, and downloads retrieved citations—all of which steps are transparent to the user. One of the advantages of *Easynet* is the great number of online services and databases available. *Easynet* can thus be used effectively when a searcher requires information from a database on an infrequently needed service. With *Easynet 2,* users can pre-select a database, and the system will tell the user which available fields may be searched before the user even types in the search line. *Easynet 3,* soon to be available, will allow users to enter commands from any online service they are familiar with, and the *Easynet* system will translate users' requests into the command language of the host system they are accessing.

Easynet provides user aids and "Help" screens, which give examples of Boolean logic, truncation, and nesting. *Easynet* also has an "SOS" function. By typing "SOS" on the keyboard, the user can bring a search specialist online to provide assistance. Unfortunately, *Easynet* has removed much of the interaction involved in online searching, as users may enter only one search line. If that search line results in any hits, *Easynet* downloads the ten most recent citations. A basic search with ten citations on *Easynet* costs $8, plus $.20 per minute. Ten additional citations cost $8, and abstracts cost $2 each. For full-text databases, the user is shown up to 15 headings or titles per search and then may choose one for display of the full text as a single search. Some expensive databases also carry a surcharge. The user receives a notice of potential costs online before charges are incurred. One way for users to circumvent the lack of interaction and the limit of one search line and to save costs is to begin their search as specific as possible and then broaden their search as much as needed until users retrieve some citations. Except for the $.20-per-minute time charge, no search charges are incurred if no citations are retrieved.

Easynet provides various password options as well as customized screens for libraries and schools. A full institutional subscription for libraries costs $550 and includes $100 in free introductory searches, posters, 25 *Easynet* user's guides, customized introductory screens, and a press kit. The library subscription also includes up to ten passwords, with charges on the monthly bill being itemized by password. The library is given a five percent credit on all searches. A more limited annual subscription costs $150. A special subscription program for secondary schools provides access to approximately 70 databases that may be relevant for high school-age students. Searches are charged at the flat rate of $3.50 per search.

A specialized version of *Easynet* produced by Addison-Wesley is available as *Einstein* on *CompuServe. Einstein,* designed for high-school students and undergraduates, provides access to 90 general interest databases. These same 90 databases are also being offered through a new service, the *Answer Machine*. Telebase Systems, the owners of the *Easynet* gateway, offer *Answer Machine* workstations where, for a fixed price, users have unlimited online access to these 90 databases through the *Easynet* interface. At a much higher price, libraries can have a workstation with unlimited access to the over 1,000 databases available through *Easynet* or make the *Answer Machine/Easynet* interface available through an institution's local area network. As a fixed-cost option, the *Answer Machine* offers a real alternative to CD-ROM.

SUMMARY

The major deciding factor in purchasing a front-end should be the user population. For instance, a library might select a package such as *Wilsearch* for an end-user search service aimed at undergraduate or novice searchers. For more sophisticated end users, librarians may wish to recommend a package such as *Sci-Mate,* which provides easy searching and includes several nice features, such as a database and bibliographic editor. For designing their own online interface, librarians might consider the scriptwriting capabilities of *Searchmaster* and *Microsoft Access.* Other considerations include the online databases and services accessed; whether assistance with database selection is provided; the package's ease of use and ease of learning; "Help" feature included; cost-saving features, such as typing ahead or uploading saved strategies; and postprocessing capabilities, such as editing a search or formatting bibliographies. Ideally, a front-end should provide varying levels of complexity so that when a user becomes more knowledgeable about system features, fewer search assisting features are required and can be bypassed easily. Although front-ends provide assistance with online search commands and, in some cases, database selection, they are no substitute for training. Users still need a basic knowledge of database indexing and structure, the ability to define their searches effectively, and some knowledge of Boolean logic.

In the future, front-ends may be enhanced through the use of artificial intelligence techniques that offer greater natural language capabilities as well as emulate expert online searchers. Front-ends will probably become increasingly important given the trend toward publishing databases on CD-ROM, especially since the search software used with each database may vary. Still, existing front-ends can be used quite effectively in many situations, such as within end-user search services, with the assistance of librarians as consultants. Front-ends also can be used effectively by more experienced online searchers for increasing the accessibility of numerous online systems and databases.

BIBLIOGRAPHY

Fenichel, Carol H., and John J. Murphy. "Using a Microcomputer to Communicate: Part 2: Specialized Software." *Microcomputers for Information Management* 2 (Sept. 1985): 155-70.

Hawkins, Donald T., and Louise R. Levy. "Front End Software for Online Database Searching. Part 1: Definitions, Systems Features, and Evaluation." *Online* 9 (Nov. 1985): 30-37. "Part 2: The Marketplace,." *Online* 10 (Jan. 1986): 33-40. "Part 3: Product Selection Chart and Bibliography." *Online* 10 (May 1986): 49-58.

Kesselman, Martin. "Front-End/Gateway Software: Availability and Usefulness." *Library Software Review* 4 (Mar.-Apr. 1985): 67-70.

Levy, Louise R. "Gateway Software: Is It for You? *Online* 8 (Nov. 1984): 67-79.

O'Leary, Mick. "Gateway Software to the Information Stars." *PC* 4 (Aug. 20, 1985): 181-86.

Chapter 11

Laser Disc-Based Services for End Users

Charles M. Peters

INTRODUCTION

Optical publishing via the use of mass-produced laser discs, also called optical discs, is being pursued vigorously by various database producers. Database producers see the use of laser-driven optical discs as an alternative distribution method for placing their information products in the hands of the end user. To date, the principal application of optical-based systems for end users appears to be in library databases. This chapter therefore focuses on the advantages and the potential these new databases have for libraries, and it reviews some of the products that are currently available. As laser disc technology is still a rapidly evolving field, this listing should in no way be considered complete. Instead, its intent is to provide examples of features to look for in selecting products appropriate for end users in libraries.

The rising costs of telecommunications from centrally located database services and the increasing costs of distributing information products in paper or microformat have made publishers look at alternative ways of disseminating their products. The optical disc offers fast replication rates, interactive operational features under microcomputer control, and inexpensive hardware, along with a compact format for storing large-scale databases. Librarians concerned with the costs of searching large, centrally located databases when the connect costs are part of the learning program may find optical discs attractive for training end users because of their fixed and predictable costs. When many databases are offered with a uniform query language, as is possible on laser disc, librarians may also find that they will spend less time instructing end users.

The library and information sciences are in the vanguard for testing the various optical-based media on the market today. These media include the videodisc, CD-ROM (Compact Disc-Read Only Memory), and optical digital disc. The first two media are based on technology developed for the entertainment industry, and the latter is based on technology used in the office automation field and in the computer industry. The differences between the two technologies are many; simply stated, videodisc and CD-ROM are optical discs manufactured for purposes requiring multiple replicas. Such discs go through a manufacturing cycle requiring a mastering and stamping process much as books go through a publishing process. In contrast, optical digital discs are written on directly by a write-once read-many (WORM) drive. As part of this process, the data goes through an error-checking process termed "direct read after write" (DRAW), which ensures the integrity of the stored data. The Library of Congress' Optical Disc Print Project is the most notable example of this type of technology applied to libraries, and there are many examples of its use in office automation schemes for document storage as well.

OPTICAL FORMATS FOR LIBRARIES

The choice between CD-ROM and videodisc—the two media currently in vogue for publishing products for the library market—is debatable. The advantages of using videodisc for optical publishing lie in its larger capacity for information storage because of its larger size of 12″ as opposed to the 4.72″ of CD-ROM. Another significant advantage of videodisc lies in the fact that a publisher can attain multimedia adjacency with pictures, sound, and textual data all on the same disc. Other benefits are videodisc's faster access time for finding information on the disc, the fact that many people can use the videodisc simultaneously, and the fact that a variety of disc manufacturers are located in the United States. Its disadvantages stem from the fact that the videodisc is an analog recording device, and the digital codes are embedded in the FM recording channels on the device. To modulate and demodulate these signals, one must use proprietary error correction and error detection codes. This feature means that videodiscs made according to one company's scheme cannot be read on another's hardware.

Compact audiodiscs (CDs) are the base upon which CD-ROM is built. A CD audiodisc is manufactured according to standards established by the N.V. Phillips and Sony Corporations and uses a player system produced under license from these companies, which makes possible the compatibility of compact discs across the entire spectrum of compact disc players. With the introduction of CD-ROM, which was designed as a computer peripheral, information brokers hope to use the economies of scale brought about by the popularity of the CD audio standard to achieve a large-scale distribution of their information products to libraries and other consumers.

Two different methods are used to embed information on the tracks of CD-ROM and on the reflective optical videodisc. The CD-ROM mode calls for what is termed "constant linear velocity" (CLV). This type of format allows for twice as much storage density over that allowed by the alternative format, known as "constant angular velocity" (CAV). The CAV format is used in the reflective videodisc calling for speed of access to data, and allows individual frames to be retrieved. CD-ROM uses timing information embedded in the CLV format to accomplish its random access capabilities, but because CD-ROM is aimed at the microcomputer market, access speeds required by mini- and mainframe computers were not built into its standards. The CD-ROM disc can be played on any CD audio player having digital output. The standardization allows discs and drives to be physically interchanged.

Standards exist for CD-ROM technology at the physical and logical level. At the application level, no standards are required, which means that each information provider can embed in CD-ROM products different protocols for logging on, different search software, and other features that would serve to make the products unique. The physical standard for CD-ROM was established by the two manufacturers who developed the technology and who now license equipment manufacturers to produce discs and drives for CD-ROM. Information is embedded in the CD-ROM disc as a spiral going from the center of the disc to its outward edge. Up to 550,000 megabytes (mega - million) of information can be stored on any CD-ROM disc. More information can be stored on videodisc, but for a variety of reasons, CD-ROM seems to have the market impetus.

A group composed of individuals representing different industry constituencies, known as the High Sierra Group, is establishing standards that will allow discs containing different database information to be read on disc players conforming to the CD-ROM physical standard. Much as MS-DOS brought about operating system compatibility for IBM and other personal computers, the High Sierra Group has recommended a formatting standard for discs for the logical placement of data on the CD-ROM disc. In order to accommodate the spectrum of already purchased personal computers and their operating systems, device drivers (i.e., programs allowing personal computers to exchange data with peripheral CD-ROM players) are now needed. The drivers were made specific at the operating system level rather than at the applications program level. This feature means that instruction on how to manipulate the data contained in the various publishing products expected to emerge from laser-based disc services will be the province of the publishers for the near future.

System integrators are those firms that stand between the publishers and the firms doing the actual pressing on the discs. Many system integrators work with both videodiscs and CD-ROM discs. The integrators take the information that is currently available and convert it to the format required by the mastering process needed to make videodiscs and CD-ROM discs. Many publishers act as their own integrators for this process. Among the independent system integrators are LaserData, Inc., in Massachusetts; Reference Technology, Inc., in Colorado; and TMS, Inc., in Oklahoma. The approaches that integrators take to fashioning a product are as varied as the products themselves. For videodiscs, the spectrum of approaches ranges from using standard consumer equipment that is available from any manufacturer to developing proprietary hardware and software in order to create a custom product.

Other optical formats being developed and of potential use to librarians include OROMs, CD-I, laser cards, and WORM technology. Optical read-only memory (OROM) is an alternative ROM disc that is 5¼" in diameter. OROM is made in the CAV mode and uses concentric rings as opposed to the spiral technology of the CD-ROM disc. The concentric rings are more closely allied to the drive formats prevalent in the computer industry. The storage capacity of such a disc is less than that of videodisc or CD-ROM, but OROM offers faster access times and faster transfer rates. Industry observers predict that OROM will be the format used for the distribution of operating systems, application programs, and general documentation of computer systems that use print or floppy disc formats at present.

Yet another format for CD is coming called Compact Disc-Interactive (CD-I). This disc is an enhanced version of the CD music format and CD-ROM. Like videodisc, CD-I will be able to use pictures, sound, and text in an interactive fashion. CD-I discs will use a different type of player than CD-ROM discs do, but CD-ROM discs will be playable on a CD-I player. CD-I is designed for the consumer entertainment market rather than as a computer peripheral. In fact, CD-I will not need a personal computer in order to use its capabilities. However, its impact on education and training may also bring CD-I into the electronic publishing field and become of interest to librarians. At this time, CD-I is still just a set of specifications that will be designed around the Motorola 68000 microprocessor.

Laser cards containing up to two million bytes of data are coming into use in the medical records field and are already being used by Blue Cross/Blue Shield of Maryland. Library applications of such cards still remain in the design stage.

The office automation field is using write-once read-many (WORM) technology in order to replace microfilm and microfiche applications in areas where speed is essential to process office documents. WORM technology may become useful in library applications when industry-wide standards are defined for it. An erasable optical disc technology is being created for the computer industry's needs. Such optical discs and drives are projected to be more economical than the magnetic tapes, discs, and drives used at present.

DATABASES AND SERVICES

The *Optical/Electronic Publishing Directory* [1] has identified 42 products in either videodisc or CD-ROM format as of the first quarter of 1986. This useful book for librarians provides information on how these optical publishing products rely on specific software and hardware products to retrieve the information embedded in the databases. This description is helpful in ascertaining how many different databases are available on the same medium for a similar system configuration. For example, if a librarian has a system using an Hitachi CD-ROM drive and an MS-DOS personal computer with 512K of memory, and wants to know if a database specifying Philips drives and an IBM personal computer with 512K will work instead, the directory gives this useful information. Datext's corporate database system, for instance, uses Hitachi drives, and *Silver-Platter* uses Philips, but the CD-ROM discs can be used on either drive and personal computer. However, one still needs to use the software system required by the differing systems. The *CD-ROM Review* [2] has identified approximately 77 published CD-ROM products but states that several publishers are still not certain that their product will be available in this format. As mentioned previously, the commitment of large amounts of money and time to place an already established product on CD-ROM might not prove economically worthwhile to a successful vendor of a printed product.

CW Communications publishes *CD-ROM Review* to be given away at various information conferences in order to bring the new technology of publishing to the attention of opinion leaders in the information services field. This periodical is now published bimonthly. *CD-ROM Review* is useful for explanations, descriptions, and reviews of CD-ROM products and for articles on how to use CD-ROM technology and where to purchase equipment and databases. Databases on CD-ROM are expected to assist librarians in their roles as intermediaries in the searching process. The use of CD-ROM for databases may give many libraries an opportunity to introduce online searching to library users at low costs. Users who might resist using more than one index in paper or microformat to find information might be more amenable to using multiple databases available on a CD-ROM disc. The first issue of *CD-ROM Review* includes an excellent discussion of *Compact DISCLOSURE,* The *DISCLOSURE* database on CD-ROM. The review makes the point that the convenience of having business data available instantaneously might be the best selling point of this CD-ROM product.

An article in *Online* compares three versions of the *ERIC* database on CD-ROM: *DIALOG onDisc, SilverPlatter,* and OCLC's *Search 450.* The authors examine how three different information providers placed the *ERIC* file on CD-ROM. Each vendor used different techniques to provide access to the information on the discs. Pricing strategy is discussed, along with the impact of using this educational database with CD-ROM products that are available from other vendors.[3]

The *Laserdisk Directory,*[4] published in the journals *Online* and *Database,* is an excellent summary of the available products published in optical format for libraries. Descriptions concerning new optically published products for use in the technical services areas of libraries are covered in the *Optical/Electronic Publishing Directory* and in the *Laserdisk Directory;* these products also have received extensive coverage in the major library publications. For further information on optically published products such as *Bibliofile* or *Books in Print plus,* see the major library journals. McGraw-Hill is placing the *Encyclopedia of Science and Technology* on CD-ROM and has plans to place several other of its important reference books and indexes in this format. The *Laserdisk Directory,* among other reference books, should keep librarians up to date on new laser disc-based products.

CD-ROM is the dominant format for optical publishing at the time of this writing. The products described here are available on CD-ROM, but some have changed distributors and others might still be in the demonstration stage only. The state of optical publishing is such that, in the near future, some of the products described here will have gone through more product testing to refine their usefulness to the end user. Other products will be withdrawn from the market for further refinements. Another problem for both publishers and distributors is attempting to gauge the potential market for these products. Digital Equipment Corporation's products were among the most valuable for the library market due to their content, but the company withdrew from the business and now offers its services to publishers as a systems integrator.

End users will purchase products on laser discs only if the discs have features that enhance their use over alternative dissemination formats. The acceptance of existing products in the marketplace will be what drives publishers to produce different products. The library is one form of end user, and librarians will have a large voice in determining the content, searching procedures, and formatting standards for these products. Librarians also will probably be the dominant purchaser of historical information on CD-ROM. *ERIC, PsycLit, Newsbank,* and *PAIS,* among other bibliographic databases, will be purchased for library use, and end users will have to be given instruction in how to use them.

The publishers of databases need to do more than take existing products, place them on CD-ROM, and offer them for sale. The two features of being able to do online searching without incurring connect costs and of devising search strategies under computer control offer many opportunities for librarians to exploit laser technology for providing bibliographic assistance to all levels of users. For example, SilverPlatter Information, Inc., is incorporating a tutorial database on all of its CD-ROM discs. Such a feature might be even more useful if it included tutorials at different levels of user familiarity with computers and online searching.

Many of the companies selling laser disc-based products provide CD-ROM hardware and software in addition to providing the databases themselves. For libraries wishing to take advantage of these services, some general information follows. The basic equipment needed is a personal computer with a minimum of 256K memory, one disc drive, a hard disc, a printer if printed listings are needed, and any database vendor's specific requirements. A good question to ask is whether the CD-ROM reader is top loading or front loading. If top loading is used, the reader will then need to be placed next to the computer to change discs. If the reader is a front loader, it can be stacked on top of the computer and under the monitor to economize on space. Various library and office equipment suppliers offer security cabinets that will keep all hardware secure. Some vendors, such as *Newsbank,* are placing the CD-ROM drive within the personal computer to be used as an internal drive.

Below are some examples of databases that are available on CD-ROM and that illustrate the diversity of products that currently exists, as well as the potential this technology holds for both libraries and end users.

SilverPlatter Information

SilverPlatter requires an IBM personal computer—either an XT or AT with 512K memory—or an IBM compatible, plus a printer supplied by the customer. SilverPlatter supplies the CD-ROM drive, controller card, discs, and search software, plus associated documentation. An "800" number is available for telephone assistance if problems develop. According to an interview with B. Hatvany,[5] president of SilverPlatter, difficult questions are handled by different support groups for hardware, software, and content problems. *SilverPlatter*'s databases are designed for use by librarians who know online searching and for end users with little knowledge of how to go about constructing a search or using a computer keyboard. An important item to note is that a uniform search language is used across all of *SilverPlatter*'s databases.

A multi-user CD-ROM system for libraries called *MultiPlatter* is being developed by SilverPlatter. *MultiPlatter* allows remote terminal access to CD-ROM databases. One module can support four simultaneous users who are searching four different databases contained within it. Four CD-ROM drives are in the module, and end-user searching can take place from remote locations via telephone or by hard wiring local monitors and keyboards up to 160 feet from the module. The advantage to this configuration for library use is in keeping all CD-ROM players and discs in a locked area and allowing end users to search from remote sites.

SilverPlatter has organized its database search and instructional software around the concept of screens that assist the user in interpreting information and data displays. There are five basic screen types: (1) information screens, which have many subscreens, (2) a database selection screen, (3) a search screen, (4) a display screen, and (5) a dictionary screen. All these screens are divided into the same four areas: the first is the status area, which displays *SilverPlatter*'s name, the version of the software used on the specific disc, and the databases currently on the disc being searched. The second item is the current display area, which lists textual information retrieved in response to commands given by the user from the third area—the menu. Fourth is the message area, which displays prompts to assist the user in his or her search and also shows user-caused error messages or system error messages.

Three types of information screens assist searchers using *SilverPlatter*'s databases: (1) the database entry screen, (2) the database-specific map screen, and (3) "Help" screens. The database entry screen describes the contents of the database, along with the copyright information concerning that particular database. This screen is closely related to the database selection screen, which lists other databases contained on the specific CD-ROM disc being searched. Additionally, the commands "Help," "Base" (to select a new database), "Xchange" (to change discs), and "Admin" (for administrative functions) are displayed in the menu area. The database-specific map screen shows the organization of the database in the current display area and defines the format of the fields in the database's record structure. Database-specific map information is provided to *SilverPlatter* by the database publisher. There are five screens of information within the map function: (1) the introduction screen, consisting of a scope note describing the database's contents and organization; (2) the vocabulary screen, listing information contained on the database's thesaurus and any special terminology used; (3) the fields screen, containing sample contents of the database and a list of which fields are not searchable; (4) the noise words screen, establishing the database's non-indexed "stop" words; and (5) the examples screen, which provides examples of sample searches along with helpful hints for searching.

There are two types of "Help" screens: command-specific and general. The command-specific "Help" screens define the use of the commands shown in the menu area: FIND, SHOW, PRINT, CLEAR, BASE, XCHANGE, GLOSSARY, MAP, OPTIONS, ADMIN. There are six general "Help" screens. These consist of: (1) an introduction screen explaining the use of the "Help" screens; (2) a commands screen, which explains how to use the commands contained in *SilverPlatter*'s system; (3) a parameters screen, which tells the user how to qualify a search by using Boolean logic (AND, OR, NOT), proximity operators (WITH, NEAR), areas within a given field, records, language, a date or a range of dates, a material type, etc.; (4) a database screen describing the general organization of a particular database and referring the user to the database-specific map screen for further information; (5) a disc screen explaining the proper care and use of the CD-ROM disc; and (6) a keyboard screen reviewing the use of a personal computer keyboard.

The search screen lists responses to the "Find" command. Results of searches, listing the number of documents retrieved along with the parameters used to retrieve them, are displayed on the search screen. Ninety nine searches can be stored and are recalled by using the "PG UP" key from the numeric pad of the computer keyboard. The display screen lists the text of the retrieval document and highlights the search words used. The total number of documents retrieved is shown on the status line of the display screen.

The dictionary screen displays the word input by the searcher, followed in alphabetical order by subsequent entries. Each entry displayed consists of the word, the number of occurrences of that word in the database, and the number of documents in the database that contain the selected word. If the desired word is not found in the database, the system software goes to the alphabetical place in the glossary where the word would typically be located, in order to give the user an opportunity to browse. The glossary can search subject fields, author fields, or other specified fields.

SilverPlatter's system is designed to allow the experienced searcher to immediately begin using the system and has many of the features of the large online systems. At the same time, menu-driven screens are embedded in the system to assist the novice user. The "Help" function is designed to put the novice user at ease and dispenses with the need to juggle a printed manual while the searcher is learning how to use the system. The use of a uniform query language for searching all of *SilverPlatter*'s databases should alleviate concern over the introduction of CD-ROM into a library.

SilverPlatter currently markets several CD-ROM databases, including *PsycLit, ERIC, EMBASE, AV ONLINE,* and *PAIS.* Some database publishers require a subscriber to return the old discs when updated discs are received, allowing database publishers to maintain control of their products and distribution. *Sociological Abstracts* is now available on CD-ROM through SilverPlatter. Retrospective discs are planned for *PsycLit, ERIC,* and *EMBASE.* The search software will allow the changing of discs from current to historical discs without the user's having to physically change discs or reformulate search strategies.

PsycLit, which includes *Psychological Abstracts* (PA) dating to 1974, is a database from the PsycInfo Department of the American Psychological Association. The database is international in scope and provides references to journal literature and technical reports from PsycInfo. *PsycLit* contains both a current database and a historical one. The current disc has material dating from 1981 to the present and is updated quarterly (the old disc must be returned to the vendor when an updated version is received). The historical disc is a separate database covering material dating from 1974 to 1980.

The *ERIC* (Educational Resources Information Center) database is also available from SilverPlatter. This widely used and comprehensive database covers the education field. Again, more than one disc is available, with two discs covering historical material dating from 1966 to 1975 and from 1976 to 1982, respectively. Citations dating from 1982 to the present are updated quarterly. The current disc has files for both "Resources in Education" (RIE) and "Current Journals in Education" (CIJE). The retrospective files are on two separate discs, and each is purchased separately.

EMBASE, a large international bibliographic database in biomedicine, is another SilverPlatter CD-ROM database. The size of this database again makes multiple discs necessary for storage of its voluminous contents and makes for different pricing structures for the discs. The current disc covers the current year, and the individual discs cover past years at the rate of one disc per year.

AV Online, the database of audiovisual materials from the National Information Center for Educational Media (NICEM), has bibliographic descriptions of over 350,000 audiovisual programs dating through March 1986, and is updated annually. This database has information about 8 mm and 16 mm films, filmstrips, videotapes, audiocassettes, records, and overhead transparencies. *AV Online* allows users to search for the distributor of any item in the database, as well as searching by title, subject code, description, or key word and Boolean combinations.

PAIS, the Public Affairs Information Service database, is being completely converted and made available on CD-ROM. This database was still being tested at the time of this writing, and the *PAIS* board of directors was awaiting results before releasing the system.

H. W. Wilson Company

The Wilson Company brought out its information products on CD-ROM in 1987 as *Wilsondisc.* The CD-ROM discs cover the full spectrum of databases offered in print and online by this established supplier of information products to the library market. The system is designed to connect to Wilson's online databases at the touch of a function key. This feature should enable librarians to assist end users in searching for the most current information on a given topic while still maintaining control over communications and connect fees incurred in doing these searches. The Wilson Company demonstrated the system extensively at library conventions throughout 1987. For more information on *Wilsondisc,* see Chapter 6.

Datext

Datext has designed a system that makes corporate information quickly available to end users. The system requires an IBM-PC, either an XT or AT, or an IBM-compatible computer with 512K bytes of memory, one floppy disc drive, and a hard disc drive with a minimum of 400K bytes (preferably 1Mb). Datext supplies the CD-ROM drive, cable, controller card, and software. Information from six online publishers is placed on CD-ROM in *Datext*'s proprietary format: Business Research Corporation's "Investext" reports in full-text format, including tables and statistics but excluding graphics materials; Disclosure Information Group's entire *DISCLOSURE II* database; Predicasts, Inc., *PROMPT abstracts* for the past two years; the most recent three years of the *ABI/INFORM* database from Data Courier, Inc; details from Media General's *MARKET FILE;* and information from Marquis' *Who's Who in Science and Industry.*

The *Datext* database consists of four CD-ROM discs with information on approximately 10,000 publicly held companies that report to the U. S. Securities and Exchange Commission. The discs reflect the manner in which *Datext* classifies these companies by line of business within 50 main industry groups. The four discs are classified as: Consumer, Industrial, Technology, and Service. All four discs contain directories for the whole database and for each disc so that a library may subscribe to all or selected discs. Discs are updated monthly, and the subscriber may keep all previously issued discs. The search software is menu driven and consists of help, information, and service screens that are retrieved in response to choices presented in the menu. The software also allows messages to be displayed on the screen in order to show what has been done, what is being done, what can be done next, and to explain errors. There are five screen message areas: path, prompt, status, database ID, and help. The first screen presented is the "Main Menu." It is divided into three areas consisting of an options window, descriptive window, and input area. The options window lists the available menu selections, which represent choices the user makes about the Company, Portfolio, Industry, Line of Business, Executive, or Quit options displayed on the screen. The descriptive window contains descriptions of the choices listed in the options window. For example, if the user selects "Company" from the options window, the company listing for the particular disc is displayed, and the user then selects a specific company. Next, a choice is made as to the type of information desired. From the *Datext* "Main Menu," company information is available for the following options: Profile, Financials, Subsidiaries, Directors, Stock Report, Recent Articles, Article Search, Investment Reports, and Report Excerpts. From the "Portfolio" menu, company information is available for the following options: Profile, Financials, Comparative Financials, Subsidiaries, Directors, Stock Report, and Recent Articles. "Comparative Financials" consists of the complete balance sheet, summary balance sheet, complete income statement, summary income statement, and complete funds flow and financial statement items for one, two, or three years. For faster retrieval, the system allows the user to type a company name instead of scrolling through the company list.

The "Company Profile Report" contains basic identification data consisting of name, address, telephone number, state incorporated in, fiscal year ending date, stock exchange where listed, number of employees, shares outstanding, and ticker symbol. A written description of the company's business; its principal line of business according to the Standard Industrial Classification (SIC) code; corporate officers, listing name, title, salary, and age; and summary of financial results for the last fiscal year are also included. The "Company Financial Report" gives, in addition to the basic identification data, recent financial data from the company's balance sheets for the past two to three years. The report also provides comments on financial results, financial ratios, quarterly income statements, the president's letter to shareholders, management's discussion of the company, and a list of recent SEC filings for proxy statements, special exhibits, etc. The "Company Stock Report" is an important listing for historical data. This report gives the last eleven years of the company's yearly high, low, and closing prices, along with its average daily volume. Weekly highs, lows, closing prices, and average daily volume are also listed, along with major ownership, dividend information, and a three-year summary of sales, net income, and earnings per share. Users can search the entire database for recent articles, investment reports, and report excerpts on a company or industry. Information about several companies' data may be gathered by selecting items on an "Industry" or a "Line of Business" menu. Article searches can be done on companies or individuals. After selecting one of these menus, the user sees a search term list displayed in the options window, and then the user selects terms from this list. Each term selected lists the number of available abstracts and pages pertaining to the option selected. The relevant articles are then displayed on the screen.

All information on *Datext*'s CD-ROM discs can be edited, printed, transferred to a hard disk, or downloaded to a floppy disk. Limited word processing facilities are available within the system's software through four "Edit" function keys, which facilitate editing and transfer tasks. Financial information can be downloaded to popular spreadsheet programs or to word processing programs via the transfer function.

The documentation is clearly presented with voluminous examples in an excellently illustrated book. The "Help" screens explaining each function and menu contribute to a system that is very user-friendly. The search software is easy to understand and gives good results from the first time a user logs on to the system. The advantages accruing to end users from using this product lie in its blending six major online products into a custom-tailored system that uses one query language at a fixed price. A useful article describing librarians' reactions to this database appeared in *Online;* however, only a limited amount of space is given to describing end users' experiences with the database.[6]

END-USER RESPONSE

A good example of the integration of CD-ROM databases into library end-user services is a program at the University of Vermont Library.

The Automated Reference Center (ARC) at the University of Vermont was discussed in two sessions at the Optical Publishing '86 conference by the principal people who established it. ARC consists of the *SilverPlatter, ERIC,* and *PsycLit* databases on CD-ROM, along with *InfoTrac* on videodisc. End users in the ARC area also have access to online databases on *Wilsonline, Knowledge Index,* and *BRS After Dark* through several microcomputer workstations. The Automated Reference Center is monitored by student assistants who answer questions from users, and it is physically adjacent to the reference area of the library should more complex assistance be needed. No direct charges are assessed to users of the Center. Completion of a CAI tutorial or attendance at a training workshop is required before a user can search any of the services in the ARC. The student monitors take care of the housekeeping details needed to keep computers, CD-ROM players, printers, and other equipment in good working order. The center is staffed whenever the library is open and, according to the reports presented at the conference, is meeting the goals established by the library staff for non-mediated end-user searching. An important aspect of the service is that students are encouraged to practice online search techniques on the CD-ROM databases before performing a search with the "clock ticking" online.

Another form of laser disc-based service for end users is that used by the Library of Congress and other government agencies. The archival storage of document images being tested at the Library of Congress uses a completely different technology from videodisc and CD-ROM. With this technology, documents are entered into the system using a document scanner for hard copy and a microfiche scanner for microfilm material. Such scanning is done at 300 points of resolution per inch. The images are converted to digital format, in conjunction with other enhancements, to allow retrieval of the images at public terminals located throughout the Library. Library users search an index computer using the Library of Congress Information System (LOCIS) and retrieve full-text images of documents that have been stored on optical digital discs. Such discs are used in the office automation field and in the computer industry for mass storage. To date, no systems employing such devices have been demonstrated for general library use. The full-text images are copied by raster scanning devices (an electronic beam is turned on or off to produce light or no light) that yield a bit-mapped image (a digitized facsimile) of the material scanned. This image dissemination technology employs a code format differing from that used by the optical disc format of CD-ROM and videodisc. The technology also uses an optical storage and retrieval device known as the jukebox, which allows many optical discs to be stored and retrieved under computer control. The jukebox technique is being used extensively in office automation schemes and for computer-assisted engineering drawing applications. It will take some time, however, before systems integrators add this new technology to commercially available systems for other libraries.

SUMMARY

The interactive features of videodisc technology brought it to the attention of people in the areas of education, business training, and publishing, because flexible programs could be tailored to the needs of the end user. The gigantic storage capacity of videodiscs was noticed by librarians concerned with the increasing costs of storing and retrieving large amounts of information on paper and microforms. The random-access and still-framing capabilities of the drive and how it controls the disc are the keys upon which the publishing concept of laser-disc services is based. The vast amount of storage—up to one billion bytes on a one-sided disc—plus its interactive capability, make the videodisc a good alternative to other methods of access, storage, and preservation of library information. Publishers of large-scale database products such as *ERIC, PAIS, Compendex,* NTIS, *AV ONLINE,* etc., have information contained in their products that is particularly valuable to libraries. Such databases already have had much added-value placed on them just by the fact that they contain some organizing system to make them efficiently and effectively accessible to a variety of library users. The storage capacity on the optical videodisc (approximately one billion bytes) or even the smaller amount available on CD-ROM (approximately 550 million bytes) makes the economies of storing quinquennial or decennial cumulations of large indexes on these devices even more favorable for libraries. The mere fact that a CD-ROM disc weighs only .07 ounces should make any librarian concerned with delivery costs consider using the system very closely.

The major drawbacks to these attractive economies of delivery and storage lie in the embedding of such valuable informational databases in hardware and software that might not be accepted by users of present on-line services. Micropublishing and electronic publishing have met with user resistance because of hardware and software concerns. Such might be the case with optical publishing: after tremendous investment in hardware and software by publishers, librarians and end users may be interested only in the content of the database without requiring any special hardware or instructions on how to access it.

Another drawback is the fact that only one user can access CD-ROM at one time with the present operating systems available. However, this situation should be alleviated when systems are developed offering multi-user access. In fact, an Apple computer CD-ROM interface along with a controller board allowing up to four workstations to be attached to one CD-ROM drive is already available. A California school district is currently experimenting with using this configuration in conjunction with the *Academic American Encyclopedia* published by Grolier Electronic Publishing Company. This experiment of using CD-ROM in a multi-user mode will need different application software than that which is currently used, and, if successful, it will have a powerful impact on the use of CD-ROM in educational institutions and in libraries. It should be emphasized that the *Academic American Encyclopedia* on CD-ROM has textual information only. The display of illustrative material on CD-ROM will come with the development of Compact Disc-Interactive (CD-I). This type of media will use the constant angular velocity (CAV) format that the video-disc uses and will allow for multimedia adjacency on the CD-ROM disc. The field of optical publishing is so vast and has such great potential that predicting future products is problematical. Optical publishing via CD-ROM, videodisc, and optical digital discs has matured to the point where commercial products are available in the marketplace. Whether these will succeed commercially remains in the hands of the end users.

NOTES

1. Richard A. Bowers, *Optical/Electronic Publishing Directory* (Westport, Conn.: Meckler, 1986).

2. *CD-ROM Review,* a bimonthly, regularly features information about CD-ROM products.

3. Jean Reese and Ramona Steffey, "ERIC on CDROM: A Comparison of Dialog On-Disc, OCLC's Search 450 and SilverPlatter," *Online* 11 (Sept. 1987): 42–54.

4. Laserdisk Directory Parts 1, 2, 3 and 4 published sequentially in four parts in *Database* (June 1986); *Online* (July 1986); *Database* (Aug. 1986); *Online* (Sept. 1986).

5. *Information Today* 3 (June 1986): 25.

6. James Fries and Jonathon Brown, "Datext—Using Business Information on CD-ROM," *Online* 10 (Sept. 1986): 69–73.

BIBLIOGRAPHY

Allen, Robert J. "The CD-ROM Services of SilverPlatter Information, Inc." *Library Hi Tech* 3 (1985): 49–60.

CD ROM, the New Papyrus: The Current and Future State of the Art. Edited by Steve Lambert and Suzanne Ropiequet. Redmond, Wash.: Microsoft, 1986.

Connolly, Bruce, "Looking Backward—CDROM and the Academic Library of the Future." *Online* 11 (May 1987): 56+.

Helgerson, Linda W. "CD-ROM: A Revolution in the Making." *Library Hi Tech* 4 (Spring 1986): 23+.

Herther, Nancy K. "CD-ROM and Information Dissemination: An Update." *Online* 11 (Mar. 1987): 56–64.

Kesselman, Martin. "Online Update (Laser Technology)." *Wilson Library Bulletin* 60 (Dec. 1985): 40+.

———. "Online Update (Optical Publishing Conference)." *Wilson Library Bulletin* 61 (Feb. 1987): 38+.

Miller, David C. "Running with CD-ROM." *American Libraries* 17 (Nov. 1986): 754–56.

Murphy, B. "CD-ROM and Libraries." *Library Hi Tech* 3 (1985): 21–26.

Nelson, Nancy Melin. *Library Applications of Optical Disk and CD-ROM Technology.* Essential Guide to the Library IBM PC, v. 8. Westport, Conn.; Meckler, 1987.

Peters, C. M. "CD-ROM: Its Potential in Libraries." In *National Online Meeting Proceedings—1986,* comp. by Martha E. Williams and Thomas H. Hogan. Medford, N.J.: Learned Information, 1986.

_____. "Databases on CD-ROM: Comparative Factors for Purchase." *The Electronic Library* 5 (June 1987): 154–60.

Saffady, William. *Optical Storage Technology, 1987: A State of the Art Review.* Westport, Conn.: Meckler, 1987.

Tenopir, Carol. "CD-ROM Database Update." *Library Journal* 111 (Dec. 1986): 70 + .

Annotated Bibliography

Sally Lyon

During the past few years, much has been published in library litera-ture about end-user searching. This chapter is a selective annotated bibli-ography of journal articles and conference papers published since the summer of 1984, a period of substantial growth and change in online sys-tems. For earlier coverage, check "End User Searching of Online Data-bases: A Selective Annotated Bibliography," in the fall 1984 issue of *Library Hi Tech.*

Designed to serve as an overview to the literature on end-user search-ing, this bibliography does not attempt to cover all the available litera-ture. Criteria for selection were based on content and coverage in order to include a variety of end-user systems and services in a number of differ-ent types of libraries. The references cited here are not all found in the other chapters of this book, so you may want to check them for further citations.

Citations are listed alphabetically by primary author. Descriptors for major emphasis are listed after each annotation. If applicable, descrip-tors for online services and products and type of library ("PL" for pub-lic, "AL" for academic, "SchL" for school and "SL" for special) are also noted. Following the entries is a combined subject/online service/library index. Introductory articles dealing with rationale and planning for end-user searching as well as end user versus intermediary searching are in-dexed as "Background."

Allen, Robert J. "The CD-ROM Services of SilverPlatter Information, Inc." *Li-brary Hi Tech* 3 (1985): 49-60.

    CD-ROM database systems, like those produced by SilverPlatter place con-siderable searching power in the hands of end users by providing simple access, economic benefit of unlimited usage of the information, a fixed yearly subscription price, and no online connect charges. This article provides a system overview with illustrated examples, and descriptions of the equipment needed. *OPTICAL DISCS *SILVERPLATTER

Anderson, Verl A. "Simultaneous Remote Searching: An Aid to the End User." In *National Online Meeting Proceedings—1987*, comp. by Martha E. Williams and Thomas H. Hogan, 5-8. Medford, N.J.: Learned Information, 1987.

This paper describes the implementation of an online reference service by the Eastern Oregon State College Library through the utilization of a new technology called Simultaneous Remote Searching (SRS). SRS enables the end user to communicate with a "user friendly person," the librarian, who acts as an interface agent between the end user and the literature search by simultaneously transmitting the information from the searching computer terminal to a second terminal at a remote location via telephone lines. Anderson points out that equipment costs less than $200. *TRAINING *AL

Arnold, Steve. "End Users: Old Myths and New Realities." In *National Online Meeting Proceedings—1986*, comp. by Martha E. Williams and Thomas H. Hogan 5-10. Medford, N.J.: Learned Information, 1986.

Arnold describes 15 myths surrounding end users such as: they are buying microcomputers in record numbers, and will not require training to become online searchers. He compares these to the reality that the microcomputer market is soft because end users cannot use microcomputers easily and online resources efficiently. *BACKGROUND * TRAINING

Association of Research Libraries. Office of Management Studies Systems and Procedures Exchange Center. *End-User Searching Services.* Kit 122. Washington D.C.: ARL, 1986.

This kit contains the results of a survey on end-user services in major research libraries, one grant proposal, five program descriptions, four examples of publicity, nine sets of instructional aids and reference tools, six evaluations/questionnaires, and a selective bibliography. *BIBLIOGRAPHY *BACKGROUND *MANAGEMENT *TRAINING *AL

Baker, Carole A. "Colleague: A Comprehensive Online Medical Library for the End User." *Medical Reference Services Quarterly* 3 (Winter 1984): 13-26.

Baker describes *Colleague,* an online service developed for use by end-user health professionals, from BRS/Saunders. She includes specific search examples and highlights special *Colleague* features. *Colleague* is compared with both *BRS After Dark* and the regular *BRS* search system. Future directions for *Colleague* and the role of the librarian in end-user searching are also discussed. *SCIENCE & HEALTH *BRS MEDICAL COLLEAGUE

Batista, Emily J., and Deborah A. Einhorn. "Putting on a Show: Using Computer Graphics to Train End-Users." *Online* 11 (May 1987): 88-92.

The authors describe how several libraries at the University of Pennsylvania developed end-user training modules using a video projector, an IBM PC, and PC *Storyboard,* a graphics software package. *TRAINING *AL

Beltran, Ann Bristow. "InfoTrac at Indiana University: A Second Look." *Database* 10 (Feb. 1987): 48-50.

A positive reevaluation of *InfoTrac* was made by the members of the reference department at Indiana University. After a year of experience, they concluded that *InfoTrac* had the potential to extend some of the benefits of computer-assisted searching to large numbers of students without placing a crippling burden on the library staff. *INFOTRAC *AL

Branden, Shirley, and Jeffrey M. Wehmeyer. "Do-it-Yourself Computer Searching: Launching an Educational Program for the End User Searcher." *Medical Reference Services Quarterly* 4 (Summer 1985): 11–14.

The authors, librarians at the University of Florida Health Center, describe the objectives and content of an initial presentation on do-it-yourself online searching they developed and the role librarians need to take in the education of end users. *TRAINING *AL

Broering, Naomi C. "The MiniMedline System: A Library-Based End-User Search System." *Bulletin of the Medical Library Association* 73 (Apr. 1985): 138–45.

The design of *MiniMedline*, a subset of the National Library of Medicine's *Medline* file, developed as an in-house search system by Georgetown University Medical Center, is discussed. *MiniMedline* provides user-friendly access to articles indexed in over 160 medical journals from 1982 to the present. *SCIENCE & HEALTH *MINIMEDLINE

Buckingham, Sarah. "Choosing an End-User On Line Searching System." *Education Libraries* 10 (1985): 41–44.

Buckingham describes the criteria to consider before choosing an end-user search service for an academic education library including ease of use, flexibility, administrative ease, security, and compatibility with equipment. The systems evaluated are divided into the following headings: software, gateways, user-friendly vendors, and straight vendors. The article includes a directory of producers of systems mentioned in the article. *BACKGROUND *AL

Caputo, Anne G. "Online Goes to School: Instruction and Use of Online Systems in Secondary and Elementary Education." In *National Online Meeting Proceedings—1985,* comp. by Martha E. Williams and Thomas H. Hogan, 85–90. Medford, N.J.: Learned Information, 1985.

A project between DIALOG and a suburban Philadelphia school district to offer online services to high school students is described here. The issues that surface when a much neglected end-user population is targeted are explored, as well as the benefits of creating a future population of "online literate" adults. Caputo found that students' research skills and use of sophisticated research materials increased and that the status of the school librarian was enhanced by library-classroom cooperation during the project. Caputo suggests that a gateway product for the school audience would present an attractive opportunity for a vendor. Since this article was published, DIALOG has set up such a school-based service known as *Classmate.* *TRAINING *CLASSMATE *SchL

Crofts, Jayne M. "Reaching the End User: The Education and Training Program at the William H. Welch Medical Library." *Medical Reference Services Quarterly* 4 (Winter 1985/1986): 77–82.

The end-user program at Welch Medical Library, Johns Hopkins University, is described. It consists of four sessions where *BRS After Dark* and

Knowledge Index are introduced, and the mysteries of database structure and language are covered along with an opportunity for hands-on experience. The library staff found that the demands for help by end users conflicted with the reference desk schedule and it became necessary to schedule appointments. The author also describes a two-part training process, where more sophisticated skills are taught to experienced end users. *MANAGEMENT *TRAINING *BRS AFTER DARK *KNOWLEDGE INDEX *AL

Crooks, James E. "End User Searching at the University of Michigan Library." In *National Online Meeting Proceedings—1985,* comp. by Martha E. Williams and Thomas H. Hogan, 99–110. Medford, N.J.: Learned Information, 1985.

Crooks describes the end-user searching on *BRS After Dark* offered to faculty, staff, and students at the University of Michigan at no cost during the fall of 1984. Most users were given little instruction and reference librarians were not assigned to assist users during sessions. However, user aids were made available. The paper includes the questionnaire given to users and examples of log and appointment books. *MANAGEMENT *BRS AFTER DARK *AL

Des Chene, Dorice. "Online Searching by End Users." *RQ* 25 (Fall 1985): 89–95.

With the advent of personal ownership of microcomputers and the introduction of numerous gateway systems since the early 1980s, the author sees librarians emerging as consultants or instructors for users who wish to install and use online services on their own equipment. The decision libraries must face about whether to provide end-user services or not is covered along with a bibliography of 123 references. *BIBLIOGRAPHY *BACKGROUND

Dess, Howard M., and Leny Struminger. "End User Searching vs. Intermediary Searching in CAS Online—Is the Answer in the Question?" In *National Online Meeting Proceedings—1987,* comp. by Martha E. Williams and Thomas H. Hogan, 105–10. Medford, N.J.: Learned Information, 1987.

This paper covers the potential of an end-user training program at Rutgers University's Library of Science and Medicine for *CAS ONLINE (Chemical Abstracts Service Online* database). *CAS ONLINE* offers a 90 percent discount to academic institutions evenings and weekends. By studying the type of questions users requested, the authors were able to determine that an end-user online service was needed. *CAS ONLINE *SCIENCE & HEALTH *AL

Dodd, Jane. *Texas A&M University Library. A Final Report from the Public Service Research Projects. A Comparison of Two End User Operated Search Systems.* Washington, DC: Assn. of Research Libraries, 1985. ERIC ED 255 224.

The impact that end-user online information systems have on library staff and users is covered in this report summarizing a study undertaken at Texas A&M University where *BRS After Dark* and *Search Helper* were made available for end-user searching at no cost. Although most users could successfully search both systems with little instruction, it was determined that library staff was needed for the administration of the service. Included are search planners and flip charts for each of the systems, end-user and staff questionnaires, a publicity piece, and the follow-up study questionnaire. *MANAGEMENT *BRS AFTER DARK *SEARCH HELPER *AL

Elmore, Barbara. "End-User Searching in a Public Library." In *Online '85 Conference Proceedings,* 98–101. Weston, Conn.: Online, Inc., 1985.

An end-user search system at Waukegan Public Library is described, including the rationale for choosing *Search Helper.* After a test run where patrons performed their own searches on *Search Helper,* it was decided it would be more efficient for the library staff to do the searching for the public. *FRONT-ENDS *SEARCH HELPER *PL

Ernest, Douglas J., and Jennifer Monath. "User Reaction to a Computerized Periodical Index." *College and Research Libraries News* 47 (May 1986): 315–18.

In the fall of 1985, Colorado State University became a test site for *InfoTrac.* The authors point out that even though most end users are able to use *InfoTrac* without asking for assistance because it is easy to use and "help screens" provide valuable information for using the system, end users should be made aware of its limitations in order to more efficiently utilize the system. *OPTICAL DISCS *INFOTRAC *AL

Evans, Nancy, and Henry Pisciotta. "Search Helper: Testing Acceptance of a Gateway Software System." In *National Online Meeting Proceedings—1985,* comp. by Martha E. Williams and Thomas H. Hogan, 131–36. Medford N.J.: Learned Information, 1985.

This paper reviews a study conducted at Hunt Library, Carnegie Mellon University, on the use of *Search Helper* by end users without assistance other than a brief explanation about the user manual by librarians. The study found that students, as they were already operating in a computer intensive environment, were very receptive to *Search Helper.* User satisfaction was quite high, and the authors concluded that end users were pleased with online instructions as opposed to written manuals or intermediaries. *FRONT-ENDS *TRAINING *SEARCH HELPER *AL

Fenichel, Carol Hansen. "Online Communications Publications for End-Users." *Online* 9 (May 1985): 129–32.

Fenichel provides a useful list of practical online publications to help end users search databases, access bulletin boards and electronic mail and hold teleconferences. The list is organized by publication type (books, directories, newsletters, journals) and further subdivided by subject. *BIBLIOGRAPHY

Fogel, Laurence D., and Claire F. Zigmund. "End Users vs. Intermediary: A Personal Perspective." In *National Online Meeting Proceedings—1985,* comp. by Martha E. Williams and Thomas H. Hogan, 153–59. Medford, N.J.: Learned Information, 1985.

The authors describe the circumstances that arose when an experienced end user took on the responsibility of training others to perform searches in an organization with intermediary searchers. The difficulties and ultimate success and benefits of the working relationship that developed between the trainer and intermediaries are covered. *TRAINING

Friend, Linda. "Identifying and Informing the Potential End-User: Online Information Seminars." *Online* 10 (Jan. 1986): 47–56.

End-user seminars developed and taught at Pennsylvania State University on *BRS After Dark* and *Knowledge Index* are described and evaluated. The article includes examples of forms used for registration, and pre-session and post-session questionnaires. *TRAINING *BRS AFTER DARK *KNOWL-EDGE INDEX *AL

Fries, James, and Jonathan R. Brown. "Datext—Using Business Information on CDROM." *Online* 10 (Sept. 1986): 28–40.

The authors discuss *Datext,* one of the first CD-ROM products designed for end users, and its use in an academic business library. They compare *Datext* with commercial online database services for current business information and search costs. Also covered are the issues libraries face when considering the purchase of *Datext.* *BUSINESS & MISC. *OPTICAL DISCS *DATEXT *AL

Graves, Gail T., Laura G. Harper, and Beth F. King. "Planning for CD-ROM in the Reference Department." *College and Research Libraries News* 48 (July/August 1987): 393–400.

Three librarians at the University of Mississippi tell how they selected CD-ROM databases and hardware to meet their reference department's needs. Included are information on vendors and pricing for various CD-ROM databases and services such as *ERIC, PsycLit, Dissertation Abstracts, Compact Disclosure, Datext, Wilsondisc,* and *InfoTrac.* The authors also discuss the selection of microcomputers, printers, CD-ROM drives, and safety and security devices. *MANAGEMENT *OPTICAL DISCS *AL

Grivens, Mary King, and W. Ellen McDonell. "End User Instructions for Searching Medlars." *Medical Reference Services Quarterly* 4 (Summer 1985): 63–67.

The University of Tennessee Center for the Health Sciences was awarded a grant to develop a program for end-user access to the National Library of Medicine's databases. This article describes the training their library staff set up for potential end users, interested medical faculty, staff, and students and the preparation of a mini-manual for distribution to participants. The authors suggest that if the end-user program is to continue, an expanded staff is necessary, since assistance was requested by most patrons. *SCIENCE & HEALTH *TRAINING *MEDLARS *AL

Hall, Cynthia, Harriet Talan, and Barbara Pease. "InfoTrac in Academic Libraries: What's Missing in the New Technology?" *Database* 10 (Feb. 1987): 53–56.

The authors share their reservations about *InfoTrac* as a research tool in academic libraries and question whether *InfoTrac* can be used without assistance from librarians. *INFOTRAC *AL

Halperin, Michael, and Ruth A. Pagell. "Free Do-it-Yourself Online Searching . . . What to Expect." *Online* 9 (Mar. 1985): 82–84.

A free self-service search service for students on two menu-driven systems including *BRS After Dark,* at the Lippincott Library of the Wharton School, University of Pennsylvania, is described. The authors found, however, that staffing was needed to monitor and assist students with logon and search strategies and other problems that arose. When surveyed, students stated that the service was easy to use, and if charged a modest fee, were willing to pay. *MANAGEMENT *BRS AFTER DARK *AL

Hawkins, Donald T., and Louise R. Levy. "Front End Software for Online Database Searching. Part 1: Definitions, Systems Features, and Evaluation." *Online* 9 (Nov. 1985): 30–37. "Part 2: The Marketplace" *Online* 10 (Jan. 1986):

33–40. "Part 3: Product Selection Chart and Bibliography." *Online* 10 (May 1986): 49–58.

Part 1 defines terms used for describing front-end systems, covers the features of front-ends and gateways, and criteria for evaluating them. In Part 2, the authors point out that since the present market of professional search intermediaries is close to saturation, online database producers and retrieval services are looking for new markets, and are currently trying to reach end users with front-end software. Part 3 contains a detailed product selection chart that compares 12 gateway and front-end packages suitable for end-user searching. An extensive bibliography is included. *BIBLIOGRAPHY *FRONT-ENDS

Herther, Nancy K. "CD ROM Technology: A New Era for Information Storage and Retrieval?" *Online* 9 (Nov. 1985): 17–28.

This article on optical disc technology and its applications for information storage and retrieval covers history, background and development, technical features, standardization issues, current applications, and the market for CD-ROM products. Included with the article are a list of manufacturers and disc replicators, a performance comparison of storage media, a list of important factors to look for in the selection of CD-ROM technology for original applications, and a substantial bibliography. *BIBLIOGRAPHY *OPTICAL DISCS

Homan, Michael J. "End-User Information Utilities in the Health Sciences." *Bulletin of the Medical Library Association* 74 (Jan. 1986): 31–35.

MINET (Medical Information Network) is examined in depth, along with several other end-user electronic information utilities and full-text databases in the health sciences. Information on the sponsor or producer and online access, as well as a description of each service covered, is included. *SCIENCE & HEALTH *MINET

Hubbard, Abigail, and Barbara Wilson. "An Integrated Information Management Education Program. . . Defining a New Role for Librarians in Helping End Users." *Online* 10 (Mar. 1986): 15–23.

Hubbard and Wilson outline the comprehensive information management education program developed at the Houston Academy of Medicine that teaches the technology, skills, and decision-making processes necessary for independent information retrieval and management. An appendix lists seminars given with a short description of what each covers. *BACKGROUND *TRAINING *SL

Hutchins, Geraldine, Vicki Anders, and Joe Jaros. "End User Perceptions on Teaching Methods." In *National Online Meeting Proceedings—1987,* comp. by Martha E. Williams and Thomas H. Hogan, 183–90. Medford, N.J.: Learned Information, 1987.

The authors describe a survey conducted at the Texas A&M Library to evaluate three instructional programs: a slide/tape, a user's manual, and a computer-assisted instruction (CAI) program that were developed to introduce first-time users to *BRS After Dark*. On the basis of a questionnaire taken to determine the most effective instructional programs, the user manual was chosen as the preferred method of instruction. *BRS AFTER DARK *TRAINING *AL

Ifshin, Steven L., and Deborah M. Hull. "CAI Plus: A Strategy for Colleague

Training." In *National Online Meeting Proceedings—1985,* comp. by Martha E. Williams and Thomas H. Hogan, 233-40. Medford, N.J.: Learned Information, 1985.

Colleague, developed by BRS and Saunders Publishing, is an online service for physicians and other health professionals covering bibliographic and full-text biomedical databases. This paper covers the training strategy, a unified approach to the implementation of instructional materials in three training modes: computer-assisted instruction (CAI), workbook, and lecture. *SCIENCE & HEALTH *TRAINING *BRS MEDICAL COLLEAGUE

(a) Janke, Richard V. "Client Searchers and Intermediaries: The New Online Partnership." In *Online '85 Conference Proceedings,* 165-71. Weston, Conn.: Online, Inc., 1985.

Janke addresses the questions of the end user, and how the information professional as intermediary can continue to enhance professional status in an educational or counseling role. Janke also discusses various methods of educating end-user searchers. *BACKGROUND *TRAINING

(b) Janke, Richard V. "Online After Six: End User Searching Comes of Age." *Online* 8 (Nov. 1984): 15-29.

The end-user online searching program utilizing *BRS After Dark* at the University of Ottawa Libraries is discussed. Janke compares online searching by end users and trained intermediaries and discusses the implications of end-user searching in libraries. The article includes the questionnaire used to survey the end user's evaluation of the service, an extensive bibliography, and tips for libraries considering an end-user service. *BIBLIOGRAPHY *BRS AFTER DARK *BACKGROUND *AL

(c) Janke, Richard V. "Presearch Counseling for Client Searchers (End Users)." *Online* 9 (Sept. 1985): 13-26.

The similarities and differences of the traditional online interview when an intermediary performs the search are compared with the presearch counseling session a librarian provides to a client searcher. A model of steps follow in presearch counseling and an online self-service worksheet are included. *TRAINING

Jaros, Joe, Vicki Anders, and Geri Hutchins. "Subsidized End User Searching in an Academic Library." In *National Online Meeting Proceedings—1986,* comp. by Martha E. Williams and Thomas H. Hogan, 223-29. Medford, N.J.: Learned Information, 1986.

Texas A & M University Library's experience of developing and running a fully subsidized end-user search service can serve as a model for libraries considering similar services. The authors point out the problems that can befall such a service; escalating demands, unexpected costs, and the effects of cuts in funding. The use of laser technology and outside funding are two changes the authors see in the future of subsidized end-user searching. *MANAGEMENT *AL

(a) Kesselman, Martin, and Irene Perry Iwan. "Database Indexes and the End-User." In *Proceedings of the International Online Information Meeting, 8th,* 283-88. Oxford: Learned Information, 1984.

This paper reviews several online systems and database indexes, discusses the problems end users may encounter with database vocabulary, and highlights features that are of particular benefit to end users. The authors see new technological developments such as vocabulary switching systems, artificial intelligence, and front-ends as having potential for improving end-user access to database indexes. *BACKGROUND

(b) Kesselman, Martin. "Front-End/Gateway Software: Availability and Usefulness." *Library Software Review* 4 (Mar.–Apr. 1985): 67–70.

Kesselman covers several front-end software packages that offer the user aid in choosing a database and setting up a search strategy. He points out that the following considerations should be made before purchasing a package: hardware and software requirements; database costs and special features; training and documentation availability. Addresses of front-end and gateway services are included. *FRONT-ENDS

(c) Kesselman, Martin. "Online Update." *Wilson Library Bulletin* 61 (June 1987): 53–54.

DIALOG's *Classmate* service (based on *Knowledge Index*) and Addison Wesley's *Einstein* gateway service (based on *Easynet*) are compared as to ease of use, availability of classroom teaching materials, and costs. Rationales for introducing online searching to high school students are included as well. *CLASSMATE *EINSTEIN *SchL

Killion, Vicki J., et al. "Training the End User in an Academic Medical Library." In *National Online Meeting Proceedings—1987*, comp. by Martha E. Williams and Thomas H. Hogan, 229–36. Medford, N.J.: Learned Information, 1987.

Three end-user services and training programs available at the Health Sciences Library, University of Cincinnati, are discussed including *BRS Colleague, Medis*, and *Medical Information Quick (MIQ)*. *MIQ* is a prototype of an end-user search service developed as a component of the National Library of Medicine's Integratred Academic Information Management Systems (IAIMS). *BRS MEDICAL COLLEAGUE *MEDIS *SCIENCE & HEALTH *TRAINING *AL

King, Joseph, and Peter Brueggeman. "Frontends, Gateways, User-Friendly Systems, or Whatever You Want to Call Them." *Database End User* 2 (June 1986): 17–21.

The authors describe the variety of user-friendly database searching products available today and advise what to look for when considering their purchase. A detailed "Matrix of Front End Software, Gateways, and User-Friendly Systems" is included. *FRONT-ENDS

Kirby, Martha, and Naomi Miller. "Medline Searching on BRS Colleague: Search Success of Untrained End Users in a Medical School and Hospital." In *National Online Meeting Proceedings—1985*, comp. by Martha E. Williams and Thomas H. Hogan, 255–63. Medford, N.J.: Learned Information, 1985.

The subject of this paper is a study conducted at the Medical College of Pennsylvania, in which faculty and staff were asked to compare the results of their own search on *Colleague* with the results of a follow-up search on the same subject performed by a search analyst on the regular MEDLARS or *BRS* search system. *SCIENCE & HEALTH *BRS MEDICAL COLLEAGUE *SL

Klausmeier, Jane A. "Microcomputer Based System for End User Training." In *National Online Meeting Proceedings—1985*, comp. by Martha E. Williams and Thomas H. Hogan, 265–71. Medford, N.J.: Learned Information, 1985.

Klausmeier reports on the results of a user survey conducted on *MICRO-*

search, a subset of the *ERIC* database on floppy disk. The program teaches the concepts of online searching and serves as a current awareness tool in the areas of library and information science and educational technology. Included is information on using the *MICROsearch* program and discussions on its usefulness and shortcomings. *MICROSEARCH *TRAINING *AL

Kleiner, Jane P. "User Searching: A Public Access Approach to Search Helper." *RQ* 24 (Summer 1985): 442–51.

Search Helper is presented here in the context of public access at Louisiana State University. In spite of a bad beginning due to software problems, the outcome of LSU's use study concluded that patrons were satisfied with their search results, and the system's lack of sophistication made it more suitable for public access than library staff use, contrary to the findings of several other library studies. *FRONT-ENDS *SEARCH HELPER *AL

Kosmin, Linda. "Economic Pitfalls of Hi-Tech End-User Searching." In *National Online Meeting Proceedings—1986,* comp. by Martha E. Williams and Thomas H. Hogan, 257–62. Medford, N.J.: Learned Information, 1986.

This paper alerts librarians and other information professionals to the economic consequences of starting an end-user service. The author points out that the decision to decentralize searching by putting it in the hands of the end user should be based on cost, performance, and benefits and not personal judgment. *BACKGROUND *MANAGEMENT

LaBorie, Tim, and Leslie Donnelly. "Vending Database Searching with Public Access Terminals." *Library Hi Tech* 4 (Summer 1986): 7–10.

The authors describe the planning, management, and results of a self-service end-user program developed at Drexel University. *BRS After Dark* was selected as the vendor and a "BRS Search Simulator" was developed to train faculty and students to perform their own searches. Compuvend equipment was installed to provide automatic logon with password security, and collection of fees. *MANAGEMENT *TRAINING *BRS AFTER DARK *AL

Lyon, Sally. "End-User Searching of Online Databases: A Selective Annotated Bibliography." *Library Hi Tech* 2 (1984): 47–50.

Lyon's annotated bibliography covers articles and conference papers from 1981 to 1984, on end-user searching on online databases. For ease of use the bibliography is divided into three sections: "End User Search Services and Systems," "End User vs. the Intermediary," and "Training the End User." *BIBLIOGRAPHY

Mount, Ellis, ed. *Serving End-Users in Sci-Tech Libraries.* New York: Haworth Pr., 1984. Also published as *Science and Technology Libraries* 5 (1) (1984).

Six articles addressing the problems of end users of online databases in the sci-tech library are offered here. The most worthwhile sections cover database development and end-user searching, teaching university student end users about online searching, and managing effective information services for end users. *MANAGEMENT *SCIENCE & HEALTH *TRAINING *AL

Murr, Kenneth R. "Training the End User's Helper." In *National Online Meeting Proceedings—1987,* comp. by Martha E. Williams and Thomas H. Hogan, 361–65. Medford, N.J.: Learned Information, 1987.

Murr covers the necessary elements to create a successful end-user searching program such as the active cooperation of everyone involved, the proper choice of equipment and software, a comprehensive training program for staff members, and a detailed search manual. *BACKGROUND *TRAINING

Norris, Carol Brooks. "End-Users and Online Searching: Implications for Intermediaries, a Selected Annotated Bibliography." In *Library Hi Tech Bibliography,* v. 2, 49–60. Ann Arbor, Mich.: Pierian, 1987.

This bibliography attempts to answer what the implications of end-user searching are for librarians and information specialists. Library and information science literature from 1984 to 1986 is covered and is divided into four sections by library type—general, academic, business, and medical. *BIBLIOGRAPHY

Ojala, Marydee. "Views on End-User Searching." *Journal of the American Society for Information Science* 37 (July 1986): 197–203.

During the past 10 years online searching has moved from libraries into homes and offices. Ojala poses and answers the following questions: what are end-user searchers, who are end-user searchers, where are end-user searchers, how did end-user searching get started in the first place, why end users are searching, and when will everyone be searching? *BACKGROUND

(a) O'Leary, Mick. "CompuServe and the Source: Databanks for the End User." *Database* 8 (June 1985): 100–106.

O'Leary reviews and compares *The Source* and *CompuServe,* end-user online services for the home consumer that offer information and electronic mail services. *CONSUMER INFORMATION *COMPUSERVE *SOURCE

(b) O'Leary, Mick. "Dialog Business Connection: Dialog for the End User." *Online* 10 (Sept. 1986): 15–24.

O'Leary reviews the *DIALOG Business Connection (DBC),* a user-friendly, menu-driven interface to 24 key DIALOG business databases. *DBC* is compared to *Easynet,* a menu-driven gateway to *DIALOG* and several other online services. A list of databases searched by *DBC* and a sample search with screen displays are included. *BUSINESS & MISC. *DIALOG BUSINESS CONNECTION *EASYNET

(c) O'Leary, Mick. "Easynet: Doing It All for the End-User." *Online* 9 (July 1985): 106–13.

O'Leary describes *Easynet,* a menu-driven gateway service to *DIALOG, BRS, SDC, NewsNet,* and several other services. The article also includes a list of databases available through *Easynet,* examples of menu structures, and help screens. *FRONT-ENDS *EASYNET

Ostrum, G. Kenneth, and Diane K. Yoder. "Training in CAS Online for End Users." In *National Online Meeting Proceedings—1985,* comp. by Martha E. Williams and Thomas H. Hogan, 343–49. Medford, N.J.: Learned Information, 1985.

In order to meet the increasing demand for online training of end users of chemical information, the Chemical Abstracts Service developed a workshop aimed at helping end users with the *CA* file. This paper also discusses the effectiveness of the workshop in changing the information-seeking habits and practices of end users. *SCIENCE & HEALTH *TRAINING *CAS ONLINE

Peart, Peter A. "Online Retrieval: Intermediaries vs. End User." In *National Online Meeting Proceedings—1985,* comp. by Martha E. Williams and Thomas H. Hogan, 357–63. Medford, N.J.: Learned Information, 1985.

Peart presents his thesis that although online systems are increasingly user-friendly, an experienced intermediary will produce better results than an end user working alone, and keep down online costs and time. He also examines the role of the intermediary, and user-friendly systems and their impact on the intermediary and end user. *BACKGROUND

Peicschl, Thomas M., and Marilyn Montgomery. "Back to the Warehouse or Some Implications on End User Searching in Libraries." In *National Online Meeting Proceedings—1986*, comp. by Martha E. Williams and Thomas H. Hogan, 347–52. Medford, N.J.: Learned Information, 1986.

The authors address the impact that end users are making on the academic library, especially on collection management, resource allocation, staffing, and organizational structure. The potential impact that new online technologies could have on libraries is also discussed. *BACKGROUND *AL

Penhale, Sara J., and Nancy Taylor. "Integrating End-User Searching into a Bibliographic Instruction Program." *RQ* 27 (Winter 1986): 212–20.

Earlham College librarians successfully integrated online instruction into their existing instructional program. The authors cover the study they conducted in order to set up an effective instruction program that involved a comparison of manual searching methods with free online searching of *BRS After Dark* by novice student end users. *BRS AFTER DARK *TRAINING *AL

"Planting the Seed...Online in the Schools." *Online* 11 (May 1987): 15–36.

This compilation of brief articles and a selected bibliography cover online services and their educational use in elementary and secondary schools. BRS, DIALOG, and Dow Jones are online services that are discussed as to their special offerings to school programs. *BACKGROUND *BRS INSTRUCTOR *CLASSMATE *DOW JONES *TRAINING *SchL

(a) Quint, Barbara. "Format Searching...A Technique That Helps New End User Searchers Cover Huge Databases with Simplified Search Strategies." *Online* 9 (May 1985): 123–28.

A technique called searching on format, often used by professional searchers to get started tracking down information regardless of topic, is described here. Searches on format rather than subject can be made from books, dissertations, journals, magazines, reports, special databases, and full-text databases. Includes a list of major files, search services, and producers by category. *TRAINING

(b) Quint, Barbara. "Menlo Corporation's Pro-Search: Review of a Software Search Aid." *Online* 10 (Jan. 1986): 17–25.

Quint gives a positive evaluation of *ProSearch. ProSearch* is a front-end software package that simplifies telecommunications, allows cross-emulation of DIALOG and BRS search protocols, suggests alternative databases from these two services, allows other services to be searched, and maintains detailed accounting records for BRS and DIALOG search sessions. Examples of search screens are included. *FRONT-ENDS *PROSEARCH

Rainey, Nancy B., and Vareen M. Albert. "Easynet: An Undergraduate Experience." *Medical Reference Services Quarterly* 6 (Spring 1987): 41–58.

The authors, librarians at the Philadelphia College of Pharmacy and Science, evaluate the usefulness of *Easynet,* a menu-driven gateway system, for undergraduates. Student problems and their possible solutions are discussed. An appendix includes a list of vendors available on *Easynet,* sample search screens, and evaluation forms given to the students. *EASYNET *SCIENCE & HEALTH *AL

Regazzi, John. "Wilsearch: Software for Direct Patron Access to Wilsonline." In *Online '85 Conference Proceedings,* 258–63. Weston, Conn.: Online, Inc., 1985.

Wilsearch, the front-end software package designed to simplify the process of searching *Wilsonline,* is reviewed. The paper also lists the databases covered, gives a sample of the search screens, and describes each element through which a search can be made. *FRONT-ENDS *WILSEARCH

Santosuosso, Joe. "Requirements for Gateway Software for Librarians." In *National Online Meeting Proceedings—1986,* comp. by Martha E. Williams and Thomas H. Hogan, 409–13. Medford, N.J.: Learned Information, 1986.

Santosuosso suggests that gateway software developers provide support for multiple communications protocols; support for a flexible auto-dial function; an accounting structure that can break down costs into library and patron components; a reporting structure that provides library management with detailed information about the use of software; and low software costs. Also a higher level of knowledge, need, and acceptance of online technology by libraries are essential. *FRONT-ENDS

Slingluff, Deborah, Yvonne Lev, and Andrew Eisan. "An End User Search Service in an Academic Health Library." *Medical Reference Services Quarterly* 4 (Spring 1985): 11–21.

The experiences of the Health Science Library at the University of Maryland at Baltimore with *BRS After Dark* are described. An evaluation over a three-month period showed that user satisfaction was quite high, but it was observed that end users had more difficulty in constructing appropriate strategies than had been anticipated. *MANAGEMENT *BRS AFTER DARK *AL

Snow, Bonnie. "Self-Help Aids for End Users." In *National Online Meeting Proceedings—1986,* comp. by Martha E. Williams and Thomas H. Hogan, 427–31. Medford, N.J.: Learned Information, 1986.

Snow examines the need for customizing training materials and documentation for end users. She also gives examples of interfacing documentation, and discusses the desirable attributes to consider in developing end-user instructional materials. *TRAINING

Steffen, Susan Swords. "College Faculty Goes Online: Training Faculty End Users." *Journal of Academic Librarianship* 12 (July 1986): 147–51.

A training program that developed at the library of a small liberal arts college, that had few computer resources and a low level of computer literacy among its faculty before the training began, is described. The author states that the advantages of the program were greater than the problems that arose since the library's image was greatly improved, requests for bibliographic instruction increased, and librarians took on the new role of teacher and consultant. *TRAINING *AL

Tenopir, Carol. "Four Options for End User Searching." *Library Journal* 111 (July 1986): 56–57.

Tenopir covers the options available for libraries that want to offer end-user searching; end-user search systems, front-end software, gateway services, database subsets on floppy diskettes or optical discs. The advantages and disadvantages of each option are reviewed. *BACKGROUND *FRONT-ENDS *OPTICAL DISCS

Wilbur, H. L. "The Orbit Searchmaster System: A Search Management Tool." In *Downloading/Uploading Online Databases and Catalogs. Proceedings of the Congress of Librarians, February 1985, St. John's University,* 22–24. Ann Arbor, Mich.: Pierian, 1985.

Wilbur reviews *Searchmaster,* a menu-driven front-end software package developed by SDC. *Searchmaster,* through the use of scripts, facilitates logon, search formulation, search execution, retrieval and post-search processing of searches in SDC, DIALOG, BRS, and NLM. *FRONT-ENDS *SEARCH-MASTER

Williams, Martha. "Transparent Information Systems through Gateways, Front Ends, Intermediaries and Interfaces." *Journal of the American Society for Information Science* 37 (July 1986): 204–14.

Williams describes the need and design requirements for transparent information retrieval systems, and the research that is being directed toward meeting these needs, such as the development of retrieval aids and the use of artificial intelligence techniques. *FRONT-ENDS

Wood, M. Sandra, Bonnie Snow, and Ellen Horak. *End User Searching in the Health Sciences.* New York: Haworth Pr., 1986. Also published in *Medical Reference Services Quarterly* 5 (Summer 1986).

The articles in this compilation present an overview of end-user searching in biomedicine as well as the specific details and variations among programs, taking into account the type of user, institutional setting, products used, and application. The commitments of money, time, and other resources that end-user search services entail are also covered. *MANAGEMENT *SCIENCE & HEALTH

Woolpy, Sara, and Nancy Taylor. "Enduser Searching: A Study of Manual vs. Outline Searching by Endusers and the Role of the Intermediary." In *Online '84 Conference Proceedings,* 243–45. Weston, Conn.: Online, Inc., 1984.

This paper covers a study conducted at Earlham College to answer questions on planning an end-user search program. The following questions were studied: can students find a greater number of relevant citations by an online search than by using printed tools; would a librarian-conducted search be more effective, and how do the costs compare; how variable are the results of student searchers using printed tools with online databases; and, is it possible for students to produce effective online searches with only limited instruction on the mechanics of searching? *BACKGROUND *AL

Zuga, Connie, and Mary Corcoran. "Front-End Services for Business Databases." In *National Online Meeting Proceedings—1986,* comp. by Martha E. Williams and Thomas H. Hogan, 479–81. Medford, N.J.: Learned Information, 1986.

Zuga and Corcoran discuss various front-end packages designed specifically for business applications. *DIALOG Business Connection* is noted as a service that provides ease of use for those searching on a non-regular basis, a solutions orientation, and access to top business sources, making it ideal for both search intermediaries and end users. *BUSINESS & MISC. *FRONT-ENDS *DIALOG BUSINESS CONNECTION

INDEX

Books and Journals for End Users

Martin Kesselman

To help meet the need for current information on online services and databases, several popular books and magazines aimed directly at home and business end users have appeared on the market during the past few years. The annotated list that follows is intended as a guide for librarians in making buying decisions for a core collection of such materials. These resources may be used in support of an in-house end-user search program or as aids for users who wish to search from their homes or offices.

This list should be thought of as a beginning. To keep up to date with new books and magazines on end-user searching, check popular micro-computer journals, the computer book section in *Booklist,* and *Online* and *Database* magazines.

Bowen, Charles, and David Peyton. *How to Get the Most out of CompuServe.* 2d ed. New York: Bantam, 1986.
　　As a supplement to the CompuServe manual, this book provides a road map to the various services available such as special interest groups, electronic shopping malls, and business information. Also reviewed are logon, efficient use of the CompuServe menus and index, electronic mail, downloading of software, and enhancing the system. The authors have also published *How to Get the Most out of the Source.*

Bowen, Charles, and Stewart Schneider. *Smarter Telecommunications. New York: Bantam, 1985.*
　　Bowen and Schneider provide a sound overview of online information resources and search techniques with an emphasis on cost-saving strategies. Beginning chapters tell one how to "cure the modem blues" and what users can expect to find when "teletraveling online" with electronic mail, financial information, and news and shopping services. A comparative look at the large

consumer information networks and packet networks comes next with a review of *CompuServe, The Source, Dow Jones,* Telenet, and Tymnet. The final chapters review the online specialists (BRS, DIALOG, etc.) with advice on how to choose and use databases. The appendix includes a glossary, the ASCII code, area codes, modem and software manufacturers, and access telephone numbers.

Cane, Mike. *The Computer Phone Book.* 2. New York: New American Library, 1986.

Volume 1 provides a guide to using online systems. Introductory sections provide explanations of how to make a computer communicate, clear definitions of telecommunications jargon, and guidance on what to look for in selecting and purchasing modems and communication software. Online services discussed in detail include *BRS After Dark, Collectors Data Service, Compu-Serve, Delphi, Dow Jones, EasyLink, Knowledge Index, MCI Mail, NewsNet, Playnet, The Source,* and local and bulletin board systems. Control characters used by each service are highlighted and several examples are provided. Besides a general index, there is a system/command index and cross-reference index that illustrate the gateways available from each of these systems to other online services. Volume 2 consists of directories of online services with information on hours, costs, access, and available databases for each, and of U.S., Canadian, and overseas bulletin board systems. The author plans to update the information through a newsletter.

Chandler, David. *Dialing for Data.* New York: Random, 1984.

Chandler provides a popular guide to the major consumer online services and bulletin boards with emphasis on saving money online and making money using online resources. Introductory chapters discuss the purchase of computers, modems, and communications software with special "Ripoff Tipoffs" to beware of. The sections on *The Source, CompuServe,* and *Delphi* include clear illustrations with explanations of what you see and what you type. Other chapters discuss Videotex, high tech connections (*DIALOG, BRS,* etc.), newspaper libraries (VU/TEXT, Mead Data, etc.), and personal services such as the *Official Airline Guide.* The appendix includes a directory of bulletin board services and a glossary.

Chasin, Mark. *Computer Connections on a Budget.* New York: McGraw-Hill, 1985.

Budget-minded users will find out how to get more online mileage at lower costs here. Numerous savings tips are given throughout on how to use several online services cost effectively. Chasin primarily highlights the large utilities and discusses each service in great detail. Services include *CompuServe, Dow Jones, The Source,* and *Delphi.* Also included are a chapter on bulletin boards and other services, a chapter on getting started in telecommunications, and an appendix with listings of Tymnet, Telenet, and DataPac telephone numbers.

Christie, Linda. *Managing Today and Tomorrow with On-Line Information.* Homewood, Ill.: Dow-Jones-Irwin, 1986.

Christie's book emphasizes the use of online services to access business information. For corporate users, there are chapters to help the company determine the online capabilities needed, select the appropriate database service, and design and implement the online search operation. To aid in equipment selection there are sections on how to buy software and hardware, and a review of modems and communications software on the market. Online services reviewed include *Nexis, Dow Jones, Knowledge Index, The Source, CompuServe, SDC, MCI Mail, Delphi, I.P. Sharp,* and *BRS/BRKTHRU.* A glossary is included.

Database User (formerly *Database End-User*). Monthly. Westport, Conn.: Meckler, 1985– .

Besides general informative articles on searching, several columns appear each month dealing with new services and features. "News Hotline" provides short press releases of new products and "From the Editor" provides commentary on online trends. A database column goes into detail about online files and another column examines new online search features and services. "Connecting Gear" reviews new communications software, front-ends, and modems. "End User Support" includes information on training options including seminars, videotapes, and demonstration discs. A final section consists of a directory of services and manufacturers.

Davies, Owen, and Mike Edelhart. *Omni Online Database Directory.* New York: Macmillan, 1984.

This directory is arranged by broad subject areas and includes those databases that end users are most likely to search. Entries include the subject content of the database, user comments as to ease of use, audience and application, the services providing access to the database, and the address and phone number of the supplier. Beginning chapters define databases, review equipment and software for online searching, and provide help in selecting an appropriate online service and database. There are also detailed listings of major online vendors and major information utilities such as *CompuServe* and *The Source.* An online directory at the end of the book includes the address and phone number for each service, and a list of major databases.

Emmett, Arielle, and David Gabel. *Direct Connections: Making Your Personal Computers Communicate.* New York: New American Library, 1986.

This is a technical book with emphasis on setting up microcomputers for telecommunications rather than on discussing online services. Especially valuable are the case studies on how to connect otherwise incompatible microcomputers, such as the Apple IIe to the IBM PC, through modem connections. Telecommunications standards and protocols are discussed in detail as are connections to mainframes. The appendix includes information on ASCII, directories of vendors, and a glossary.

Enright, Thomas, et al. *Computel's Guide to Telecomputing on the Apple.* Greensboro, N.C.: Computel, 1985.

Although geared toward owners of the Apple II family of computers, this book contains much information for anyone getting started in telecommunications. It is arranged in three sections: "Ready," "Set," and "Go." "Ready" contains general information on modems, communications software, bulletin boards, and *The Source* and *CompuServe.* "Set" reviews Apple microcomputers. "Go" includes technical information about online searching, including chapters on protocols and downloading software. Also included are a glossary, a communications software program for the Apple in BASIC that can be keyed in, and a brief directory of the major online services.

Ferrarini, Elizabeth. *Infomania: The Guide to Essential Electronic Services.* Boston: Houghton, 1985.

Ferrarini discusses a wide variety of online services and databases. There are chapters on topics such as money, news, careers, job hunting, computers, shopping, and people. For example, the chapter on learning includes information on such services as *Telelearning* and the *Educational Events Data Base.* Some of the more unusual online services covered in the book include *Telepsych, Fantasy Plaza,* and the *Venture Capitol Network.* More traditional end-user services are also discussed, including *DIALOG* and *Knowledge Index, BRS After Dark,* and *BRS BRKTHRU,* and even foreign online services. One chapter includes local online services and bulletin boards arranged by state. The appendix offers a directory of phone numbers, helpful online hints, and a discussion on how to buy modems and software with a list of manufacturers.

Gilreath, Charles. *Computer Literature Searching: Research Strategies and Databases.* Boulder: Westview, 1984.

Gilreath's book is aimed at the "wired scholar," such as a faculty member, graduate student, or other serious researcher. The basics of computer literature searching as well as database indexing and organization are discussed. Special emphasis is placed on the role of the search analyst as a partner in the online research process. The remaining chapters deal with searching and databases in agriculture and life sciences, social sciences and education, physical sciences and engineering, business, humanities, arts and architecture, and legal research. A glossary is included.

Glossbrenner, Alfred. *The Complete Handbook of Personal Computer Communications.* New York: St. Martin's, 1986.

Glossbrenner's book begins by telling how to get started in telecomputing by choosing modems and communications software. Subsequent chapters cover *BRS, DIALOG, SDC,* and *NewsNet;* consumer services such as *CompuServe* and *The Source;* free computer bulletin boards; shopping and banking online; teleconferencing; and telecommuting (working away from the office via computers). In addition there is a chapter on the technical aspects of data communications. The appendix discusses troubleshooting, the use of the Telenet and Tymnet telecommunications network, and electronic mail. A glossary is included.

———. *How to Look It Up Online.* New York: St. Martin's, 1987.

A companion volume to the book reviewed above, this work explains the techniques and services to access online information. Online services discussed include *DIALOG, Knowledge Index, DIALOG Business Connection, BRS, BRS/BRKTHRU, BRS After Dark, Nexis, SDC, Dow Jones, VU/ TEXT, NewsNet* and *Wilsonline.* Special emphasis is placed on questions dealing with access to full-text information, investment and competitive intelligence, sales and marketing, and government information. Useful advice is provided by "Online Tip" boxes throughout the chapters as well as chapters on search aids and special features available from online services. The appendix includes a discussion on how to import downloaded data into *Lotus 1-2-3, dBase,* and other programs.

Goldmann, Nahum. *Online Research and Retrieval with Microcomputers.* Blue Ridge Summit, Pa.: TAB, 1985.

Rather than emphasizing the various services and databases available online, this book deals primarily with search techniques for serious researchers. Goldmann stresses the need for using a graphic form in formulating effective search strategies. Careful planning before going online is also stressed, along with discussion on the types of databases available (i.e., bibliographic, full-text), online records, fields and indexes, and search techniques such as Boolean logic and truncation. Emphasis is placed on free-text versus controlled vocabulary searching and the effective use of thesauri and other search aids. Librarians should note there is also a chapter on end users, intermediaries, and information evaluation that reviews the role of intermediaries in the search process. The book also includes chapters on selecting equipment and communications software, the use of the IBM PC for information gathering and online do's and don'ts including "Goldmann's Golden Rules of Successful Information Retrieval." Illustrations from a variety of online services including *BRS, Chemical Abstracts Service, DIALOG,* and *MEDLARS* are used throughout.

Hansen, Carol. *A Microcomputer User's Guide to Information Online.* Hasbrouck Heights, N.J.: Hayden, 1984.

While not offering much detail on particular databases, this book does provide a sound introduction to the workings of online systems, information that can be obtained online, and the online search process. Information utilities and online services are treated in some depth and there is information on obtaining subscriptions, training and system commands, and protocols. These sections also include some case studies, providing examples of each system's usefulness. Other chapters deal with equipment and communications software, transferring files (uploading and downloading), and software for use with offline files. Also included are a glossary, bibliographies, and lists of database producers and manufacturers.

Helliwell, John. *Inside Information.* New York: New American Library, 1986.

Businesspersons and other professionals will find this book to be a sensible guide to using online resources for improved productivity. The first part of the book is an introduction to hardware and software needed for communications. This section provides assistance with the selection of modems, features to look for in communications software, and how to make connections online. General search strategy techniques are discussed next, followed by discussions of some advanced features. Much of the rest of the book is devoted to locating and using business information, for example, from the *Disclosure* and *Predicasts* databases. The *DIALOG* service is stressed but there is also information on how consumer services such as *CompuServe* can be used as a source of business information. Other chapters discuss full-text databases on the *VU/TEXT* and *NewsNet* services, directory databases such as *Electronic Yellow Pages* for making lists, numeric databases, and the use of the report feature on

DIALOG. The appendix provides details on the *Crosstalk* communications software, *DIALOG,* Mead Data, editing downloaded information, and addresses of online services.

Howitt, Doren, Marvin Weinberger. *Databasics.* New York: Garland, 1984.

Databasics includes a wealth of online information, with a slant toward business-related sources. Part 1, "All About the Information Industry," explains the concepts of databases, indexing, database producers, and online systems. It also discusses costs, tips on database searching, and electronic mail. Part 2, "A Guide to Selected Business Databases," reviews broad-coverage business databases, general news databases, and databases in other areas such as advertising and marketing, science and technology, and energy and the environment. Part 3 discusses online services in detail. Part 4 reviews the nuts and bolts of using microcomputers for online searching, communications software, and modems. Part 5, on online information in the future, looks at networking and gateways, speech synthesis, and artificial intelligence. An appendix includes a bibliography, a directory of information brokers, a listing of terminals, communications software and modems, and coupons for discounts on many online services and products.

Humphrey, Susanne, and John Biagio. *Databases: A Primer for Retrieving Information by Computer.* Englewood Cliffs, N.J.: Prentice-Hall, 1986.

This is a fairly complete sourcebook for the online information consumer. Beginning chapters provide a solid background on the value of computerized information retrieval, how information is stored and organized online, and the principles of searching. Other chapters discuss controlled vocabulary, database indexes, free-text searching, saving strategies, downloading, and the quality of subject indexing. The book ends with a section on how to select an appropriate service, a directory of selected online services, and a bibliography of selected books, periodicals, directories, organizations, conferences, and readings. A glossary is also included. This book may be used as a classroom text as each section provides exercises for review.

Lambert, Steve. *Online: A Guide to America's Leading Information Services.* Bellvue, Wash., 1985.

Lambert provides a sound introduction to seven major online services including *MCI Mail,* the *Official Airline Guide, CompuServe, NewsNet, Western Union, DIALOG,* and *Dow Jones.* Included for each are descriptions of services, how the service can be accessed, and basic search techniques. The section entitled "Starting Out and Setting Up" provides an overview of equipment needed for online searching, including modems and communications software. The last section of the book reviews common communications problems. Coupons for online discounts are included.

Lesko, Matthew. *The Computer Data and Data Base Source Book.* New York: Avon, 1984.

Lesko's book serves as a "road map" to commercial and government databases and public data sources. The first section provides several examples and uses of online databases in fulfilling information needs. Most of the text following is a directory of databases, arranged alphabetically. Each entry includes information on subject, source, contents, inclusive dates, the database producer, the online system(s) on which the file is available, and approximate costs. The "Public Data Sources" section includes data in printed publications and on computer tape. Lesko also provides advice on obtaining needed information and data from government agencies.

Lewis, Sasha. *Plugging In.* Radnor, Pa.: Chilton, 1984.

Plugging in shows the microcomputer user how to set up a computer system for telecommuncations with checklists for hardware and software. Next discussed are the information utilities—*CompuServe, The Source, Delphi,* and *Dow Jones.* The section on "bargain basement databases" compares *Knowledge Index* and *BRS After Dark.* The section on "Caviar Databases" reviews *DIALOG, BRS, SDC, Dow Jones, Nexis,* and *NewsNet.* Other topics cover protocols, advice for developing effective search strategies, and bulletin boards. The appendix includes a list of ASCII codes, brief descriptions of DIALOG databases, a short directory of major services, and a glossary.

Link-Up. Monthly. Medford, N.J.: Learned Information, 1984– .

This news magazine is aimed at business, educational, and personal end users. Each issue contains several news items and feature articles. A recent issue included articles on online employment services, bulletin board software, and online resources for the handicapped. Regular departments include book and software reviews, information on different online special interest groups, and "On Board," a monthly listing of new bulletin boards throughout the country.

Ness, Dan. *Fast Facts Online: Search Strategies for Finding Business Information.* Homewood, Ill.: Dow-Jones-Irwin, 1986.

The intended purpose of this book is to make choosing a database and online service easier for beginning searchers. Introductory chapters list sources of business information and types of online databases, and tell how to evaluate databases and structure an information search. Most of the book is a subject directory that ranks databases for coverage. Each entry includes the vendor, database name, beginning date, number of records online, updating frequency, geographic coverage, and searchable fields. Databases are also arranged alphabetically with more detailed information. A final section, "Database Notes," illustrates special uses and access paths for major business databases. The appendix includes an annotated bibliography and glossary.

Newlin, Barbara. *Answers Online: Your Guide to Informational Databases,* New York: McGraw-Hill, 1985.

Newlin concentrates on databases and the information one can expect to get from them. Chapters are devoted to business databases, scientific databases, and news, general information, and social science databases. Each entry includes database content as well as a sample online record. Newline also reviews electronic mail, *BRS After Dark, Knowledge Index,* full-text services and databases, basic and advanced online search techniques, and document delivery. A nice feature is the chapter on evaluating services and databases.

Online Access. Bimonthly. Chicago: Online Access, 1986– .

Featured articles in recent issues of this new journal have included coverage of information about foreign companies and markets online, free online information about foreign companies and markets online, free online information services from the U.S. government, and new telecommunications equipment.

Some regular departments and columns include "Hands On," with expert comments on online products and services; "Windows" a look at online innovations; "Online Investing"; and "Online Travel." An especially valuable feature is the "Online Access Guide," a selective descriptive list of the best online services and products.

Online Today. Monthly. Columbus, Ohio: CompuServe, 1981– .

This magazine, free to subscribers of CompuServe, stresses the CompuServe service and contains many articles on various databases available through CompuServe's *IQuest* and *Einstein* gateways. A recent issue contained articles on gateways, accessing online services from overseas, and cellular modems. Regular features include hardware, software, book reviews, a beginner's corner, new products, and a shopper's guide.

Sandler, Corey. *How to Telecommunicate: A Personal Computer User's Guide.* New York: Holt, 1986.

Sandler begins with a review of telecommunications hardware, standards, modems, protocols, and communications software. A section on database "department stores" that reviews the features of *CompuServe* and *The Source* and how to navigate through them follows. *Dow Jones* and other business online resources such as *DIALOG, NewsNet, VU-TEXT* and Mead Data are also discussed. Other chapters of interest review search commands, electronic mail, telex, micro-to-mainframe communications, and security and new communications technology such as cellular telephone and modems, fiber optics, and CD-ROM. The appendix includes a directory of selected databases and online services and a glossary.

Stone, M. David. *Getting Online.* Englewood Cliffs, N.J.: Prentice-Hall, 1984.

Most of Stone's book deals with preparations before going online, reviewing decisions concerning terminals, modems, and communications software, and putting them all together. The rest of the book is a catalog of utilities and online systems including access, price structure, description, and detailed listings of available databases. Stone also includes information on bulletin boards, an overview of Videotex, and advice on staying current in the online field.

Wood, Robert. *Connections: Telecommunications on a Budget.* Glenview, Ill.: Scott, Foresman, 1986.

Written for the novice searcher, chapters stress how online services can be accessed inexpensively. It's no wonder, then, that most of the book is devoted to searching free bulletin board systems and the *CompuServe, The Source,* and *Delphi* information utilities. For research online, the book stresses the use of *Knowledge Index* and only briefly mentions *BRS After Dark, EasyNet, Dow Jones,* and *Nexis.* Cost-saving measures are also reflected in the chapters on getting started with telecommunicating and include advice on finding and joining a user's group and the use of "free" communications software in the public domain. The appendix includes a telecommunications dictionary, an annotated directory of online services, selected local services and bulletin boards arranged by state, a directory of user groups, and directories of national bulletin boards and other online services.

Appendix

Directory of Online Products and Services for End Users

AMA/NET
Softsearch Inc.
1560 Broadway
Suite 900
Denver, CO 80202
(800) 426-2873

BIOSIS (BIOSIS BITS, BIOSIS Connection)
Biosciences Information Service
2100 Arch St.
Philadelphia, PA 19103
(800) 523-4806

Books in Print Plus
R. R. Bowker
205 E. 42 St.
New York, NY 10017
(212) 916-1605

BRS (BRS After Dark, BRS Colleague, BRS Educator, Tech Data)
E. Lancaster Ave.
St. Davids, PA 19087
(800) 468-0908

CAS ONLINE
2540 Olentangy River Rd.
P.O. Box 3012
Columbus, OH 43210
(800) 848-6538

Chemical Information Systems
7215 York Rd.
Baltimore, MD 21212
(800) 424-9600

Classmate
see DIALOG

Colleague
see BRS

Compact Cambridge
Cambridge Scientific Abstracts
5161 River Rd.
Bethesda, MD 20816
(800) 843-7751

CompuServe
(Einstein, IQuest)
5000 Arlington Centre Blvd.
P.O. Box 20212
Columbus, OH 43220
(800) 848-8199

DataTimes
Datatek Corporation
818 N.W. 63 St.
Oklahoma City, OK 73116
(405) 843-7323

Datext
444 Washington St.
Woburn, MA 01801
(617) 938-6667

220

Delphi
General Videotex Corporation
3 Blackstone St.
Cambridge, MA 02139
(800) 544-4005

DIALOG
(Classmate, DIALOG Business
Connection, DIALOG Medical
Connection, DIALOG onDisc,
Knowledge Index)
3460 Hillview Ave.
Palo Alto, CA 94304
(800) 334-2564

Dow Jones News/Retrieval
P.O. Box 300
Princeton, NJ 08540
(800) 257-5114

Ebsco
see Medline-CD

Easynet
Telebase Systems Inc.
134 N. Narbeth Ave.
Narbeth, PA 19072
(800) 327-9638

Einstein
see CompuServe

GEnie
General Electric Information Services
401 Washington St.
Rockville, MD 20850
(800) 638-9636

Grateful Med
see MEDLARS

**Human Resources Information
  Network**
Executive Telecom Systems Inc.
9585 Valparaiso Court
Indianapolis, IN
(800) 421-8884

InfoGlobe
444 Front St.
Toronto, Ontario, Canada M5V 2S9
(416) 585-5250

InfoMaster
Western Union Telegraph Company
1 Lake St.
Upper Saddle River, NJ 07458
(800) 525-6000

Information Access Company
(InfoTrac, Search Helper)
11 Davis Drive
Belmont, CA 94002
(800) 227-8431

InfoTrac
see Information Access Company

IQuest
see CompuServe

Knowledge Index
see DIALOG

Lexis
see Mead Data Central

Mead Data Central
(Lexis, Medis, Nexis)
P.O. Box 933
Dayton, OH 45401
(800) 227-4908

Med-Base
(Q Base)
Online Research Systems
2901 Broadway
Suite 154
New York, NY 10025
(212) 408-3311

Medis
see Mead Data Central

MEDLARS
(Grateful Med)
National Library of Medicine
4600 Rockville Pike
Bethesda, MD 20209
(800) 638-8480

Medline-CD
Ebsco Electronic Systems
P.O. Box 13787
Torrance, CA 90503
(213) 530-7533
See also BRS, DIALOG, SilverPlatter

microDISCLOSURE
Disclosure
5161 River Rd.
Bethesda, MD 20816
(800) 638-8076

Microsoft Access
Microsoft Corp.
13221 S.E. 26th
Bellevue, WA 98005
(800) 426-9400

MiniMedline
Dalgren Memorial Library
Georgetown University Medical
    Center
3900 Reservoir Rd. N.W.
Washington, D.C. 20007
(202) 625-7577

NewsNet
945 Haverford Rd.
Bryn Mawr, PA 19010
(800) 345-1301

Nexis
see Mead Data Central

OCLC
6565 Frantz Rd.
Dublin, OH 43017
(800) 848-5878

Official Airline Guide
2000 Clearwater Dr.
Oak Brook, IL 60521
(800) 323-4000

Paper Chase
Beth Israel Hospital
330 Brookline Ave.
Boston, MA 02215
(800) 722-2075

PC Net/Link
Informatics General Corporation
6011 Executive Blvd.
Rockville, MD 20852
(800) 638-6595

Pergamon Orbit Infoline
1340 Old Chain Bridge Rd.
McLean, VA 22101
(800) 336-7575

ProSearch
Personal Bibliographic Software
412 Longshore Dr.
Ann Arbor, MI 48105
(313) 996-1580

Q Base
see Med-Base

Questel
1625 Eye St. N.W.
Washington, D.C. 20006
(800) 424-9600

Sci-Mate
Institute for Scientific Information
3501 Market St.
Philadelphia, PA 19104
(800) 523-4092

Searchmaster
see Pergamon Orbit Infoline

Searchware
22458 Ventura Blvd.
Woodland Hills, CA 91364
(818) 992-4325

SilverPlatter Information
37 Walnut St.
Wellesley Hills, MA 02181
(617) 239-0306

The Source
Source Telecomputing Corporation
1616 Anderson Rd.
McClean, VA 22102
(800) 336-3366

Tech Data
see BRS

TEX
American Mathematical Society
P.O. Box 6248
Providence, RI 02940
(800) 556-7774

VU/TEXT
1211 Chestnut St.
Philadelphia, PA 19017
(800) 258-8080

WESTLAW
50 W. Kellogg Blvd.
P.O. Box 64526
St. Paul, MN 55164
(800) 328-0109

Wilsearch
(Wilsondisc)
H. W. Wilson Co.
950 University Ave.
Bronx, NY 10452
(800) 462-6060

Wilsondisc
see Wilsearch

Index

This index covers chapters 1-11. Page numbers in italic denote entries of major emphasis.

224

Contributors

MARTIN KESSELMAN (co-editor) is Coordinator of Online Services and Bibliographic Instruction at the Library of Science and Medicine, Rutgers University. Kesselman holds an M.L.S. from Pratt Institute and an M.S. in Botany from the University of Akron. His numerous articles and presentations have been in a variety of areas: online searching, end-user searching, database products and services, reference statistics, and bibliographic instruction. He has been author of the bimonthly "Online Update" column in *Wilson Library Bulletin* since 1984 and is a former associate editor of *Library Hi Tech.*

SARAH BARBARA WATSTEIN (co-editor) is Head, Reference Division, Hunter College Library, City University of New York. Watstein's articles span many subject areas: reference statistics, artificial intelligence, the psychology of women, and burnout. She is co-editor of a forthcoming bibliography on the status of women in librarianship to be published by the American Library Association. She holds an M.L.S. from the University of California, Los Angeles, and an M.P.A. from New York University. Watstein will be on leave from her current position for the academic year 1988/89 to participate in The Council on Library Resources Academic Library Management Intern Program.

DEBRA KETCHELL is Information Systems/State Resource Librarian, Health Sciences Library and Information Center, University of Washington, Seattle. Her numerous publications and presentations have been in the areas of online searching by health professionals, searching with microcomputers, and the electronic library. She holds and M.L.S. from the University of Washington.

PRISCILLA KRONISH is Physical Sciences Librarian at the Dr. Jerome S. Coles Science Library, Elmer Holmes Bobst Library, New York University. Kronish was instrumental in developing the library's online search service in the early 1970s. She holds an Ed.D. from New York University.

229

IDA BRANDWAYN LOWE is Acting Assistant Dean for Research and Program Development, School of Education and Educational Services, Baruch College, City University of New York. She holds an M.L.S. from Columbia University, an M.A. in Latin American Studies from the New School for Social Research, and an M.B.A. from Baruch College. Her publications span such topics as online information retrieval, information research in business and volunteering and the aged.

SALLY LYON is Chief, Reference Division, City College, City University of New York. She has written articles and reviews on online searching and databases and has been active in the ALA RASD Machine Assisted Reference Section.

STANLEY D. NASH is Information Services Librarian at the Alexander Library, Rutgers University. He holds an M.L.S. from Long Island University, and a Ph.D. in English History from New York University. His publications are in the areas of end-user searching, bibliographic instruction, and social history.

LAURA M. OSEGUEDA is Agriculture and Life Sciences Reference Librarian and Coordinator, Reference Retrieval Services, D.H. Hill Library, North Carolina State University. She holds an M.L.S. from the University of California, Berkeley, and has published in the areas of online searching, databases, computer applications, library instruction, and the reference process.

CHARLES PETERS is Microforms Librarian at University of Arizona Libraries. He received his MLS at the University of Michigan. Peters has been a frequent speaker on the topic of CD-ROM in libraries at the National Online and Optical Publishing conferences.

SUZANNE J. REDALJE is currently Head, Chemistry Library and Information Services, University of Washington, Seattle. She has authored several publications on end-user searching and organized and chaired a discussion group dealing with online searching and databases in the sciences as part of ACRL's Science and Technology Section. She holds an M.L.S. from the University of California, Los Angeles.

ROSEMARIE RIECHEL is Head, Information and Telephone Reference Division, and Online Search Specialist, at the Central Library, Queens Borough Public Library. She holds an M.L.S. from Columbia University as well as a D.L.S. from Columbia. Riechel's publications have focused on public libraries, especially online searching and reference services in public libraries.

STEPHEN SMITH administers the Federal and State Documents Depository Collections at the Spartanburg County Public Library in Spartanburg, South Carolina. He holds an M.S. in Library and Information Science from the University of Illinois. He has written in the areas of online business and news sources and compiles "Search Strategy Index" for *Library Hi Tech News*.